North American Horse Travel Guide

The complete travel resource book for horses & riders

Featuring hundreds of stables, ranches, farms, fairgrounds and trails for the traveling horse

By Bruce McAllister

Roundup Press, Boulder, Colorado

First Edition
ISBN # 0-9638817-2-8

Printed in the United States of America

Cover
Cover Design by BOOKENDS, Boulder, Colorado
Flying Horse Art by Samuel Van Meter (all rights reserved)

Design & typography by
ONE WORLD Graphics, Boulder, Colorado

ROUNDUP PRESS
P.O. Box 109
Boulder, CO 80306-0109

IF YOU ARE UNABLE TO OBTAIN ADDITIONAL COPIES
FROM YOUR DEALER, WRITE DIRECTLY TO
THE PUBLISHER AT ADDRESS SHOWN ABOVE.

Printed by
Johnson Printing Company
1880 South 57th Court
Boulder, CO 80301

Distributed by
Johnson Books
1880 South 57th Court
Boulder, CO 80301

Table of Contents

CANADA (CANADIAN PROVINCES ARE PRINTED ALPHABETICAL-
LY WITH STATES, BUT LISTED HERE SEPARATELY FOR THE CON-
VENIENCE OF USERS)

This guide includes symbols to make reading easier as you go cross country with your horse(s). In each facility listing there are symbols for everything from mechanics to tack shops to vet schools. And on each state/ provincial map, the first letter of the designator (like F-3, S-1) lets you know what kind of facility it is.

FACILITY SYMBOLS

BED & BREAKFAST (which boards horses)

CAMPGROUND
CAMPER RV HOOKUPS

FARRIER

FISHING

FOOD

FUEL

MAILING ADDRESS

MECHANIC

MUSCLE THERAPY
MASSAGE

PHONE/ FAX NUMBER

SIGHTSEEING DETOUR

STALLS	⇌
SWIM / HYDRO THERAPY	🐟
TACK SHOP	⛑
TRAILS	🐎
VETERINARIAN	✚
VET SCHOOL	⌂

SYMBOLS FOR COST PER STALL

Under $10 per night per horse	$
$10-15	$$
Over $15	$$$

MAP DESIGNATORS

C	SCENIC DETOUR
D	HORSE TRAILS
F	FAIRGROUND
R	RANCH
S	STABLES
TS	TACK SHOP
VS	VET SCHOOL/ EMERGENCY

DISCLAIMER! READ BEFORE USING THIS BOOK!

The publisher has attempted to be accurate in listing facilities, services, trails, recreational opportunities for horses in Canada and the U.S.A.. There may be both typographical and/or content mistakes. The author and Roundup Press shall have neither liability nor responsibility to any person or entity with respect to any injury, loss or damage caused or alleged to have been caused directly or indirectly by the information throughout this book. We have made every effort to be as accurate and thorough as possible. ALWAYS CALL AHEAD TO VERIFY SERVICES AND DIRECTIONS! Listing of all medical services, vet schools, farriers, stables, ranches, fairgrounds, farms, parks, mechanics, fuel stops, restaurants and campgrounds is NOT AN ENDORSEMENT of those facilities and/or services. This information was mostly supplied by horse facility operators.

Fairgrounds, in particular, cannot guarantee the security of horses left unattended. It is strongly recommended that security be provided 24 hours a day. Guard dogs can be helpful.

The publisher cannot be held responsible for any accidents or incidents at any facilities or with services provided. And the reader is to use the information in this book at his/her own risk. If you do not wish to accept these conditions, you can return this guide to the publisher for a full refund within 14 days of purchase. Enclose a sales receipt for verification.

BEFORE USING ANY FACILITY, SERVICE, OR TRAIL, IT IS VERY IMPORTANT TO CALL OR WRITE FIRST. A FACILITY COULD BE FULLY BOOKED OR OWNERSHIP CHANGED. FACILITIES AND RECREATION AREAS COULD BE CLOSED DUE TO AN ACT OF GOD OR FOR ANY REASON WHATSOEVER.

Acknowledgments

A million thanks to Claire, Margot, Jackie, and Lucy for putting up with the data gathering phase of this book. And we are indebted to all the facilities, horse councils, and government agencies across North America who gave us the information and photos that made this book possible. Thanks to Ron of ONE WORLD ARTS for introducing me to the world of desktop publishing! And my longtime friend Karl Kocivar gave me invaluable suggestions on how to publish a book.

Hauling Horses

- Check all states you plan to visit ahead of time for health requirements and driver's license requirements. As many as a dozen states might now require a commercial driver's license if your horse trailer is more than 25 feet long.

- Unless horses have had a bad experience, they are normally good travelers. Horses being transported should be tied securely with a quick release knot. The knots should be tied short enough to prevent horses from getting a foot over the rope, but still giving them enough slack to reach hay and water.

- Always travel with leather or breakaway halters-- and take along spares and extra lead ropes. It is a good idea to take two water buckets per horse, double-ended snaps, screw eyes, twine, a long water hose, and a hammer. These items will make temporary stabling much easier-- especially at fairgrounds. Recommend a third bucket for grain for each horse.

- Hauling a load of horses requires extra care. Take corners slowly and avoid quick starts and sudden stops. Whatever you use to convey horses should have a floor with good footing. Two inches of sand works well in a stock trailer, while rubber mats with a non-slip tread and shavings should be used in horse trailer.

- A green horse will load better if preceded by an experienced animal. Practice with them before you plan to start your trip. Offer them grain to get them into the trailer. Once in, allow the horse to stand quietly and eat. Then take a 5 to 10 minute trip. Increase the time of your practice trips until you feel your horse is comfortable in the trailer. A horse must always have good footing when loading or unloading.

- At every gas stop, offer water to horses. Make sure that they have grass hay in net or bag at all times. For non- drinkers, try giving them apples and/or carrots. Every 8 hours try giving the horses bran mash with electrolytes.

- Have a blanket or sheet available for sudden temperature changes. Use fly spray on horses if you are traveling in a hot climate.

- On trips of five hours or more, it might be a good idea not to put on shipping wraps-- they can decrease circulation in the horses' legs and/or come loose and tangle. Bell boots are fine on the front feet.

- ALWAYS make sure the trailer has good ventilation!

- Do not give traveling horses dusty hay-- it might cause respiratory problems. Wet down the hay if necessary before hitting the road.

- Your vet might consider giving the horses a rhino flu booster shot or an Equistem™ booster shot before big trips.

Truck & Trailer Checklist

- Always have properly inflated spare tires, lug wrench, hydraulic jack, and flashlight easily accessible for flat tires. Remember to have some wheel chocks for both sides of your trailer. 4x4s sawed diagonally with ropes connecting make good permanent chocks.

- Make sure tire pressures are correct-- low pressures shorten tire life and decrease gas mileage. Before long trips, check all fluid levels, brake pads, wheel bearings, turn/running lights on both truck and trailer. This is especially important for trips through mountainous areas.

- Complete road maps, a vehicle compass, and CB radio come in handy for navigation. Some truckers now even have GPS (Global Positioning Satellite) navigation for precise navigation in remote areas or you can use topographical maps which show longitude and latitude. This will become more popular as GPS road maps become available. Currently many general aviation aircraft and pleasure boats use GPS for navigation. Handheld GPS units go for as little as $700.

For winter and/or long term storage for horse trailers that have living quarters built in, it's a good idea to do the following:

1- Disconnect any auxiliary batteries, check their levels, and store in a warm place- its a good idea to make sure that they are also charged. Partially discharged batteries can freeze, if stored at low temperatures.

2- Drain gas tank for any gasoline powered generators- over several months, the gas could age and gum up the fuel system. For this purpose, NAPA Auto Parts sell Gas Siphon Kits @ $ 2.79. They come with a 6.5 foot siphon tube which you can prime by squeezing. Or you can buy gasoline additives which will keep the fuel "fresh" over the winter. Make sure to run the engine a few minutes after you have put in the additive.

3- Drain any water tanks in trailer.

4- Turn off propane tank valves. It might be a good time to check the date of manufacture on the propane tank. By law, they must be pressure checked 11 years after date of manufacture and then every 5 years thereafter. The pressure check can be done by fire extinguisher or propane dealers who have the proper test equipment. It's also a good idea to keep your propane tanks filled up-- then there is less chance for rust in them.

Back Country Tips & Manners

- A good mountain horse needs to be trained to deal with whatever it is likely to encounter in the back country, including, but not necessarily limited to the following:

   loading & hauling

   standing tied

   hobbles

   picket rope

   crossing water and streams

   rope under the tail

   crossing downed trees and other obstacles

   crossing boggy areas

   crinkling noise of maps or plastic rain gear

   fly repellent spray bottles

   sudden movement of birds, wildlife and dogs

   sudden appearance of hikers with large bright packs

   motorcycles or mopeds

   tolerating other animals on the trail, including llamas
- For emergency tack repairs, take along a knife with a leather punch, pliers, small rolls of stove wire and electrical tape, and leather (or nylon) boot laces will make most emergency tack repairs.

- Short-cutting across switchbacks on the trail should not be done. It creates a new tread, which is usually steep, causing erosion and gullies. Cutting switchbacks also constitutes abuse of our resource and the hoof prints that remain are a signature of who is to blame. The key word is "gentle". Be gentle to the back country!

- Tying horses to trees is a no-no. A high picket line between trees away from the campground is the recommended method of confining stock. Where the line goes around the tree, the bark should be protected by padding such as a cinch, gunny sack, or 2 inch wide nylon tree saver strap. The line should be approximately seven feet above the ground and lead ropes tied so that the halter snap is two feet from the ground. This allows the horse to lie down yet not get tangled. A rule of thumb is: tie horses shorter when you will not be nearby or be able to see them such as at night. Horses seem more relaxed when tied to a high picket line than with other methods.

PLEASE NOTE! There should be a swivel in the lead rope or it could become twisted or unraveled as the horse moves around. If the lead is tied too long, the horse may get a leg over the lead or may become tangled if it rolls. And if the picket line is too low, a saddled animal may catch the saddle on the high line and damage the saddle.

- Campsites should be at least 200 feet from the edge of lakes, rivers, and streams. Select authorized campsites that are not heavily used. These will give you better grazing and more privacy in addition to reducing impact. Carry out everything you bring in, and leave only your footprints!

- The effort to stop the spread of noxious weeds into the back country has caused prohibition on packing hay or unprocessed grain into many federal lands, including wilderness areas and parks. Always check ahead with the proper agency for the latest camping regulations, numbers of horses and people allowed in a group, and trails open to horses!

- Never leave any campfire unattended, and always abide by fire regulations! Many campsites do not allow open fires.

- Never leave horse manure or hay in camp areas, trailheads, or loading areas.

- If you picket horses, move them often.

- Take only the minimum number of animals needed.

A SHADOW CAST

I hate to admit to the company I'm in
But a back country jerk too often I've been.
You have seen the shadow on the mountains I cast
Because the marks I have left there last and last.
When you see that lone tree with its root laid bare
You know me and my string have often been there.
But really, does tying up to a tree overnight spell its doom?
I've done it often you know, even when there is other room.
Wait a minute, I seem to recall a high mountain pass
With its cool, clear water and lush, green grass,
And there in the middle of this picturesque scene
Is a tall lone fir tree that's lost all its green.
What could have killed it I thought, hikers, bears, or...
Then it hit me, my god, I've been here before.
Mother Nature made that tree to stand the wind and the snow,
It has stood the test of time and continues to grow.
She made that tree to take the worst of her work,
But she didn't plan on me, the back country jerk.

By Dan Plummer

Dan Plummer's poem and some of the information in the Hauling Horses and Back Country Tips and Manners sections is reprinted with permission from the publishers of BACK COUNTRY HORSEMAN GUIDEBOOK which is published by the Back Country Horsemen of America, P. O. Box 597, Columbia Falls, MT 59912. If you would like copies of the guide or are interested in joining a chapter, or starting one, please write to the address above. There are also chapters in Missoula, Montana; Leavenworth, Washington; Salmon, Idaho; and Visalia, California.

About the Author

Bruce McAllister is a photo journalist and has covered such diverse stories as the Green River Rendezvous in Wyoming, a wagon train trek in Quinter, Kansas, the Sourdough Rendezvous in Whitehorse, Yukon, a travel story on the Amazon, and a climb up Cotopaxi, one of the highest peaks in the Americas. He has also almost frozen his fingers off in the Alaskan Arctic and once did a back flip off a gondola into a canal in Venice. An experienced mountain pilot, he has flown over most of North America, the Arctic and Mexico in his Cessna T210. He is married and has three daughters--and cooked up this book with help from the eldest of his daughters, Margot McAllister Dippert. She is an accomplished dressage rider who has competed at the Grand Prix level in the Rockies and the east coast. She also is a dressage instructor.

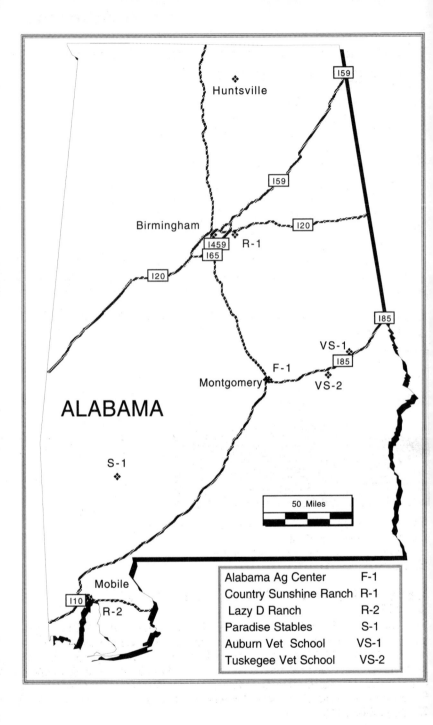

Alabama Agricultural Center / Garrett Coliseum / Montgomery (F-1)

At 1555 Federal Blvd. ⚏ 600 stalls available. This big complex is an equine and sales facility. ✚ Vet on call.
◡ ⬛✕ These services are nearby. 🚐 Camper/RV hookups available.
⌖ *P.O. Box 70026, Montgomery, AL 36107.*
☎ **(205)242-5597 or FAX (205)240-3242.**

Auburn University College of Veterinary Medicine / Auburn (VS-1)

Emergency horse care. Call only for emergencies! May require referral from a vet. NO STALLS FOR TRANSIENT BOARDING.
⌖ *100 McAdory Hall, Auburn University, AL 36849*
☎ **(205) 844-4490**

Country Sunshine Ranch / Leeds Area (R-1)

2 miles to I-2 and I-459. Call for directions.
⚏ 5 stalls with straw @ $10/night. No stallions and requires health papers. Medium-size arena ✚ Dr. Murray in Pell City at (205) 338-1111 is only 15 minutes away. ◡ Farrier on call. ⋛ Fishing in area. ⛽ Fuel in Leeds.
✕ 4 miles away. 🚐 Electric hookups. ⊨ Have full bed and break-fast. $55 to $65 per night.
⌖ *Route 2/ Box 275, Leeds, AL 35094.*
☎ **(205) 699-9841**

Lazy D Ranch / Mobile Area (R-2)

Near Mobile. Call for directions. Off Highway 98 and I-65. ⚏ 15 stalls with feed, requires neg cog/ health papers. Call in evening/ask for Susan Schwartz. ✚ 20 minutes away. ✕ Try the Ol' Heidelberg Restaurant 3.5 miles west of Mobile on US 72 ☎ (205) 922-0556 or the Olive Garden closer in on US 72 ☎ (205) 539-1954.
⌖ *Stone Road End/ Box 1084, Semmes, AL 36575*
☎ **(205) 649-7715**

Paradise Stables / Grove Hill (S-1)

≋⚡❚✖

Off Rt. 43, Hebron Road (4 miles), then go right on dirt road 1 Mile; Stable on the left. ≋ 45 stalls, wood, including feed. ❚ On call. ⓘ Grove Hill--6 miles. ✖ Larry's Family Restaurant, Grove Hill--6 miles.

⌂ *Route 3/ Box 367, Grove Hill, AL 36451*

☎ **(205) 275-3983**

Tuskegee University School of Veterinary Medicine / Tuskegee (VS -2)

⌂

Emergency horse care 24 hours a day, 7 days a week. Call only for emergencies! May require referral from a vet. NO STALLS FOR TRANSIENT BOARDING. Facility on the campus. Get final directions when you call..

⌂ *Patterson Hall, Tuskegee, AL 36088*

☎ **(205) 727-8461**

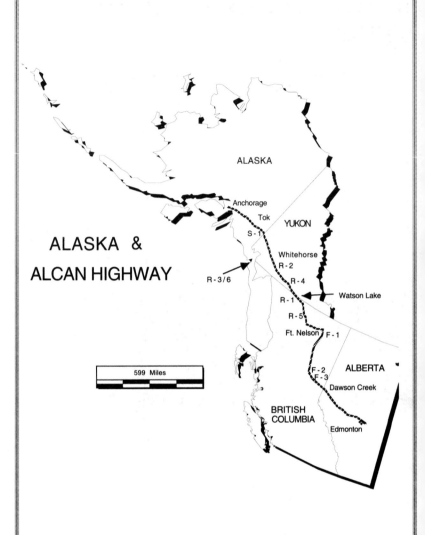

ALASKA & ALCAN HIGHWAY

ALASKA

Anchorage
Tok
S - 1

YUKON

Whitehorse
R - 2

R - 3/6

R - 4

Watson Lake

R - 1

R - 5

Ft. Nelson   F - 1

F - 2
F - 3

ALBERTA

Dawson Creek

BRITISH
COLUMBIA

Edmonton

599 Miles

The Stage Stop S-1	Ft. Nelson Fairground F-1
Bar None Ranch R-1	Ft. St John Rodeo F-2
Circle D Ranch R-2	Dawson Creek Fairgr. F-3
Donna/Wally Stock R-3	
Doug S. March R-4	
Stone Mt. Ranch R-5	
Macintosh Lodge R-6	

The Stage Stop / Tok, AK / ALCAN Highway (S-1)

1.7 miles from Tok Junction/Mile 122.9. 2nd mailbox on right from Tok, turn right onto driveway 200 feet and you are at the Stage Stop. If you pass Sourdough Campground you went too far! 2 - 10x12 stalls in new log barn and have 3 pole corrals. Bedding supplied. $15 per stall per night and $10 per corral. Stallions allowed. Require health papers. Bed & breakfast starting at $36 per night. Large country breakfast served before 8 a.m.--continental breakfast after 8 a.m. Camper/RV hookups @ $15 per night. Have showers. Saveway Store in Tok. Fast Eddys in Tok. 883-4411.

P.O. Box 69/ Mile 122.9 Tok Cutoff Road, Tok, AK 99780

☎ **(907) 883-5338**

Bar None Horse Ranches / Watson Lake, Yukon / ALCAN Highway (R-1)

Near KM 1015.3 ALCAN Highway across from truck scales. 4 stalls, 10X12 & running creek, private corrals, feed available. Cost per night up to customer. Stallions allowed. ➕ Vet nearby. Camper/ RV, without hookups. Esso Watson Lake. Plenty of mechanics in Watson Lake. Recommend Watson Lake Iron Works. ❌ Watson Lake Hotel has good food. ➤ Excellent fishing in numerous lakes, including Watson Lake.

Box 502, Watson Lake,YT YOA 1CO, CANADA

☎ **(403) 536-7501**

Circle D Ranch / Whitehorse, Yukon ALCAN Highway (R-2)

West of Whitehorse on ALCAN Highway (KM 1512). 5 corrals, , incl. bedding @ $5 per night. Stallions allowed and do require health papers. ➕ Vet in Whitehorse. Farrier available. At Husky Fuel. Mechanic Art Lock, 1 mile away at KM 1510 ☎ 633-5036. ❌ Porter Place good place to eat in Whitehorse. ➤ Plenty of fishing in area.

Box 4942, Whitehorse, YT Y1A 4S2 CANADA.

☎ **(403) 668-1045**

Donna & Wally Stock /Haines Junction Yukon / ALCAN Highway (R-3)

≠$$

3/4 mile north of Haines Junction. **≠** 2 small corrals @ $10 per night. Please call first.

☏ *Box 5464, Haines Junction, YT YOB 1L0 CANADA*

☎ **(403) 634-2606**

Doug S. March / ALCAN Highway / Teslin Yukon (R-4)

≠

Overnight corral 9 miles south of Teslin. Call in advance for directions.

☎ **(403) 390-2559**

Stone Mountain Safaris / Toad River, BC Mile 675 / ALCAN Highway (R-5)

≠⊨$

Must call ahead for availability/reservations. Open area suitable for horses and supposed to be a good layover stop. Latest information: 2 or 3 corrals. Rates and availability not verified--owner not available at press time. ⊨ Bed and breakfast available.

☎ **(604) 232-5469**

Macintosh Lodge / Haines Junction / Mile 1022 / ALCAN Highway (R-6)

≠🚗🐎➕☽✸🛢❌$

6 miles out of Haines Junction. You can take the ferry from there or make it by road in 10 hours to Anchorage. **≠**Accommodations for horses with quite a bit of room to move around in, according to operator. 🚗 Motel accommodations. Tenting is free with showers at $3 per person. 🐎 Gateway to one of Canada's finest parks, Kluane National Park (pronounced Clue-an-ee). ➕ Vet is Wendy Royle at ☎ (403) 633-6137. ☽ Farrier is Cliff Hanna at ☎ (403) 633-4071. ✸ Mechanic in residence. 🛢 Fuel available at Lodge. ❌ Cafe and bar at the Lodge.

☏ *Mile 1022 ALCAN Highway, YT Y1A 3V4 , CANADA*

☎ **(403) 634-2301**

Fort Nelson Fairgrounds / Ft. Nelson / BC / ALCAN Highway (F-1)

≠✸🛢❌

At milepost 292 on the ALCAN Highway. Call ahead for availability. **≠** Corrals with water free of charge. Feed not included but that can be purchased locally. ✸🛢❌ These services available. For food, try the Coach House Inn at Milepost 300. ☎ **(604) 774-3730**

☎ **(604) 774-6827**(Mr. & Mrs. Lauren Bumstead) **or (604) 774-6408**

Fort St. John Rodeo Grounds / Ft. St. John / BC (F-2)

On west side of road. Locals recommend Ft. St. John horse layover only for emergencies. Could not verify availability of corrals. These services available in Ft. St. John. For food, try the Pioneer Inn in the center of town at 9830 100th Ave.
Contact Tammy Webb at ☎ **(604) 789-9096.**

Dawson Creek Fairgrounds / Dawson Creek, BC (F-3)

Fairgrounds near airport/Auction Mart. 7 barns with stalls, water, hay, and caretaker. Availability good during summer, sometimes tight in winter. Stalls @ $10 per night and that includes free use of indoor arena. These services available in Dawson Creek. For food, try the Alaska Cafe on 10th Street near Milepost "0" ☎ **(604) 782-7040.**
☎ **(604) 782-2704**(caretaker) **or (604) 843-7788** (Larry Fosum)

Fairbanks Homestead, circa 1968   © Bruce McAllister

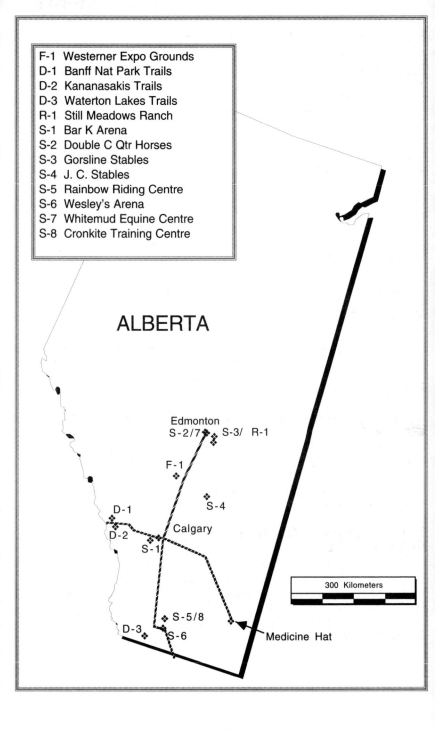

F-1 Westerner Expo Grounds
D-1 Banff Nat Park Trails
D-2 Kananasakis Trails
D-3 Waterton Lakes Trails
R-1 Still Meadows Ranch
S-1 Bar K Arena
S-2 Double C Qtr Horses
S-3 Gorsline Stables
S-4 J. C. Stables
S-5 Rainbow Riding Centre
S-6 Wesley's Arena
S-7 Whitemud Equine Centre
S-8 Cronkite Training Centre

ALBERTA

Edmonton
S-2/7   S-3/ R-1

F-1

S-4

D-1

D-2   Calgary

S-1

300 Kilometers

S-5/8

D-3   S-6

Medicine Hat

Bar K Arena / Calgary (S-1)
≋✚⊍⌂✕

4 miles east of city limits. Call for directions. Contact: Lyle Keeler.
≋ 19 wood stalls with bedding. 68X108 arena. ✚⊍ Vet and farrier
available. ⌂✕ These services within 10 miles.
☏ *RR #6, Calgary, AB T2M 4L5 CANADA*
☎ **(403) 285-9126**

Cronkite Training Centre / Lethbridge (S-8)
≋⌐⊂✚⊍⌂✕

Off #4 highway 10 minutes southeast of Lethbridge. ≋ Several stalls
with bedding. Stallions allowed. Contact: Fred Cronkite. ⌐⊂ Camper
RV hookups and showers available. ✚⊍ Vet and farrier available in
Lethbridge. ⌂✕ These services available within 10 miles.
☏ *RR #8-10-6, Lethbridge AB T1J 4P4 CANADA*
☎ **(403) 327-9380**

Double C Quarter Horses/ Edmonton (S-2)
≋✚⊍⌂✕

On Highway 2N/NW of Edmonton. Call for directions. ≋ 18 wood
stalls with bedding. 168 acres, 60X160 indoor arena, 15 outdoor pens
with shelters. ✚⊍⌂✕ These services available-- large urban area.
☏ *RR #8 / 15519 156th Street, Edmonton, AB T5L 4H8 CANADA*
☎ **(403) 447-2915**

Gorsline Stables / Sherwood Park (S-3)
≋⌐⊂✚$$

East of Sherwood. Call for directions. 65 wood stalls with bedding
@ $15 per night. ⌐⊂ Campground 7 minutes away. ✚ Vet within 5
minutes' drive.
☏ *52358 Range Road #223, Sherwood Park, AB T1C 1B1 CANADA*
☎ **(403) 922- 3915**

J. C. Stables / Stettler (S-4)
≋⊰⊍⌂✕

Call ahead for directions. This is a commercial thoroughbred breeding
farm. Contact: Ted Connor. 30 stalls with bedding. Check ahead if you
have a stallion. ⊰ This is a good fishing area. ✚ Clinic with 4 vets
nearby. ⊍ Farrier nearby. ⌂✕ These services available in Stettler.
☏ *Box 1150, Stettler, AB T0C 2L0 CANADA*
☎ **(403) 742-2275**

Camping in the High Country near Banff

Wranglers from Warner Guiding
Banff

Rainbow Riding Centre / Lethbridge (S-5)

≣⊒⚘⊕∪▯▨⊠$$

3 miles east of Lethbridge. Call for directions. ≣⊒ 32 12X12 stalls
with bedding @ $ 15 per night. ⚘ Electric hookups @ $5 per night.
⊕Vet in Coaldale at ☎ 345-2000. ∪ Farrier available in Taber at
☎ 223-1689. ▨⊠ These services available within 5 miles.
   ⊕ *RR #8 - 24-6, Lethbridge, AB   T1J 4P4 CANADA*
☎ **(403) 328-2165**

Still Meadows Ranch / Sherwood Park Area (R-1)

≣⊒⚘▼⭐⊕∪▯▨⊠$$

Call for directions. ≣⊒ Box and tie stalls @ $ 10 per night. Pens also
available. This has been a family business since 1981 and Brian and
Maxine Rusnack also have ▼ a tack shop on the premises.
⚘ Camper RV hookups 2 miles away at Kawtikh. ⭐ Trail riding
available. ⊕ Vet available. ∪ Farrier on the premises. ▨⊠ These services available in Tofield or Sherwood Park.
   ⊕ *General Delivery, N. Cooking Lake, AB   T0B 3N0 CANADA*
☎ **(403) 922-5566**

Wesley's Arena / Raymond (S-6)

≣⊒⚘⊕▯▨⊠

5 miles west of Highway #4. Call for directions. 50 miles north of the
border. Owner Arnold Wesley very helpful! ≣⊒ 12 wood stalls and
outside pens. Stallions allowed. ⚘ Electric hookups. ⊕ Vet in
Raymond. ▨⊠ These services available in Raymond.
   ⊕ *Box 537, Raymond, AB T0K 2S0 CANADA*
☎ **(403) 756-3986**

Westerner Exposition Grounds / Red Deer (F-1)

≣⊒⚘⊕∪▯▨⊠

On Highway 2, south of Red Deer. Call ahead for reservations. Open
8:30-4:30 daily. Host many horse shows, so stalls not always available.
≣⊒ 400 metal stalls and 2 outside rings. ⊕∪ Vet and farrier in the
area. ▨⊠ These services available in Red Deer.
☎ **(403) 343-7800**

Whitemud Equine Centre / Edmonton (S-7)

≣⊒≣⊕∪▯▨⊠$$

#16 west of #2 to Whitemud Freeway. Exit at Fox Drive. Go 3 blocks
and turn at Keiller Road. Contact: Jean Archer. ≣⊒ 110 wood stalls
with straw bedding @ $15 per night for box stalls and @ $12 per night
for tie stalls. Stalls range from 10X10 box to 10X15 tie.

No stallions allowed and must have neg cog/ current health papers.
≋ Fishing in the area. ✚ Vet in Sherwood Park at ☎ (403) 467- 3765.
♾ Farrier on site at ☎ 467-3264.⚒ Mechanic 1 mile away at Grandview
Esso at ☎ (403) 436-4192. Open 7 a.m.-10 p.m. 🛢 Husky Truck Stop in
Edmonton at ☎ (403) 434-7020. ✖ On Fortieth in Edmonton at
☎ (403) 430-7171.
⌖ *12505 Keillor Road, Edmonton, AB T6G 2L6 CANADA*
☎ **(403) 435-3597**

Banff National Park / Banff (D-1)

≋🐎≋🛢⚒✖

Easiest way to Banff is Route 1 from Calgary. This national park has some nice horse trails for day or overnight trips. There are scenic trips to the following places in the Park: Johnson Canyon, Elk Lake Summit, and Mystic Lake. In Banff, the Parks Information office is at 224 Banff Avenue, ☎ (403) 762-4256 and they are open daily from 8 a.m. to 10 p.m. ≋ On Birch Avenue Brewster Stables might have a stall available if you make advance arrangements. ☎ (403) 762-2832. An excellent guide service is Warner & MacKenzie Guiding and Outfitting at ⌖ Box 2280, Banff, AB T0L 0C0. Their office in Banff is in the Trail Rider Store at 132 Banff Avenue. ☎ **(403) 762-4551 or (800) 661-8352**

Kananasakis Country / Canmore (D-2)

🐎≋🛢⚒✖

Pine forests, granite peaks and big stands of aspen. And the jumping off place, Canmore, is more reasonable during the summer season than Banff. Canmore is 25 miles east of Banff and this area is less regulated than the national parks. For helpful trail information, contact Boundary Stables, Box 44, Kananasakis Village, AB T0L 2H0. ☎ (403) 591-7171.
✖ Pepper Mill on 9th Street ☎ 678-2292.
⌖ *Kananaskis , # 412/ 1011 Glenmore Trail SW, Calgary, AB T2V 4R6 CANADA*

Waterton Lakes National Park / Waterton Lakes (D-3)

🐎 ⛺🚐≋

This park is the meeting of prairie and mountains and it's partners with its U.S. neighbor, Glacier National Park. 🐎 Park authorities say that most trails are open to horses-there are mandatory horse guidelines. 3 RV sites: Townsite, Crandell Mountain and Belly River.
☎ **(403) 859-2262 or 859-2224**

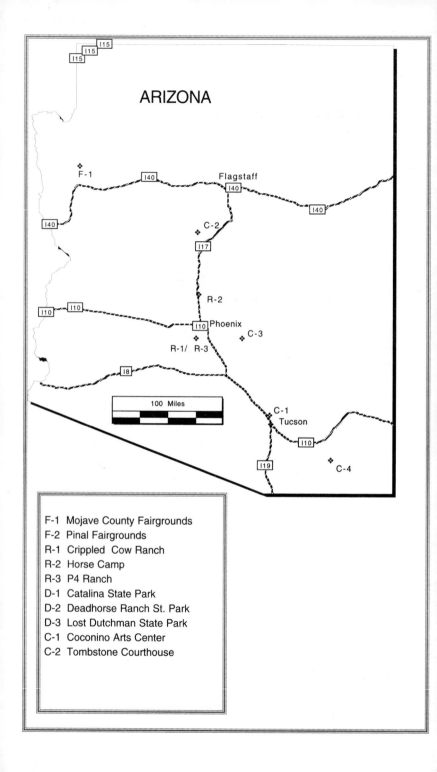

ARIZONA

F-1

I40   Flagstaff

C-2

I17

R-2

I10   Phoenix

C-3

R-1/ R-3

I8

100 Miles

C-1
Tucson

I10

I19   C-4

F-1 Mojave County Fairgrounds
F-2 Pinal Fairgrounds
R-1 Crippled Cow Ranch
R-2 Horse Camp
R-3 P4 Ranch
D-1 Catalina State Park
D-2 Deadhorse Ranch St. Park
D-3 Lost Dutchman State Park
C-1 Coconino Arts Center
C-2 Tombstone Courthouse

Crippled Cow Ranch / Laveen (R-1)

5 miles from I-10. From I-10 take 51st Ave. south, Dobbins east, 43rd Ave. south to 43rd and Elliot. ▬ 4 30X30 metal stalls with bedding and auto H20. Price per night negotiable. ⛟ Camper/RV hookups with water. Price per night negotiable. ≽ Fishing in the area. ➕Ʊ Vet and farrier in Laveen. ▧▨ These services available within 3 miles.
⚕ *4232 West Sunrise, Laveen, AZ 85339*
☎ **(602) 237-4351**

Horse Camp / Phoenix Area (R-2)

27624 North 42nd Street in Cave Creek. 10 miles north of Scottsdale and 10 miles east of Deer Valley. 15 miles north of Phoenix on I-17. ▬ 40 stalls ranging in size from 16X21 to 24x24. No stallions nor bedding provided. Metal stalls with auto H20 @ $10 per night. Health papers are required. Horse Camp is a 12 acre operation. ➕ Good vets in Cave Creek and Phoenix. Ʊ Farrier available from Phoenix. ⛟ Have Camper/RV hookups (8 available) ✎ Mechanic within 10 miles. ⛽ Fuel at Cave Creek and Phoenix. ▨ Cave Creek and Phoenix.
⚕ *27624 North 42nd Street, Cave Creek, AZ 85331*
☎ **(602) 585-4628**

Mojave County Fairgrounds / Kingman (F-1)

1 mile west of I-40 in Kingman/ take the Fairgrounds Exit. ▬ 200 metal stalls. Stall per night @ $7. ➕ Vet in Kingman. Ʊ Farrier in Kingman. ≽ Fishing in Kingman area. ⛟ Camper/RV hookups and showers. ⛽ Plenty of gas stations in Kingman. ✎ Good mechanic within 1 mile. ⛽ Fuel up at the Circle K 1/2 mile away. ▨ Golden Corral 1/2 mile away.
⚕ *P.O. Box 6115, Kingman, AZ 86402*
☎ **(602) 753-2636**

P4 Ranch/ Phoenix Area (R-3)

Located at 29448 North 53rd Street in Cave Creek. Call for directions. ▬ 8 wood box stalls with bedding. Stalls @ $15 per night and accept American Express Cards. This includes use of entire facility. Have outdoor 150X275 arena plus round and square pens. Have fly control, tack room and wash racks, trailer parking, customer lounge, courtyard and barbeque grill. Bill & Jo Paige are native Arizonians and have been at this location since 1986. Stallions are allowed. ➕ Vet on premises/14 years. experience. Ʊ Farrier on premises. ✎ Nearest mechanic is J. Scurnopoli at 992-3030. Nearest trailer dealer is J. Page at 585-0855. ▮ Kwikstop gas station at 585-6539.☒ Best place to eat is Harold's Corral at 488-1906. 🚐 Good lodging at Tumbleweed Motel at 488-3668. 🐎 Good trail rides from P4 Ranch or north of Cave Creek.

🛈 *29448 North 53rd Street, Cave Creek, AZ 85331*
☎ **(602) 585-0855**

Pinal County Fairgrounds / Coolidge (F-2)
⇌$

Located at 11 Mile Corner Road. ⇌ 60 stalls @ $5 per night. Contact: Terry Haifley.

🛈 *P.O. Box 3110, Casa Grande, AZ 85222*
☎ **(602) 723-5242**

Catalina State Park / Tucson Area (D-1)
🐎📷$

Park is located at base of NW slopes of Catalina mountains, 9 miles north of Tucson on Route 89. Equestrian Center at Park has stalls, charges $7 per vehicle. Many interesting cactus and pictographs at nearby Saguaro National Monument.

🛈 *Catalina State Park, Box 36986, Tucson, AZ 85740*
☎ **(602) 628-5798**

Dead Horse Ranch State Park / Clarkdale (D-2)
🐎🚐🎣

The park is across the river north of Cottonwood/North 5th Street off Route 89A. There are 2-3 corrals, 2 areas for horse camping. 12 horses maximum. Good access to Pecks Lake and Coconino National Forest.🚐 There are 45 campsites available. 🎣 Trout, bass, catfish in either park lagoon or Verde River.

🛈 *Dead Horse Ranch State Park, Box 144, Cottonwood, AZ 86326*
☎ **(602) 634-5283**

Lost Dutchman State Park / Phoenix (D-3)
🐎📷

Northeast of Phoenix and 6 miles NE of Apache Junction on Route 88. 4 stables in area (OK Corral, Superstition Stables, Don Donnelly Ranch, and Meanwhile Back At the Ranch). The last one is a fancy dude ranch. This is a day-use-only park and best trailhead is Cholla. There are good pull through parking areas, good variety of cactus, and great views of the Sonora Desert.

🛈 *Lost Dutchman State Park, 6109 North Apache Trail, Apache Junction, AZ 85219*
☎ **(602) 982-4485**

Coconino Center for the Arts / Flagstaff (C-1)
📷

Just north of Flagstaff on US 180. Every spring the Center presents a cross section of cowboy life. The cowboy art includes saddles, buckles, boots, oil paintings, and photographs. There are also some workshops. Called "Trappings of the American West", the exhibit usually opens in late April and runs into early June.

✝ *P.O. Box 296, Flagstaff, AZ 86002*
☎ **(602) 779-6921**

Tombstone Courthouse State Historical Park / Tombstone (C-2)
📷

Located at 219 East Toughnut Street in town off Route 80. Noted for Earp-Clanton gun fight. Walk through Boot Hill Graveyard and get a slice of western history!

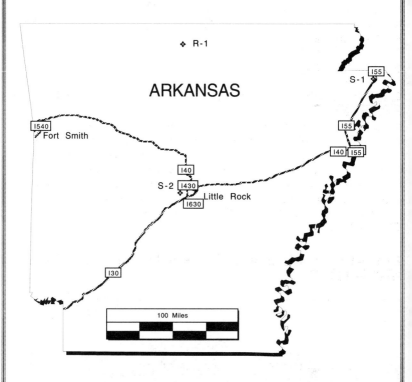

ARKANSAS

R-1

S-1

I55

I540
Fort Smith

I55

I40 I55

I40
I430
S-2
Little Rock

I630

I30

100 Miles

Carter Creek Farm S-3
Circle S Horse Motel S-1
Daystar Arabians S-4
Double S Oaks Ranch R-1
Economy Feed & Tack TS-1
Fox Creek Farm S-2
Stonegate S-5

Carter Creek Farm/ Mena (S-3)

In Mena. Near Routes 30 and 40. Call for directions and reservations necessary. 20 wood stalls with bedding @ $10 per night. Current health papers required. This facility backs onto the Wichita mountains which have 1000's of acres of trails. Camper RV hookups in town and in nearby state park. 2 vets in Mena. Several farriers in the area. These services available in Mena. For food, try the Lime Tree at the Best Western.

Route #1/ Box 181-A, Mena, AR 71953

☎ **(501) 394-2874 or 394-7356**

Circle S Horse Motel / Blytheville (S-1)

From I-55, take Exit 63, go south on Route 61 10 miles to 3344 north US Highway 61. 15 stalls with bedding. Lighted indoor arena. Current health papers required. Stallions allowed. Vet 2 miles away. Farrier 3 miles away. Grecian's Steakhouse on other side of town a good place for dinner. Camper RV hookups available at extra charge. Roadrunner Gas Station 1/2 mile away.

3344 North U.S. Highway 61, Blytheville, AR 72315

☎ **(501) 763-9203**

Daystar Arabians / Ft. Smith Area (S-2)

8.5 miles south of Hackett on Highway 45. Facility .5 miles west of road and not visible from it. Large abandoned pit/ open area at turnoff. Call for directions if not coming from Hackett.

26 12X12 stalls @ $5 per night. Neg. cog/ health papers required. 60X100 indoor and outdoor arenas. This is an excellent facility and has a tack shop. Owner is quite progressive and this a good place to layover. She also buys and sells horses. Plenty of trails nearby. This is hilly country with plenty of open fields. Vet 20 minutes away. These services available in Hackett, on Route 71, and in

Ft. Smith. Calico County in Ft. Smith has good hamburgers and, for the budget minded, plenty of fast food places in same area.
⌕ *P.O. Box 349, Hackett, AR 72937*
☎ **(501) 639-2401**

Double S Oaks Ranch/ Mt. Home (R-1)

Off Highway 5, 6 miles north of Mt. Home. Must call in advance.
50 stalls with metal piping @ $6 per night and feed @ $2 per day. Have 90 acres of pasture- this is a working cattle ranch. Health papers are required and stallions are allowed. ✚ Vet in the area. ⚒ Farrier in the area. ⚓ Fishing and swimming. ⤜ Trails at Bull Shoals Lake.
⌕ *Route 1/ Box 52, Midway, AR 72651*
☎ **(501) 481-5225**

Economy Feed & Tack / Ft. Smith (TS-1)

2 miles south of Ft. Smith on Highway 71 on the west side of the road. Well stocked store with about anything you might need and some good values in used saddles. Hay and bedding. Worth a detour! Owner very helpful with finding vets, etc.
⌕ *11318 Highway 71 South, Ft. Smith, AR 72916*
☎ **(501) 646-5043**

Fox Creek Farm / Little Rock (S-2)

Take Exit #4 off I-430 and turn west on Col. Glenn Road. Go approximately 200 yards until you reach first black top road (Bowman Road). Take a right and go 1/4 mile.Farm will be on your left. 28

8X10 concrete block/ wood stalls with bedding @ $12.50 per night. Current health papers are required and stallions are allowed. ✚ Vet in Little Rock. We will call them if you are staying with us. These services readily available in the Little Rock area.⌕ *4100 Bowman Road, Little Rock, AR 72210*
☎ **(501) 225- 9384**

Stonegate Center / Ft. Smith Area (S-5)

Call for directions and reservations. paddock boards and planning to build stalls. Nice layout but important to call ahead. Owned and run by a vet. Require neg. cog/ health papers within past 6 months. Farrier available from Alma. These services available in Ft. Smith (see Daystar listing).

3718 East Highway 451 Rye Hill, Ft. Smith, AR 72901

☎ **(501) 649-0612**

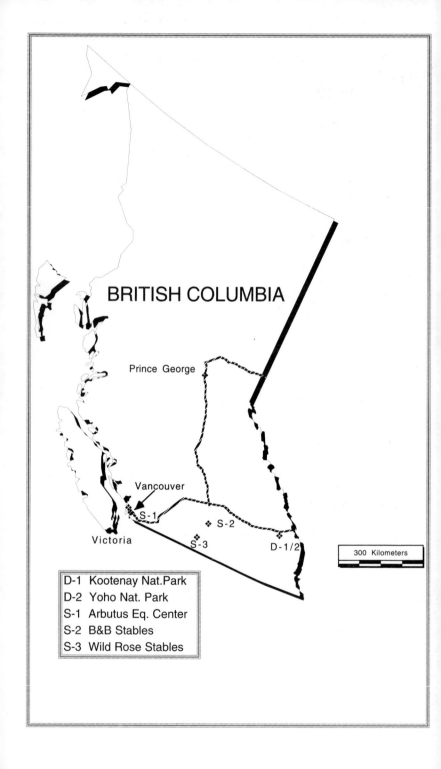

BRITISH COLUMBIA

Prince George

Vancouver

S-1

S-2

Victoria

S-3

D-1/2

300 Kilometers

D-1 Kootenay Nat.Park
D-2 Yoho Nat. Park
S-1 Arbutus Eq. Center
S-2 B&B Stables
S-3 Wild Rose Stables

Arbutus Meadows Equestrian Center / Nanoose Bay (S-1)

=== 🚐 ≡🔲🔪⊠ $$$

On Vancouver Island. Call for directions. === 10 wood outdoor covered stalls with bedding @ $25. 200X300 indoor arena with jumping ring. 🚐 Plenty of beautiful campgrounds on the island-as well as motels and lodges. ≡ Salmon at different times of the year.
🔲 Vet within 15 miles. 🔪⊠ These services all within 2 miles.
🕆 *1515 Island Highway, Nanoose Bay, BC V0R 2R0 CANADA*
☎ **(604) 468- 2345**

B & B Stables / Kelowna (S-2)

=== 🚐 ≡🔲🐎🔪⊠ $$

West of Highway 97 north to S. Smith-right on Curtis-right on North Valley Road. Call for final directions. === 27 wood stalls with bedding @ $10 per night. Require health papers and stallions allowed.
🚐 Electric hookups and showers @ $ 10 per night. ≡ Fishing in the area. 🔲 Vet in Kelowna at ☎ 491- 0969. 🔪⊠ These services available in Kelowna.
🕆 *840 Valley Road, RR#1/ Site 22/ Comp. 10, Kelowna, BC V1Y 7P9 CANADA*
☎ **(604) 861-5775**

Wild Rose Stables / Naramata (S-3)

=== ⊨🐎

Call for directions and reservations. === 5 paddocks with shelters.
🐎 "Leave our covered paddocks and arena for a ride into the Okanagan Mountain Park which includes 70,000 acres."
⊨ 1 suite available but only with advance notice. Includes breakfast.
🕆 *RR# 1, S4 C5, Naramata, BC V0H 1N0 CANADA*
☎ **(604) 496-5720**

Kootenay National Park / Radium Hot Springs Area (D-1)

🐎≡

 Over 100 miles of trails to alpine meadows, mountain lakes and snow fields. Camping is available at Redstreak, McLeod Meadows, and Marble Canyon campsites.
🕆 *Superintendent, Kootenay National Park, Box 220, Radium Hot Springs, BC V0A 1M0 CANADA*
☎ **(604) 347-9615**

North American Horse Travel Guide

Yoho National Park / Field Area (D-2)

🐎

Follow Route 1 west of Lake Louise. Yoho means "awesome" in Indian language and the park does include some of the most dramatic terrain in the Canadian Rockies. This park includes lofty peaks, glacial lakes, primitive forests, waterfalls, and alpine meadows.

🐎 The following trails are open to horses in this beautiful park: From Amiskwi Pass south to Kicking Horse FireRoad (35.5 km); Ottertail Fire Road to Goodsir Pass (14 km.) and Ice River Fire Road to Hoodoo Creek (17.5 km) which has campgrounds.

⚲ *Superintendent, Yoho National Park, Box 99, Field, BC V0A 1G0*

☎ **(604) 343-6324**

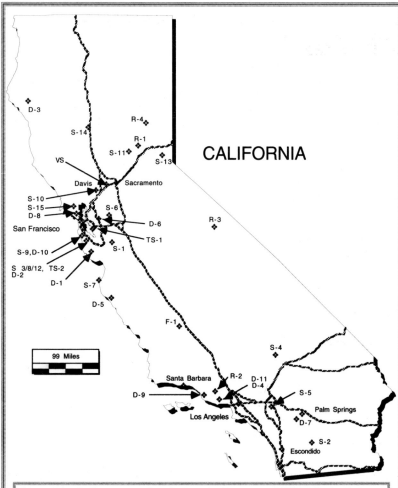

CALIFORNIA

99 Miles

Grant Ranch S-1	R & R Ranch R-2	CTETA Park D-2
Horse & Human TS-1	The Ranch S-9	Humboldt Area D-3
Hungry Horse R-1	Ranchotel S-10	Malibu SP D-4
Lazy Circle K S-2	Raptor Stables S-11	Molera Rides D-5
Lost Hills KOA F-1	Sierra Meadows R-3	Mt Diablo SP D-6
Mar-Son's Farm S-3	Springdown S-12	Mt San Jacinto D-7
Martinez Motel S-4	Squaw Valley S-13	Mt Tamalpais D-8
Menifee Ranch S-5	Sun Hunter S-14	Pt Mugu SP D-9
Nebergall's S-6	Sunset Corral S-15	Seahorse D-10
Olsen Nolte TS-2	UC/Davis VetS VS	Topanga SP D-11
Pebble Beach S-7	Whitehawk R-4	
Portola Farms S-8	Big Basin Area D-1	

California

Grant Ranch Stables & Equestrian Center / San Jose (S-1)
≡◘U▯❋◙≋$$$

10 miles from Highway 680 at 18415 Mt. Hamilton Road. From 680 go east to Alumrock Ave, then south to Mt. Hamilton Ave. ≡ 21 stalls, 11 metal, remainder wood with bedding (at $20 per night). Most are 12X12. Stallions allowed. ◘ Nearest vet is in Milpitas at ☎ (408) 946-6888. U Nearest farrier is Tom Richey in San Jose at ☎ (408) 274-1481. Showers, water available, but no RV hookups. ❋ Nearest mechanic is 10 miles away (Evergreen Auto at 2983 S. King Road). ☎ (408) 238-1003 and he's open M-F, 8-6. ▮❋ San Jose (9 miles away).
⌂ *18415 Mt. Hamilton Road, San Jose, CA 95140*
☎ **(408) 274-9258**

Horse & Human Connection Center / Hayward (TS-1)
▼

Tack, hay, and grain. ⌂ *3871 Breakwater Avenue, Hayward, CA 94545*
☎ **(510) 591-4403**

Hungry Horse Guest Ranch / Stallion Springs Ranch / Nevada City (R-1)
≡◘U⬤≋▮❋$$

There are two ranches in this operation. One is 2.5 miles from Highway 49 at 16254 Grizzly Ridge Road, Nevada City. The other further off Highway 49 at 18292 Oak Tree Road in Nevada City. Call ahead for complete directions. ≡ 38 12X12 stalls with many pastures. 8 are wood and 30 are metal and include bedding. Stalls @ $10 per night and incl. auto H2O. Need health papers and stallions are allowed. ⬤ Camper RV hookups on 700 acres and solar showers available. Hookups @ $10 per night. ≋ Fishing in the area is good. ❋ Dick Turnbow Auto at 19987 Oak Tree Road. ☎ 292-3429. Open 7 days a week. ▮ Closest gas station is UNOCAL. ❋ Peterson's Corner at north San Juan at ☎ (916) 292-3311.
⌂ *Sharon Butler, P.O. Box 1390, Nevada City, CA 95959*
☎ **(916) 478-9058**

Lazy Circle K Farm/Borrego Springs (S-2)
≡◘U❋▮❋$$

West of S-3. Call for directions. 7 metal stalls with bedding @ $15 per night. Range in size from 12X12 to 12X16. Stallions allowed and require current health papers. Vet in Brawley at ☎ (619) 344-3531. U Farrier in Ranchita. ❋ Nearest mechanic--4 miles away. ▮ Fuel in Borrego Springs. ❋ Food at La Casa Del Zorro Resort in Borrego Springs at ☎ 767-5323. ⌂ *P.O. Box 335, Borrego Springs, CA 92004*
☎ **(619) 767-3200**

Lost Hills KOA Campground / Lost Hills (F-1)

≣ 🚐 🄌 🕊 🐎 $

Call for directions ≣ 4 12X24 metal stalls with no bedding @ $7.50 per night. Stallions allowed. 🄌 Vet 20 miles away. 🚐 80 camper RV hookups with water, showers, laundry, and children's playground @ $20 per night. 🕊 Good mechanic is Roy Johnson 20 miles away at ☎ (805) 758-2683.

✝ *P.O. Box 276, Lost Hills, CA 93249*

☎ **(805) 797-2719**

Mar-Son's Charter Oak Farm / Woodside (S-3)

≣ 🄌 🕊 🄌 ✖

Off Route 280 near Woodside. Call for reservations. Access can be confusing, so get directions at same time. Located at 880 Runnymede Road quite near 280. ≣ 63 stalls, 12X12 with shavings, auto H2O and current health papers required. A first class operation! 🄌🕊 Vets and farriers on call. 🕊✖ These services available in Woodside.

✝ *880 Runnymede Road, Woodside, CA 94062*

☎ **(415) 851-4011**

Martinez Horse Motel / Barstow (S-4)

≣ 🚐 🐎 🄌 🕊 🄌 ✖ $$

From I-15 go 3.5 miles west on Route 58. ≣ 15 stalls w/o bedding @ $10 per night. Range in size from 18X18 to 24X24. Stallions allowed. 🚐 Electricity and water available for Camper /RVs. 🐎 Open BLM land nearby. 🄌 Vet 6 miles away. 🕊 Farrier available. 🕊 Nearest mechanic 3 miles away at City-Metro ☎ (619) 256-5007. 🄌✖ Fuel and food within 1 mile.

✝ *27702 Waterman Street, Barstow, CA 92311*

☎ **(619) 256-3671**

Menifee Valley Ranch / Menifee (S-5)

≣ 🄌 🕊 🄌 ✖ $$

From Corona and Highway 91 take Freeway 15 south towards San Diego. Get off at Bundy Cyn and take Scott Road east to 28940 Scott Road--ranch will be on your left. ≣ 40 12X12 wood/metal stalls with bedding @ $12 per night. Require health papers and stallions are allowed. 🄌 Vet in Temecula. 🕊 Farrier in Menifee at ☎ (909) 672-8113. 🕊 5 miles away at ☎ (909) 928- 9699.

✝ *28940 Scott Road, Menifee, CA 92584*

☎ **(909) 672-8113 or FAX (909) 672-8119**

Mar- Son's Indoor Arena

Nebergall's Stables / Tracy-Stockton Area (S-6)

On Highway 4 between Brentwood and Stockton and Tracy. Call for directions. ▰ 2 10X12 stalls with shavings. No stallions allowed. ☐ Camper/RV hookups available. ☐ Vets in Oakley/ Pleasant Hill. ♨ Farrier available.☰ Delta fishing. ⚒ Closest mechanic 1.5 miles away.
⌂ *2650 Sellers Avenue, Brentwood, CA 94513*
☎ **(510) 634-2535**

Olsen Nolte Saddle / San Carlos (TS-2)

Excellent merchandise, custom saddles and tack.
⌂ *1580 El Camino Real, San Carlos, CA 94070*
☎ **(415) 591-4403**

Pebble Beach Equestrian Center / Pebble Beach (S-7)

Call for directions. At press time, this beautiful facility is planning new stalls, so might have something available but must make reservations. ⤳ Excellent trail rides on 30 miles of heavily forested country down to beach. Will supply maps free of charge--but call ahead for arranging access to trails--might need keys, etc.⛓ Hudson and Company in Pebble Beach has an excellent selection of horse blankets and boots.
⌂ *P.O. Box 1498, Pebble Beach, CA 93953*
☎ **(408) 624-2756**

Portola Farms / Woodside (S-8)

3 miles west of 280 Freeway on 1545 Portola Road on north side of road. Specialize in hunter-jumper. ▰ 100 12X12 stalls with shavings, nice layout, friendly people! Large outdoor arena. ☐♨ Vets and farriers on call.. ⚒ Closest truck mechanic is in Woodside at Chevron. ⛽ Available in Woodside. ☒ Variety of restaurants in Woodside.
⌂ *1545 Portola Road , Woodside, CA 94062*
☎ **(415) 851-2676**

R & R Ranch / Moorpark (R-2)

1 mile off Freeway 118. Take one way only from Freeway 118 to 4302

Hitch Blvd. 4 inside stalls with bedding and auto H20 @ $15 per night. Outside stalls @ $10 per night. Camper RV hookups available @ $12 per night. Vet in Moorpark/Somis at ☎ (805) 386-4291. Farrier available in Moorpark at ☎ 529-0965. Mechanic at Ralph's Automotive 5 miles away at 2180 First Street in Simi Valley. Open 7:30 a.m. - 6:00 p.m. Mon-Fri.

☎ (805) 522-5769. Fuel at J. E. Clark Corp. in Moorpark at ☎ (805) 525-1525. Try the Coffee Grinder in Moorpark at ☎ (805) 529-2288.

⌂ *4302 Hitch Blvd., Moorpark, CA 93021*

☎ **(805) 523-7681**

The Ranch / Moss Beach (S-9)

Nice layout near Half Moon Bay. 10 stalls. Call ahead for directions and reservations. Access could be a problem for extra-long trailers so check with them first! Good vet nearby.

⌂ *1591 Sunshine Valley Road, Moss Beach, CA 94038*

☎ **(415) 728-9538**

Ranchotel Horse Center / Vacaville (S-10)
〓⊞♘≋✦✖▼ $$

On Interstate 80, 1 mile west of Vacaville.
〓 12 12X12 stalls with wood shavings @ $15 per night. Stallions may be allowed with advance notice. Large 80X120 indoor arena, 2 outdoor arenas with grandstand. ▼ Have tack store on the premises. ⊞ Vets in Vacaville or at University of California at Davis. ♘ Farriers on call. ≋ Fishing in the area. ✦ Good mechanic at Wayne's Auto Clinic 1 mile away. ☎ (707) 446-4343/ open 8 to 5, 5 days a week. ⛽ Fuel available in Vacaville (1 mile away). ✖ Nut Tree Restaurant (3 miles away).
✝ *P.O. Box 6, Vacaville, CA 95696*
☎ **(707) 448-2435**

Raptor Stables / Grass Valley (S-11)
〓

Call for directions and reservations. 11402 Idaho Maryland Road In Grass Valley on Idaho Maryland Road. 〓 Have 115 stalls.
✝ *P.O. Box 532, Rough & Ready, CA 95975* ☎ **(916) 272-4920**

Sierra Meadows Ranch / Mammoth Lakes Area (R-3)
〓⊞♘≋🐎✖🚐 $$

Located at 1 Sherwin Creek Road. Call for directions.
〓 Up to 100 24X24 pipe corral stalls with water in barrels @ $15 per night .Bedding extra. No stallions allowed. ⊞ Nearest vets: 2/ Mammoth, 4 /Bishop. ☎ (619) 873-5801.
♘ Several farriers avail-

able.  Campers that are self contained can stay at our facility overnight for no charge. ✎ On premises/Kirk Robertson at ☎ 934-6161 or Perea Bros. at ☎ 934-2202. For trailer repair try Coach & Camper Service. at ☎ (619)872-4921. ▮ 5 gas stations within 1 mile. ☒ Ranch House Cafe on premises good place to eat. ⚞ This ranch is located in the Inyo National Forest where there are many trailheads that lead to back country and hay meadow riding. Currently the ranch is working with Mammoth Lakes and USFS to survey and map all horse trails in the area.

⚐ *Gail Fetherston, P.O. Box 4058, Mammoth Lakes, CA 93546*
☎ **(619) 934-6161**

Spring Down Equestrian Center / Woodside Area (S-12)

Take Portola Exit west from 280 past town and then a sharp right after 1 mile past church. ▰ MUST CALL IN ADVANCE TO CHECK ON AVAILABILITY. Box stalls @ $25 per night.
⚐ *755 Portola , Woodside, CA 94062*
☎ **(415) 851-1114**

Squaw Valley Stables / Squaw Valley (S-13)

▰◐☗⚒✎▮☒$$$

Open May 20th to Sept. 10 every year. From I80 Truckee south 12 miles on Highway 89. ▰ 20 Stalls, 12X20, no bedding @ $16 per night. ◐ Vet in Truckee at ☎ 587-7200. ☗ Farrier on premises. ✎ Truckee Automotive.☎ 587-5705. ▮ At Shell/Truckee. ☒ Food at Squaw Creek Resort in Squaw Valley.

⚐ *1525 Squaw Valley Road, Olympic Valley, CA 96146*
☎ **(916) 583-6187**

Sun Hunter Riding School / Orland (S-14)

▰◐☗⟐☗✎☒$$$

MUST BOOK 24 HOURS IN ADVANCE! 3 Miles west of I-5, take Black Butte Exit from I-5, west 3 miles.▰ 10 12X14 wood Stalls, 7 pipe pens, bedding provided, stallions allowed. Stalls @ $20 per night. ⟐ No Camper/RV hookups but do have water and showers @ $10

per night. ❏ Vet in Orland at ☎ 865-4478. ♉ Farrier nearby.
≋ Fishing in the area. ✎ Mechanic at Petros Truck Stop/ 9 miles.
✗ Good food at Berry Patch in Orland ☎ 865-8484.
⚐ *Star Route/ Box 6, Orland, CA 95963*
☎ **(916) 865-5246**

Sunset Corral / Novato (S-15)
≋❏♉🐎🔋✗

Highway 101 to Novato, Exit at San Marin Drive to Salto to Vineyard
and take a right to the Ranch/ 2901 Vineyard Drive. ≋ 72 stalls,
12 wood, 60 metal with auto H2O. Health papers required.
❏♉ Vet and farrier on call. 🐎 Many trails in state owned open space
in nearby tree covered hills--great scenery! 🔋 Fuel available in Novato.
✗ Food available in Novato.
⚐ *2901 Vineyard Drive, Novato, CA 94947*
☎ **(415) 897-8212**

University of California/ Davis School of Veterinary Medicine / Davis (VS)
⌂

Emergency horse care 24 hours a day, 7 days a week. Call only for
emergencies! May require referral from a vet. No stalls for transient
boarding. Located at junction of Highway 80 and Highway 113.
⚐ *1018 Haring Hall, Davis, CA 95616*
☎ **(916) 752-0290 or after hours (916) 752-5438**

Whitehawk Ranch & Equestrian Center / Graeagle (R-4)

≋❏✎🐎≋🚐✗$$

6 miles south of Graeagle on Highway 89 (1137 Highway 89/
Chino).≋ 12 12X12 wood stalls with shavings, auto H2O @ $15 per
night. ❏ Vet in Beckwourth at ☎ (916) 832-4485. 🚐 2 miles down

the road River's Edge Trailer Park. ☜ Mechanic, Eric, on premises.
❌ Good restaurants within 10-15 miles. 🐎≋ Within 10 miles good
fishing and riding in the Lakes Basin Recreation Area (see Big Basin
listing).
☗ *P.O. Box 800, Blairsden, CA 96103*
☎ **(916) 836-0866 or FAX (916) 836-1204**

Big Basin Recreation Area / Graeagle Area (D-1)
🐎≋

Many trails and lakes in this area, including Plumas Eureka State Park
west of Graeagle. Steeped in the legend of the California Gold Rush is
Gold Lake. According to history buffs, a Thomas Stoddard proclaimed
during the Gold Rush that he had stumbled onto a lake with shores
covered with gold. Good fishing throughout the area. Ask for a free
LAKES BASIN RECREATION map from Plumas Chamber of Commerce.
It locates some of the good fishing and shows all the trails.
☗ *Big Basin Redwoods State Park, 21600 Big Basin Way, Boulder
Creek, CA 95006*
☎ **(408) 338-6132**

CTETA Horse Park / Woodside Area (D-2)
🐎

Take Sandhill Road Exit off #280 and go west to top of hill (3674
Sandhill Road). On your right is the main gate to facility which may or
may not be locked. Write or call for days that gate open or events
scheduled. ☎ There is a pay phone near gate. This facility includes
many acres of beautiful cross-country riding.
☗ *CTETA Horse Park (Western American Performing Arts Education
Center, P.O. Box 620010, Woodside, CA 94062*
☎ **(415) 851-2140**

Humboldt Redwoods State Park / Miranda Area (D-3)
🐎📷≋🚐

Horseback riding permitted. Features redwoods over 300 feet tall-
some trees over 1000 years old. Trails wind through redwood groves
and open meadows. 🚐 There are over 200 campsites--for any additional details on restricted trails and/or campsites for horses, contact
the Park. Good fishing including trout, salmon, and steelhead.
☗ *Humboldt Redwoods State Park, P.O. Box 100, Weott, CA 95571*
☎ **(707) 946-2409**

Malibu Creek State Park / Agoura (D-4)

4 miles south of U.S.101 on Las Virgenes/Malibu Canyon Road in Calabasas. Horses permitted on 30 miles or fire roads--this area has been used in filming of many movies and it includes a M*A*S*H set on Crags Road. There are over 50 campsites and water. But trailers are limited to 18 feet or less. Fishing for stocked trout, catfish, and bass. Recent major fire could delay access for 1-2 years. Check ahead!

☝ *Malibu Creek St. Park, 28754 Mulholland Hgwy., Agoura, CA 91301*
☎ **(818) 880-0350**

Molera Trail Rides / Big Sur (D-5)

Call for directions. Good contact for information on the many great trails in State Forest near this facility. Good stopover point and some spectacular views!

☝ *P.O. Box 167, Big Sur, CA 93920*
☎ **(408) 625-8664**

Mt. Diablo State Park / Danville (D-6)

Park is east of San Francisco. Go east 5 miles from Danville on I-680E. Horses allowed but check for restrictions ahead of time. On a good day you can see the Golden Gate and some of California's highest peaks. There are over 50 campsites, but they must be booked ahead-- unknown whether there are any horse facilities.

☝ *Mt. Diablo State Park, P.O. Box 34159, San Francisco, CA 94134*
☎ **(510) 837-2525**

Mt. San Jacinto Wilderness State Park / Palm Springs Area (D-7)

From Palm Springs, go on Route 111 north to Palm Canyon, then left on Tram Drive. Equestrian sites by PERMIT ONLY. Permits required for campsites.

☝ *Mt. San Jacinto Wilderness SP, P.O. Box 308, Idyllwild, CA 92349*
☎ **(714) 659-2607**

Mt. Tamalpais State Park / Mill Valley (D-8)

Go 6 miles west of Mill Valley on Panoramic Highway. 50 Miles of fire roads open for horses, and Muir Beach is a good place to unload your horse. There is also a concession stable at Muir Beach ☎ 388-8295. Park surrounds Muir Woods National Monument and Golden Gate Nat. Rec. Area to the south. Some campsites but no water.

☝ *Mt. Tamalpais State Park, P.O. Box 34159, San Francisco, CA 94134*
☎ **(415) 726-8800**

Point Mugu State Park / Oxnard Area (D-9)

15 Miles south of Oxnard on Route 1. Best horse entrance is at La Jolla Canyon. Horses welcome on back country trails-- but not beaches or campgrounds. Horses can also enter at Newbury Park.

🏕 *Pt. Mugu State Park, 9000 Pacific Coast Hgwy., Oxnard, CA 93033*
☎ **(805) 488-5223**

Sea Horse-Friendly Acres Ranch / Half Moon Bay Area (D-10)

North of Half Moon Bay on Highway 1 (1828 Cabrillo Highway) on your left. Caters to tourists but friendly and could give you the ins and outs of going beach riding--beautiful coastline and beaches!
☎ **(415) 726-9903**

Topanga State Park / Los Angeles (D-11)

North from Pacific Coast Highway #1 to Entrada Road-- look out for Sassafrass Nursery to find entrance to Park, then follow Entrada Road 1 mile and you will be at main entrance/ 20825 Entrada Road. This is the country's 2nd biggest urban park and there is horseback riding on the fire roads. Fire in 1993 could delay access indefinitely--check ahead.

🏕 *Topanga State Park, 20825 Entrada Road, Topanga, CA 90290*
☎ **(213) 455-2465**

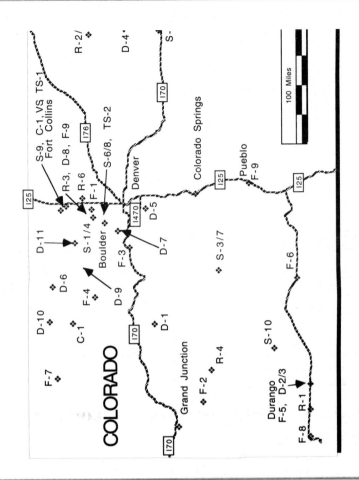

COLORADO

100 Miles

Fort Collins
S-9, C-1, VS, TS-1
C-1, D-8, F-9
R-3, D-8, F-9
R-6
F-1
S-6/8, TS-2
Denver
Colorado Springs
Pueblo F-9
Boulder
D-5
D-7
F-3
S-3/7
F-6
D-11
S-1/4
D-6
F-4
D-9
D-10
C-1
D-1
F-7
R-4
F-2
S-10
Grand Junction
Durango
F-5, D-2/3
R-1
F-8
R-2
D-4
S-

Blue Cloud Farm S-1	Moffat Fairgrds. F-7	Chatfield Rec Area D-5
Boulder Fairgrds. F-1	Montezuma Frgr F-8	Colo St Forest D-6
Castillo Caballero S-3	Morningstar Rch. S-9	Golden St. Park D-7
Colo St, Fairgrds F-9	Mt Ridge Eq Ctr S-6	Lory State Park D-8
CSU Vet School VS	Mt. Shadows S-7	Lion Gulch Trail D-9
Delta Arena F-2	RMD Ranch R-2	Mt. Zirkel Area D-10
Echo Basin Rch. R-1	Rocky Lazy BarS R-3	Rocky Mountain
Fly. Heels Arena F-3	Ryan's Roost S-10	State Park D-11
HiView Acres S-4	Saddle Mt Ranch R-4	Steamboat Carnival C-1
Horse Motel S-5	Seward Ranch R-5	Anheuser Brewery C-2
JR Shin. Star R-6	Shavano Farm S-8	Happy Horse Tack TS-1
Kremmling Fairgr.F-4	Hill's Guide Svc D-1	The Corral TS-2
LaPlata Fairgrds F-5	Over Hill Outfitters D-2	
Larimer Fairgrds F-9	Rapp Guide Svc. D-3	
Monte Vista Frgr F-6	Bonny State Rec D-4	

Blue Cloud Farms / Longmont (S-1)

≥≣✚♘♞⛔✗

6069 Prospect Road- call for directions. ≥≣ 4 wood stalls for transient horses--with bedding. Stallions are allowed. ✚ Vet 7 miles away. ♞ Mechanic at Del Camino/12 miles away. ♞✗ in Longmont.
⛨ *6069 Prospect Road, Longmont, CO 80503*
☎ **(303) 443-5918**

Boulder County Fairgrounds / Longmont (F-1)

≥≣♞✚♘⛟♞✗

Southwest Longmont just north of shopping center at Hover Road / Diagonal Highway intersection. ≥≣ 174 metal 10X10 stalls and several arenas. ✚ Vet nearby. ♘ Farrier 1/2 mile away. ⛟ Camper RV hookups. ✗ 4B's Restaurant 1/4 of a mile good place to eat.
⛨ *Boulder County Fairgrounds, 9595 Nelson Road, Longmont, CO 80501*

☎ **(303) 678-6235.** (ask for Rhonda Balsamo)

Castillo de Caballeros / Salida (S-3)

≋ 🐎 ⊨ $$

Call for directions. Southeast of Salida on 6720 Paradise Road.
≋ 4 stalls, 12X12 pens, with bedding provided @ $10 per night.
⊨ Bed & Breakfast provided with prices ranging from $37 per couple

per night to $85 for the honeymoon suite. Amenities include hot tub on the deck with panoramic view of the mountains, piano, chess set, wood stove, down comforters, and bottomless pot of coffee. 🐎 Plenty of good trails in this area with access to BLM and San Isabel

Forest Trails. And good fishing in this area.
🖂 *Castillo de Caballeros, P.O. Box 89, Salida, CO 81201*
☎ **(719) 539-2002**

Colorado State Fairgrounds / Pueblo (F-9)

≋ 🚐 ⚡🏨❌ $

In south Pueblo. Take Abriendo exit off I-25. Call ahead for reservations. The State Fair, a big drawing card, is late August every year.
≋ Over 350 stalls @ $5 per night. 🚐 Camper RV hookups available @ $5 per night. ⚡ Car Doctor mobile service 24 hours a day/ 7 days a week at ☎ (719) 542-0457 or for trailer repair RV PLUS at ☎ (719) 547-2009. 🏨 Many in Pueblo area. ❌ For good Italian food, try Gaetano's (Take Exit 101 off I-25) Call ☎ (719) 546-0949. It's 2 blocks west on #910/50W. Or the Country Kitchen on north Elizabeth ☎ (719) 545-3179. For a deluxe dinner, try La Renaissance which is located in a renovated church off Abriendo Avenue. ☎ (719) 543-6367. Closed Sundays and holidays.
☎ **(719) 561-8484**

Colorado State University College of Veterinary Medicine / Ft. Collins (VS)

⚕

Emergency horse care 24 hours a day, 7 days a week. Call only for emergencies! May require referral from a vet. NO STALLS FOR TRANSIENT BOARDING. Located at 300 West Drake Street.
🖂 *W102 Anatomy Building, Ft. Collins, CO 80523*
☎ **(303) 221-4535**

Delta Horse Country Arena / Delta (F-2)

Southeast part of Confluence Park in Delta off Route 50. ≋ 10 metal stalls, no bedding, free of charge. Must call ahead to Tom Brown to

make reservations. Wash rack, large arena (which is open daily at no charge. ✚ 2 Vets on call. ☘ Farrier in the Area. ✌ In Delta, there are 2 feed stores. ⚞ There are many trails in the area and some run along the Gunnison and Uncompahgre Rivers.

✝ *Delta Horse Country Arena, P.O. Box 19, Delta, CO 81416*
☎ **(303) 874-0923**

Echo Basin Dude Ranch / Mancos (R-1)

Call for directions. On county road 4 miles northeast of Mancos. ≋ Unlimited outside pens @ $15 per night. Access to La Plata high country and Mesa Verde area. ⛺ Cabins and RV hookups available. Contact : Johnny Green
☎ **(303) 533- 7000**

Flying Heels Arena / Granby (F-3)

1 mile south of Granby on Highway 40. ≋ Arena pens with water free of charge. ✚ 2 vets in area: Larry Peterson ☎ 887-3848 and Mike Brooks ☎ 887-2417. All nearby in Granby. Contact: Mrs. Linke
☎ **(303) 725-3559**

HiView Acres / Hygiene (S-4)

On Highway 66 to Estes Park/11 miles west of I-25 on Highway 66-- take Exit 243 off I-25. Address is 6796 McCall Drive. ≋ 6 stalls (pole barn/ metal siding/ range from 12x12 to 14x16/ all with bedding--@ $12 per night. Stallions allowed. Must have neg cog and innoculation papers. ✚ Nearest vet is in Longmont at ☎ (303)

North American Horse Travel Guide

678-VETS. ♒ Farrier nearby. 🚐 Camper/RV hookups @ $10 per night and they include water and showers. There is a sewer dump within 5 miles. ✎ Closest mechanic is Lyons Tire in Lyons on #66. ☎ 823-6064, open M-F 7-6, Saturdays 7-3. 🍴 In Lyons. ✖ Andrea's Homestead in Lyons ☎ 823-5000.

⚲ 6796 McCall Drive, Longmont, CO 80503

☎ **(303) 651-3070 or FAX (303) 776-8430**

Horse Motel / Burlington (S-5)
�🔌♒✎🐎🍴📱✖

1.5 miles north of Burlington on #385 at 670 7th Street. � 7 metal stalls with bedding. 🔌 Vet 6 miles south. ♒ Farrier in Burlington. 📱✖ These services available in Burlington. 🎣🐎 Plenty of trails and fishing at Bonny Reservoir 24 miles north (see Bonny State Recreation area listing at end of Colorado section).

⚲ Joan Chandler, 670 7th Street, Burlington, CO 80807

☎ **(719) 346-8955**

JR Shining Star Ranch / Greeley Area (R-6)
�🚐🔌♒📱✖$

From I-25 go east on Highway 34 (Loveland Exit) to County Road 25 and then go 1 mile south. 7.5 miles from interstate. � 6 wood stalls with bedding @ $5 per night. 4 have auto H20. Current health papers are required. Preferably not stallions. Instruction in roping, riding, and barrel racing. 🔌 Vet available in Greeley. ♒ Farrier on the premises. ✎ Nearest mechanic is 8 miles away at Johnson's Corner which is near Loveland exit on I-25. It's open 24 hours a day. 🍴 Mini Stop in Greeley or at Johnson's Corner. ✖ Red Lobster in Greeley.

⚲ 26445 Weld County Road #25, Milliken , CO 80543

☎ **(303) 339-9520**

Kremmling Fairgrounds / Kremmling (F-4)
�🚐🎣$

Southeast corner of Kremmling--follow the signs and look for caretaker to get the key. � 5 stalls @ $5 per night. Covered stalls, open pens, and 2 Arenas. 🚐 No RV Hookups, but you can camp nearby. 🎣 Southeast part of town on highway going to Dillon, there is a feed store on your left as you approach lumber mill.

La Plata Fairgrounds / Durango (F-5)
�✎📱✖$

North of main street and west from Ft. Lewis College. � 60 stalls, 12X12 stucco @ $3 per night. Must book Mon.-Fri. between 8 and 5. 🔌 Vet across the street. ✎ Mechanic across the street at Firestone or Big O Tire. 📱✖ These services across the street.

⚲ P.O. Box 807, Durango, CO 81302

☎ **(303) 247-2308**

Larimer County Fairground / Loveland (F-9)

From I-25 take Exit 402 to Roosevelt and then take a right to the fairgrounds (1/2 mile). Stalls available @ $6 per night. For $5 per night you can stay with your camper on the grounds but no RV hookups available- no water or electricity hookups.
☎ (303) 669-6760

Ski Hi Fairgrounds / Monte Vista (F-6)

On east edge of town- 1 mile from center of Monte Vista. 50 stalls with water @ $7 per night. Need one week's notice if possible. Home of the San Luis Valley Fair and the Ski Hi Stampede in July (fairground name is pronounced "Sky High".
✝ *Ski Hi Fairground, 720 First Avenue, Monte Vista, CO 81144*
☎ (719) 852-2692 (City of Monte Vista)

Moffat County Fairground / Craig (F-7)

East edge of town at 790 East 4th Street/north of the airport and off Route 40. 100 stalls with auto H2O @ $5 per night. 2 outdoor arenas and race track.
☎ (303) 824-5708

Montezuma County Fairground / Cortez (F-8)

On Route 160, 2 miles east of Cortez (30100 Highway 160). 64 panel stalls with dividers and water @ $8 per night. MUST MAKE RESERVATIONS IN ADVANCE. At least 2 or 3 vets in the area. Farriers nearby. No hookups but rest area nearby with RV dumps and within 1 miles there is an RV park. Contact: Dante Sena.
☎ (303) 565-6379

Morning Star Ranch / Ft. Collins (S-9)

1 mile east of I-25 on East Highway 14 (main Ft. Collins Exit). Morning Star will be on your left. 60 12X12 stalls with rubber mats and shavings @ $10 per night. Stallions allowed and require neg cog/health papers. Nearest vet in Ft. Collins at ☎ 484-9151. Farriers in the Ft. Collins area. Poudre Valley

Automotive ☎ 221-5300 . It is at 225 NW Frontage Road in Ft. Collins and also has fuel. ☒ Try the Charco Broiler in Ft. Collins ☎ 482-1472.
⌖ *5400 East Highway 14, Ft. Collins, CO*
☎ **(303) 224-4335**

Mountain Ridge Equestrian Center / Boulder Area (S-6)
⚏✚🖑🐎☒$$

On Highway 3, go 8 miles north of Boulder. Approximately 15 miles from I-25. Mountain Ridge Ranch is on west side of highway.
⚏ 34 stalls--8 available for transient horses. Stalls with bedding @ $15 per night. ✚🖑 Vets and farriers in the Boulder area. Stallions are allowed.
🐎☒ These services available in Boulder and Longmont.
⌖ *9417 North Foothills Highway, Longmont, CO 80503*
☎ **(303) 442-8922**

Mt. Shadows Animal Hospital / Salida (S-7)
⚏✚

On Highway 50, 5 miles north of Salida. ⚏ 2 stalls. ✚ Vet on premises.
⌖ *Mt. Shadows Animal Hospital, 9171 Highway 50 West, Salida, CO 81201*
☎ **(719) 539-2533**

RMD Ranch / Wray (R-2)
⚏✚🔪☒

South of Wray 2 miles, call for directions.⚏ 11 wood stalls with bedding. Stallions allowed. 90X200 outdoor arena. Plans for an indoor arena. Contact: Ray Johnson. 🔪 7-11 Store in Wray.
☒ Sandhiller Motel has good food, lunch and dinner buffets.
⌖ *RMD Ranch, P.O. Box 341, Wray, CO 80758*
☎ **(303) 332-5541**

Rocky Mountain Lazy Bar S Ranch / Loveland (R-3)
⚏✚🖑🐎☒

3756 West County Road 16, call for directions. ⚏ 5 wood stalls with bedding and fencing on runs. Heated indoor arena, runs with shelters, and an outdoor show arena. ✚🖑 Vet and farrier in Loveland. Carr Animal Clinic at ☎ (303) 667-2422.
🐎☒ These services available in Loveland. Try Perkins or Village Inn for breakfast.
⌖ *3756 W. County Road #16, Loveland, CO 80537*
☎ **(303) 669-1349**

Ryan's Roost / Lake City (S-10)

Hidden away at 8600 feet above sea level in some of Colorado's San Juan mountains, Ryan's Roost offers scenery and seclusion. Call for directions- the Roost is 8.5 miles from Lake City. Guests who stay at this bed & breakfast can put up their horse free of charge in the inn's corral. Hay-in-a-Bag is available. Rooms range from $45 to $65 for singles, $55 to $75 for doubles and include full breakfast. They also have two cabins which range from $60 to $125 per night. The great room has a wood burning fireplace and there is a hot tub in the solarium. The operator, Therese Ryan, is quite helpful. Plenty of good trails in the San Juan mountains! One mile away is the trailhead into the Powderhorn Primitive Area (Gunnison National Forest). An excellent source for trail information is Sandy Thompson, USFS District

Ranger, in Lake City at ☎ (303) 944-2500. Vets and farrier available in Gunnison which is about 55 miles away. These services available in Lake City.

🖋 *P.O. Box 218, Lake City, CO 81235*
☎ **(303) 944-2339**

Saddle Mountain Guest Ranch / Crawford (R-4)

80 miles from Grand Junction and 60 miles from Montrose. 6 miles east of Crawford on Route 92. 10 paddocks. Health papers required and stallions allowed. Plenty of trails. This ranch is surrounded by wilderness, and is as close as you can get to Gunnison National Forest with someone else doing the cooking! Ranch provides lodging for two for $37.50 with meals extra. Ranch has 3 cabins and 24 rooms total. Buffet style and, according to the owner Arnold Watson, his chow is better than restaurant food. Vet 12 miles/ Hotchkiss. Farrier on premises.

🖋 *Saddle Mt. Guest Ranch, 4536 E. 50 Drive, Crawford, CO 81415*
☎ **(303) 921-6321**

Seward Ranch / Wray (R-5)
〰️➕🐴✖️ $$

4.5 miles east of Wray on Highway 34. 〰️ 12 wood stalls (6 have runs) and 11 pens. Bedding provided. Stalls @ $10 per night. This ranch specializes in raising quarter horses. ➕ Vet nearby. 🏪 7-11 store in Wray. ✖️ La Familla and Sandhiller Restaurants good bets for decent food. Contact: Norma Seward.

☍ *Seward Ranch, 35537 US Highway 34, Wray, CO 80758*
☎ **(303) 332-5149**

Shavano Farm / Boulder (S-8)
〰️➕🔱🐴✖️ $$

Call for directions. 5137 Independence Road is just between Foothills Parkway and where the Diagonal Highway to Longmont starts. This facility just north of the Boulder Airport.

〰️ 12 12X12 wood stalls with bedding in brand new facility which also includes indoor arena. Each stall @ $15 per night. ➕ Vet in Boulder at ☎ 442-6262. 🔱 Farrier in Boulder at ☎ 772- 8450.
🏪✖️ These services all within 2 miles. For food recommend The Cork Restaurant at ☎ 443-9505.

☍ *5137 Independence Road, Boulder, CO 80301*
☎ **(303) 530-1968**

Hill's Guide Service / Collbran (D-1)
〰️🐎🚐

60 miles east of Grand Junction. Take Plateau Canyon exit off Interstate. Call for exact directions. Have operated guide service for 28 years, taking groups into the high country.
〰️ Corrals & sheds.
🚐 Camper/RV hookups 1 mile away at the Rainbow Motel.
☍ *Route 1 / P.O. Box 189, Collbran , CO 81621*
☎ **(303) 487-3433**

Over The Hill Outfitters / Durango (D-2)

4 miles north of Durango on County Road #203. Guided trail rides, big game hunts, and breakfast rides. No horse boarding but can help find boarding facilities. Have been high country guides for 23 years. Can also supply horses with a wrangler. This part of Colorado has often

been called "Little Switzerland" in honor of its beautiful and distinctive mountains. ⚑ *Over The Hill Outfitters, 3624 County Road #203, Durango, CO 81301* ☎ **(303) 247-9289**

Rapp Guide Service / Durango (D-3)

Call for directions. Guide service with over 50 horses, mules, draft horses. Knows all of the top ranches in southwest Colorado, Has camp equipment. ▰ No stalls available but good resource for places to layover in SW Colorado. Pastures available by prior arrangement.
⚑ *47 Electra Lake Road, Durango, CO 81301*
☎ **(303) 247-8923**

Bonny State Recreation Area / Burlington Area (D-4)

23 miles north of Burlington on Route 385, then east on County Road

2 & 3 1.5 miles to the lake. Good riding around lake which has sandy beaches and good shade from abundant cottonwoods.
🚐 210 campsites and holding tank dump stations are located at Wagon Wheel and Foster Grove campgrounds.
📫 *Bonny State Recreation Area, Box 78-A, Idalia, CO 80735*

Chatfield State Recreation Area / Denver Area (D-5)

South of Denver on Wadsworth Blvd. past County Line Road (C470), then turn west to Deer Creek entrance. Or go south on Santa Fe Drive to Titan Road, go west until Roxborough Road, then north to Park entrance. Horseback riding on over 20 miles of trails. Open April through October and the daily access fee is $3. Open 5 am-10 pm.
📫 *Chatfield Recreation Area, 11500 North Roxborough Park Road, Littleton, CO 80125* ☎ **(303) 791-7275**

© Bruce McAllister

Colorado State Forest Park / Walden Area (D- 6)

Take Highway 14 from Ft. Collins over Cameron Pass, following the Poudre River . Park entrance off this highway. Park prefers dispersed horse camping with $3 daily fee. Many unloading areas in Park with good wide roads.
🚐 Park includes 6 cabins and 3 unique yurt tructures.Yurt reservations at ☎ (303) 484-3903 (NEVER SUMMER NORDIC in Ft. Collins). park also has 104 campsites in diverse locations, incl. many lakes. All roads in park are gravel and elevations range from 8,000 to 12,000 feet. There is a KOA campground located outside the entrance to the park ☎ (303) 723-4310. ☎ (303) 723-4310.
📫 *Colorado State Forest Park, Star Route/ Box 91, Walden, CO 80480* ☎ **(303) 723- 8366**

Golden Gate State Park / Golden (D-7)

$

From Denver take I-70 west to Colorado Exit 58- then 5 miles west to Golden Exit (Washington Ave.). Then 1.5 miles and turn left on Golden Gate Canyon Road. There is a good, large parking area to unload horses in the Rimrock Loop, and you can purchase for $2 per night a camping permit for the back country. This park has old cabins, lots of timber and mountains ranging in elevation from 7,000 to over 10,000 in elevation. There is also a horse campers' campsite at Deer Creek.

✝ *Golden Gate Canyon State Park, Route C / Box 280, Golden, CO 80403*

☎ **(303) 592-1502**

☎ **(303) 493-1623**

Lory State Park / Ft. Collins Area (D-8)

From Ft. Collins, follow Route 287 to LaPorte. At Bellvue exit, go left 1 mile to County Road 23; then left 1.4 miles to County Road 25--then right for 1.6 miles. This park is situated on edge of Horsetooth Reservoir and has 25 miles of trail available for horseback riding. There is a concession stable at ☎ (303) 224-4200.

✝ *Lory St.Park, 708 Lodgepole Drive, Bellvue, CO 80512*

Lion Gulch Trail / Arapaho & Roosevelt Nat. Forests / Estes Park (D-9)

Trailhead is located on Highway 36, 13 miles west of Lyons and 8 miles east of Estes Park. Ample parking available at this trailhead and 3 mile ride takes you from elevation of 7320 feet to 8400 feet. Old wagon road becomes a trail after 1.5 miles and you will end up in Homestead Meadows area (use USGS Panorama Peak map). This is a nice day trip and there are some great views. No permit needed.

✝ *USFS, 2995 Baseline Road, Boulder, CO 80303*

☎ **(303) 444-6600**

Mt. Zirkel Wilderness / Clark (D-10)

Take Route 129 from Steamboat Springs to Clark-- cross the Elk River and take first right (Seedhouse Road) and follow that to Hinman Park. You can park there and have good access to the Mt. Zirkel Wilderness Area where there is excellent fishing. You can get further information from USFS/Hahn's Peak District.
☎ (303) 879-1870

Rocky Mt. National Park / Estes Park (D-11)

In Rocky Mountain National Park 80 percent of the trails are open to horseback riding. For overnight use, permits are required. Horse camp-sites approved for use by individual parties of no more than five (5) private horses or other stock and riders include: Koenig (Corral Creek Trailhead), Lawn Lake (Lawn Lake Trailhead), Thunder Lake (Wild Basin Area, 1/4 mile from the highway), Finch Lake (Wild Basin Ranger Station), Hague Creek (Corral Creek Trailhead), and Ditch Camp (Colorado River Trailhead). Groups of no more than twenty (20) horses or other stock and twelve (12) people may use the following locations: Lost Meadow (Lost Lake Trailhead), North Inlet (North Inlet Trailhead), Tonahutu (Tonahutu or Green Mountain Trailhead), and Bighorn Mountain (Twin Owls Trailhead). There is a "Back Country Camping Guide" for locations of overnight camps and obtaining a back country permit. Please remember that grazing is not permitted in the park. Feed must be packed in.
☎ (303) 586-2371

Steamboat Springs Winter Carnival / (C-1)

Ski joring in mid-winter combines horse and skier for exciting races down the main-street of Steamboat Springs. This beautiful mountain area also features chariot races every summer For further details, contact Steamboat Springs Central

Reservations/Information at ☎ (800) 922-2722

Anheuser-Busch Brewery /Ft. Collins (C-2)

North of Ft. Collins take I-25 to Mt. Vista Drive (Exit 271), go west, then turn right on to Busch Drive. Tour the Brewery and that includes seeing the Clydesdales--this group is one of four Budweiser Clydesdale hitches based at a Bud brewery.

Anheuser- Busch Brewery, 2351 Busch Drive, Ft. Collins, CO 80524
☎ **(303) 490-4694**

Demonstration at Brewery by Zoro

Happy Horse Tack Shop/ Ft. Collins (TS-1)

English and western tack. Custom saddle shop and tack repair. Ask for Rusty. Highly recommended by locals.

113 Peterson, Ft. Collins, CO 80524

☎ **(303) 484-4199**

The Corral/ Boulder (TS-2)

English tack. Variety of gifts for horse lovers. Good store for dressage, event, and jumper riders. Custom boots and chaps.

1711 15th Street, Boulder, CO 80302

☎ **(800) 764-0090 or (303) 443-0090**

Sheepherder Camp at Sunrise   © Bruce McAllister

Mills Craig (deceased)

Sleeping Rider- Steamboat Springs Dressage Show
© Bruce McAllister

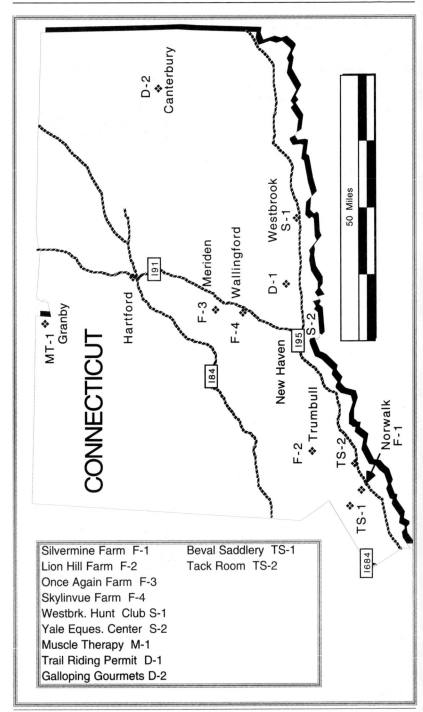

CONNECTICUT

MT-1 ❖ Granby

Hartford

D-2 ❖ Canterbury

191

184

F-3 ❖ Meriden

F-4 ❖ Wallingford

Westbrook S-1

D-1 ❖

195 S-2

New Haven

F-2 ❖ Trumbull

TS-2

Norwalk F-1

TS-1 ❖

1684

50 Miles

Silvermine Farm F-1
Lion Hill Farm F-2
Once Again Farm F-3
Skylinvue Farm F-4
Westbrk. Hunt Club S-1
Yale Eques. Center S-2
Muscle Therapy M-1
Trail Riding Permit D-1
Galloping Gourmets D-2

Beval Saddlery TS-1
Tack Room TS-2

Lion Hill Farm / Sweetbrier Ltd. / Easton (F-2)

Call for directions. 40 stalls. 80X180 indoor ring with heated viewing area. Shows, horse trials, hunter/pacing clinics. 100X200 outdoor sand ring. Current health papers required.

⚑ *1020 Sport Hill Road, Easton, CT 06612*

☎ **(203) 268-0089 or FAX (203) 459-8122**

Once Again Farm / Meriden (F-3)

$$$

Call for directions-- easy access to all major highways. 15 wood stalls with bedding @ $20 per night. Training, dressage, and boarding. 20X60 outdoor dressage arena and 80X180 indoor arena. Vet within 2 miles. These services all nearby.

⚑ *750 Allen Avenue, Meriden, CT 06450*

☎ **(203) 238-3553 or 284-8368**

Silvermine Farm / Norwalk (F-1)

Call for directions. 40 10X12 stalls with bedding. Nearest vet is in Brewster. Farrier available from Norwalk. Gas stations in Norwalk. Silvermine Tavern in Norwalk.

⚑ *94 Comstock Road, Norwalk, CT 06850*

☎ **(203) 846-2098**

Skylinvue Farm / Wallingford (F-4)

Call for directions, requires reservations. 48 wood stalls, varying from 10X12 to 12X12 with bedding. 60X180 indoor arena, 90X260 outdoor ring and outside hunt course. Blankets and other washables cleaned and repaired. Show tack room and stall drapes. ☎ (203) 269-3055.

⚑ *866 North Farms Road, Wallingford, CT 06492*

☎ **(203) 265-4638**

Westbrook Hunt Club / Westbrook (S-1)

Call for directions, availability of stalls. Reservations mandatory. 55 wood stalls. Neg cog/health papers required. Instruction and showing. Vet on call. Farrier nearby. These services within 5 minutes drive.

⚑ *Pond Meadow Road, Westbrook, CT 06498*

☎ **(203) 399-6317**

Yale Polo & Equestrian Center/ New Haven (S-2)

Call for directions and reservations. Contact: Heather Lombardi for OK. 60 wood stalls. Health papers required. Instruction, training, polo, centered riding and combined training. Open to the public. Summer training available.

⚐ *Central Ave./ Box 402A, New Haven, CT 06510*

☎ **(203) 432-0873**

Muscle Therapy for Horse & Rider/ Granby (MT-1)

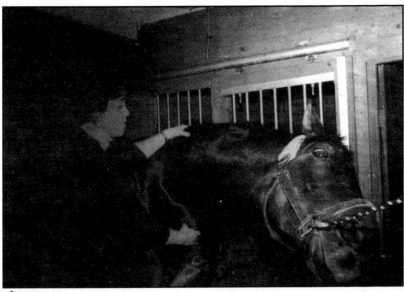

Treatments, clinics, training courses. Trains others in Equine Trigger Point Myotherapy which is therapeutic massage to seek taut muscle bands and muscular knots referred to as "trigger points." Compression of these using various techniques, passive stretch by the therapist to promote free range of motion to an affected area, and a prescription of corrective movements to keep muscles lengthened. All of this is done only after seeing the horse in action without rider and in consultation with its vet. Myotherapy is used by some of the members of the U.S. and Canadian Equestrian Teams. Contact: Margie Amster Herr, TPM

⚐ *249 Mountain Road, North Granby CT 06060*

☎ **(203) 653-9150**

Trail Riding Permits for Regional Water Authority (D-1)

Bethany Area--hilly/trails around lakes and reservoirs. Contact the Bethany Horseman, c/o Sharon Huxley.
☎ **(203) 393-3475**
Guilford Area--scenic trails around lakes and reservoirs. Contact Trail Riders of the Shoreline, c/o Lisa Toman
☎ **(203) 269-5205**
or Terry Holland Buckley
☎ **(203) 457-0529**

Galloping Gourmets (D-2)

Group goes on rides through beautiful forests, other areas in east Connecticut and Rhode Island on weekends (every other weekend through November). ☏ For details and information packet, send self addressed, stamped envelope to Galloping Gourmets, P.O. Box 57, Canterbury, CT 06331.

Beval Saddlery / New Canaan (TS-1)

English saddlery, riding attire, custom riding coats and boots, sportswear, repairs and alterations, stable supplies, and gifts.
☏ *50 Pine Street, New Canaan, CT*
☎ **(203) 966-7828**

The Tack Room / Westport (TS-2)

Specialists in hard--to--fit and find items; custom saddlery. This is a full service tack store.
☏ *153 Post Road East, Westport, CT 06880*
☎ **(203) 227-6272**

W. J. Barry / East Norwalk

Service, repairs, refurbishing on 2 horse trailers, goosenecks, and horse vans. Basic safety check, periodic maintenance, and pre-purchase inspection of used equipment. By appointment only.
☎ **(203) 834-0790** or Shop **(203) 852-0811**

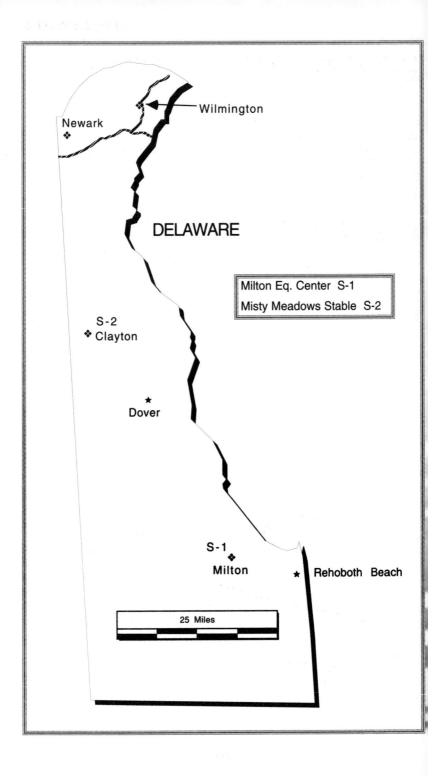

Milton Equestrian Center / Milton (S-1)
≋ ⚞ ✚⚷◪✖$$

Easy to find. Call for directions. Just outside of town of Milton on Route 5. ≋ 27 wood stalls @ $10 per night. Stallions allowed and require neg cog/current health papers. Large parking lot and water available for those who want to stay in rigs overnight. Indoor/outdoor arenas. ⚞ Cross country riding, layups, and arena available by reservation. ✚⚷ Vet and farrier within 20 minutes.

☖ *RD #2/ Box 280, Milton, DE 19968*

☎ **(302) 684-1818**

Misty Meadows Stables / Kenton (S-2)
≋✚⚷◪✖$

On Chance Road close to Kenton. Call for directions. ≋ 26 wood stalls with bedding @ $6 per night. Require current health papers and stallions are allowed. Have been at this location for over 10 years. ✚ Several vets close to Misty Meadows. ⚷ Farrier available. ◪✖ These services within a few miles.

☖ *RD# 2, Box 704, Clayton, DE 19938*

☎ **(302) 653-5701**

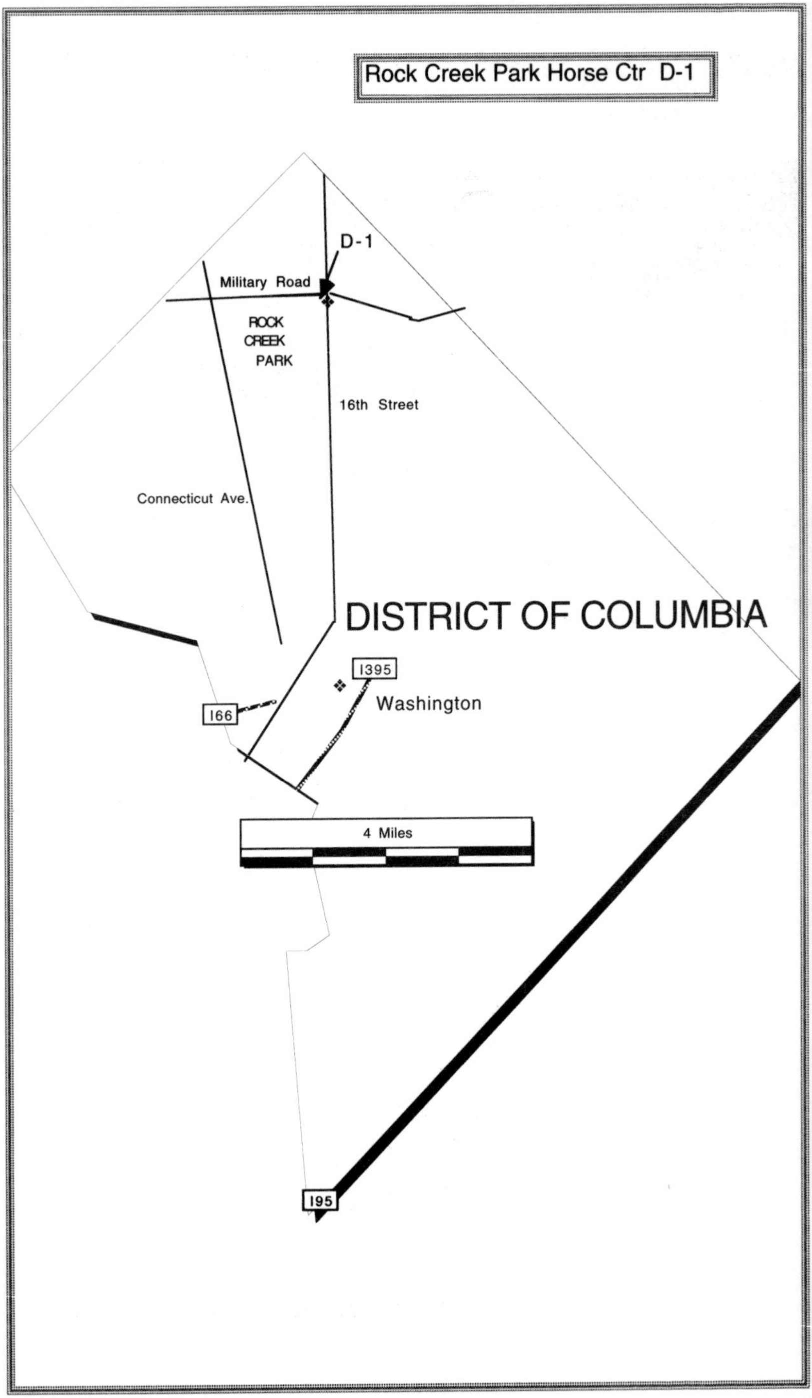

Rock Creek Park Horse Ctr D-1
D-1
Military Road
ROCK
CREEK
PARK
16th Street
Connecticut Ave.
DISTRICT OF COLUMBIA
I395
Washington
I66
4 Miles
I95

Rock Creek Park Horse Center/
Washington (D-1)

Photo courtesy of NPS

Located within Rock Creek Park, north of the National Zoo, off Military Road NW. Easy to find via 16th Street or Connecticut Ave. Concession Stable has information ☎ (202) 362-0117. This national park has 11 miles of wide, dirt and gravel bridle trails which crisscross the wooded northern section of the park. Near Picnic Area 25 is an equitation field.

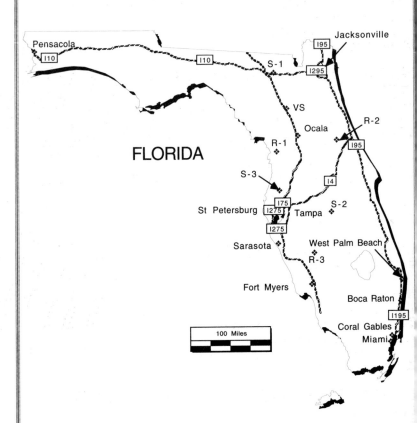

Cherokee Farms S-1   Renab Ranch R-1
Hickory Hammock S-2   Spring Garden Ranch R-2
Iron Horse Ranch R-3   Univ of FL Vet School VS
Land O Lakes Stable S-3

Pensacola
I10
I10
S-1
I195 Jacksonville
I295
VS
Ocala
R-2
I195
FLORIDA
R-1
S-3
I4
I75
St Petersburg
I275
Tampa
S-2
I275
Sarasota
West Palm Beach
R-3
Fort Myers
Boca Raton
I195
Coral Gables
Miami

100 Miles

Cherokee Farms / Lake City (S-1)
≈≈❑♨☎🚐🏨✖$

Right off I-90, call for directions. ≈≈ 42 12x14 concrete stalls and shavings first night. Stalls @ $5 per night. Big outdoor arena and training track 1/4 mile long. Hot walker. Stallions allowed. This facility grows its own hay. ❑ Vet at ☎ 752-7720. ♨ John Lee ☎ 755-0294. 🚐 3 camper/RV hookups @ $12 per night. 🏨✖ Major strip of restaurants, hotels, and gas stations just a couple of miles away. Contact: Lindsay Roberts.

⌂ *Pinemount Road/ Highway 252, Lake City, FL 32055*
☎ **(904) 752-1777**

Hickory Hammock Stables / Lake Wales (S-2)
≈≈$$

3 miles north of Lake Wales on Alternate 27. Call for directions. ≈≈ 17 10X10 wood stalls with bedding and turnout @ $15 per night. Outdoor arena. This is a hunter-jumper training and teaching facility. Owner is quite friendly, was born on the property and has been running this stable for 25 years. Will board a stallion if it is moderately well behaved (have 1 stall for transient stallions).

⌂ *313 Hickory Hammock Road, Lake Wales, FL 33853*
☎ **(813) 676-5736**

Iron Horse Ranch / Arcadia (R-3)
≈≈🚐❑♨🏨✖$

On Route 72. Call for directions and reservations. ≈≈ 4 paddocks available--price negotiable. 🚐 Peace River KOA Campground nearby (On Highway 70, 2 miles west of ranch on U.S. 17. ☎ (813) 494-0214. ❑♨ Plenty of vets and farriers in the area. 🏨✖ These services available in Arcadia which is about 3 miles away.

⌂ *3900 Highway 72W, Arcadia, FL 33821*
☎ **(813) 494-1953**

Land O Lakes Riding Stables / Land O Lakes (S-3)
≈≈

Call for directions! ≈≈ At press time planning brand new 200 stall barn. Might have stalls, but call ahead for reservations!!

⌂ *23619 Rolling Meadow Lane, Land O Lakes, FL 34639*
☎ **(813) 996-4948** or FAX **(813) 996-2124**

Renab Ranch / Lecanto (R-1)

Off Route 44 go south on #491 (Lecanto Highway). Across from Withlacoochee State Forest. ⚏ 4 12X12 stalls with bedding and water @ $5 per night and pastures @ $10 per night. Stallions not allowed. Outdoor arena 60X90. ✚ Vet 10 miles away and vet college 75 miles away. ☎ (904) 746-7171. ♀ Farrier available ☎ (904) 795-5795. ⛺ Camper RV hookups available @ $5 per night. ✎ Mechanic at JC Auto and Marine Service ☎ (904) 746-9054. Also works on trailers. ▌Texaco Homosassa ☎ 628-2599. ✖ Mr. Wang's Chinese ☎ 628-6366 or many seafood places available.
▼ Ranch also owns Old Country Store in Homosassa Springs (on Route 19 take exit 490A east on Grover Cleveland Blvd (7120 West Grover Cleveland). It has tack, saddles and vet supplies.
🐎 Withlacoochee State Forest across from Ranch (with equestrian crossing) and trail maps available. Forest includes 40,000 acres, many trails, 100-- mile endurance rides and many 1/2 day rides. Ranch includes premium pastures and fencing. Owner lives on the premises.
⌂ *5338 South Lecanto Highway, Lecanto, FL 34461*
☎ **(904) 628-9816 or 628-2716**

Spring Garden Ranch Training Center DeLeon Springs (R-2)

From I-95 Exit Ormond Beach/Ocala exit and go west towards Ocala (Rt. 40). At Brazzaville light (#17) turn left. Go 7 miles to Spring Garden Ranch Road. Turn left. Ranch is 1 mile on right/enter at gate #1. From I-4/Orange City/Deland. Go 2.5 miles, turn right on 17/92. Go 1 mile, turn left on 15A (bypass.). Go 7 miles, turn left on 17/92. Go 4 miles, turn

right on Spring Garden Ranch Road. Ranch is 1 mile on your right. Enter at Gate #1. 🏇 750 concrete 12X12 stalls @ $10 per night(including bedding). Stallions allowed. Outdoor arena, 200X300 plus 2 dressage rings. 60 half--acre paddocks, blacksmith shops, harness shops and 120 tack rooms/offices. Indoor arena planned. "We are a harness training facility and our entire operation is for the safety and convenience of our riders and horses. This facility is like no other. ✚ Excellent vet ☎ 985-4902. ♆ 3 or 4 farriers on grounds October-May. 🚐 15-20 Camper/RV hookups @ $15 per night. ✎ Mechanic at Hiatt Motors 1.5 miles away ☎ 985-5161. ⛽ Gas stations nearby. ✖ Restaurant on premises. 🐎 Ocala National Forest nearby has good horse trails. Contact: Linda Colley.
☗ *P.O. Box 367, DeLeon Springs, FL 32130*
☎ **(904) 985-5654**

Univ. of Florida/ College of Veterinary Medicine / Gainesville (VS)
⌂

Emergency horse care. Call only for emergencies! May require referral from a vet. NO STALLS FOR TRANSIENT BOARDING. Located at 2015 SW 16th Avenue.
☗ *P.O. Box 100125, Gainesville, FL 32610*
☎ **(904) 392-4069**

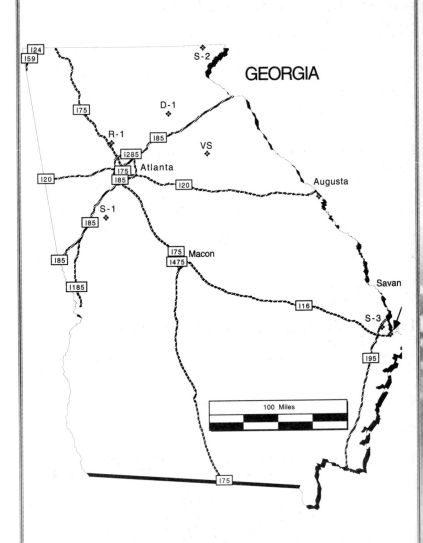

GEORGIA

Bar M Stables	S-1
Dillard House Stables	S-2
Double TK Ranch	R-1
Hi Ho Hills Farm	S-3
Univ. of GA Vet School	VS
Chattahoochee Nat Forest	D-1

Bar M Stables / Senoia (S-1)

1.5 miles north of Senoia on Route 85. ▤ 20 wood stalls with bedding. Stallions allowed and require neg cog/health papers. Owner says it's well kept but not fancy. Has 4 hot walkers, 3 round pens, arena, and 175 acres of pasture. ✚ Vet within 30 minutes' drive. ♈ Farrier available. 🚐 Electric hookups. ✖ Crossroads Restaurant 1.5 miles.

✝ *Highway 85, Senoia, GA 30276*

☎ **(404) 599-3303**

Dillard House Stables / Dillard (S-2)

Call for directions. Route 441 is the nearest highway. ▤ 14 10X12 wood stalls with bedding @ $15 per night. Only well behaved stallions allowed. Require neg cog/health papers. ✚ Vet within 7 miles. ♈ Many farriers in the area. 🚐 Camper/RV hookups nearby. ≋ Trout fishing in lakes nearby. ✖ Restaurant on the premises. ▮ These facilities within 1/2 mile. 🐎 Excellent trails and national forest nearby.

✝ *P.O. Box 10, Dillard, GA 30537*

☎ **(706) 746-2038**

Double TK Ranch / Marietta (R-1)

15 miles north of Atlanta. From I-75 take Exit 114A to Shallowford Road. ▤ 200 stalls with bedding & stallions allowed. 🐎 75 acres of trails and have an arena. ✚ 3 vets in the area. ♈ Farrier in the area. ▮ These facilities within 5 minutes. ✖ Good food within 15 minutes.

✝ *1231 Shallowford Road, Marietta, GA 30066*

☎ **(404) 926-3795**

Hi Ho Hills Farm / Savannah (S-3)

5 miles off I- 95/ take Exit 19. Call for directions. ▤ 12 12X12 stalls with shavings, auto H20 @ $15 per night. Neg cog/health papers required. ✚ 3 vets within 20 miles. 🚐 1 Camper/RV hookup @ $10. 🐎 1600 acres of trails. Much dressage riding. ▮ Within 5 miles there is Fuel City and they have a mechanic. ✖ This is a resort type area--good

restaurants, hotels, golf, tennis, and swimming. Beach is only 30 miles away.

☖   *Route 1 / Box 365A, Savannah, GA 31408*

☎ **(912) 826- 2163**

University of Georgia / College of Veterinary Medicine / Athens (VS)

⌂

Emergency horse care. Call only for emergencies! May require referral from a vet. NO STALLS FOR TRANSIENT BOARDING. Located at 343 Carlton Street..

☖   *Athens, Georgia 30602*

☎ **(706) 542-3223**

Chattahoochee / Oconee National Forests (D-1)

🐎

These two forests contain more than 500 miles of trails for horseback riding. The Chattahoochee National Forest is in North Georgia east of Dalton, and the Oconee National Forest is southeast of Atlanta.
The USDA publishes a 23--page trail guide (complete with maps) which goes into great detail on the many trails in both forests.

☖   *Chattahoochee-Oconee National Forest Supervisor, 508 Oak Street NW, Gainesville, GA 30501*

☎ **(404) 536-0541**

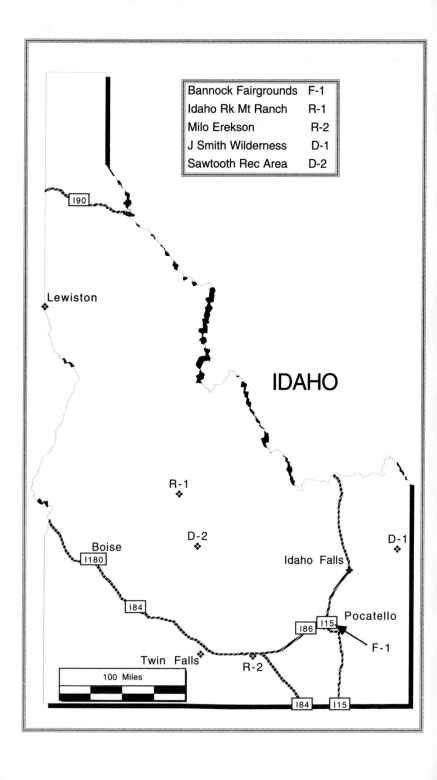

Bannock County Fairgrounds / Pocatello (F-1)
≋ ⊝▥▨⊠$

Exit 3 off Route 91, take Alameda to intersection. Then go up Fairway.
≋ 300 stalls/no bedding @ $5 per night. ⊝ Camper/RV hookups
with water and electricity @ $5 per night. ▥ Texaco, Circle K and
Chevron stations nearby. ⊠ Sandpiper Inn has good food.
⌐ *P.O. Box 4777, Pocatello, ID 83205*
☎ **(208) 237-1340**

Idaho Rocky Mountain Ranch / Sun Valley Area (R-1)
≋❶⊁▭

50 miles north of Sun Valley off #75. ≋⊨ 4 pastures. We have a
modified American plan and guests' horses are welcome/ must stay
here for them to put up your horse. This is a working cattle ranch with
main lodge and cabins built in 1930. It's in excellent condition with a
guest capacity of about 40. ⊁ This facility is on the edge of a wilderness area and has great views of the Sawtooth Range. For more
detailed information on Sawtooth National Forest see separate listing at
the end of this section. ❶ Vet is 50 miles away.
⌐ *HC 64 / Box 9934K, Stanley, ID 83278*
☎ **(208) 774-3544**

Milo Erekson / Declo (R-2)
≋❶⊌⊱⊝▥⊠$

1/4 mile south of I-84. ≋ Pastures with water @ $5 per night.
Stallions allowed. ❶ Several vets in Burley. ☎ (208) 678-5509.
⊌ Farrier in Declo ☎ (208) 654-2085. ⊝ Camper RV hookups within
1/2 mile. ▥ These facilities all within 10 miles. Gas within 3 miles.
⊠ Good food in Declo (3 miles).
⌐ *Route 1/ Box 32, Declo, ID 83323*
☎ **(208) 654-2085**

Jedediah Smith Wilderness / Targhee National Forest (D-1)
⊁≋

On the west slopes of the Tetons and named after Jedediah Smith,
who was a mountain man, explorer, and trapper in the early 1800s.
This area features breathtaking views of the Tetons and sub-- alpine
lake basins. Maximum number of pack/saddle stock permitted is 25.
Hay/straw prohibited.
⌐ *P.O. Box 208, St. Anthony, ID 83445 or Teton Basin Ranger, North
Main Street, Driggs, ID 83422*
☎ **(208) 624-3151 or (208) 354-2312**

Sawtooth National Recreation Area
Stanley Area (D-2)

The Ponderosa Pine Scenic Highway #21 comes out of Boise and Highway 75 from Ketchum and Sun Valley. Camps just off Highway 75 just south of Stanley. This country resembles Wyoming's Tetons and is quite spectacular-- with lakes and fishing to match. Most of the forest open to horseback riding but some trails can be hazardous. So get a map and information before heading in! Some of the best rides are the following : Amber Lakes Trail # 130 (7 mile trip/ use USGS Amber Lakes Map), Cabin Creek Trail # 191/day trips/ use Snowyside Peak USGS map, Norton Lakes Trail # 135/use Baker Peak USGS map, and Toxaway Loop (use Snowyside Peak USGS map). Mr. Mose Shrum, at the number below is the trails expert for the National Forest.

✝ *Sawtooth National Recreation Area Headquarters, Star Route, Ketchum, ID 83340*

☎ **(208) 726-7672**

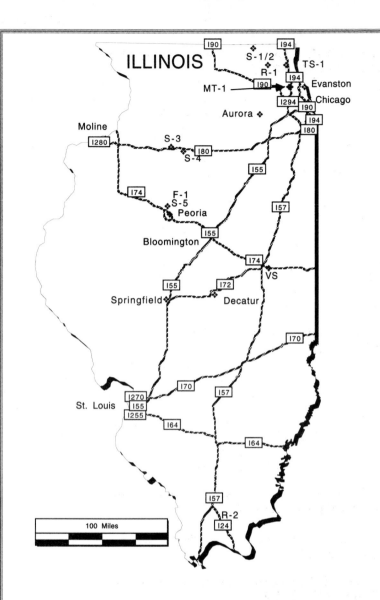

ILLINOIS

190	S-1/2	194	TS-1
R-1	MT-1	190	194	Evanston
I294	Chicago
Aurora	190	194	I80
Moline	I280	S-3	I80	S-4	I55
I74	F-1 S-5	I57
Peoria	I55
Bloomington	I74	VS
I55	I72
Springfield	Decatur
I70
St. Louis	I270 I55 I255	I70	I57
I64	I64
I57	R-2 I24

100 Miles

Black Oak Stable S-5	Libertyville Tack TS-1
Deer Lake Farm S-1	Prairie Hill B&B S-4
Echo Acres S-2	Timmerman's Ranch R-1
Equine Massage MT-1	Triple T Ranch R-2
Heart of Illinois Arena F-1	Univ. of IL Vet School VS
Huskey's Horse Motel S-3

Black Oak Stables / Peoria (S-5)

A few minutes from I-71 northwest Peoria. Call ahead for availability and directions. 35 large box stalls @ $10 per night. Have indoor arena. Require all shots/ health papers. RV hookups available. 30 minutes to Jubilee State Park which has plenty of trails. Feed for sale. Vet and farrier available. These services available.

⌂ *4213 Charter Oak Road, Peoria, IL 61615*
☎ **(309) 691-8257**

Deer Lake Farm / Hebron (S-1)

Call for directions. 18 wood stalls with bedding @ $12 per night. Stallions allowed. Current health papers required. At nearby Glacial Park there are 7 miles of trails. Vet and farrier nearby. These services are available, and a Day's Inn 6 miles away.

⌂ *8417 Regnier Road, Hebron, IL 60034*
☎ **(815) 648-4044**

Echo Acres / Harvard (S-2)

Call for directions. 2 miles from Harvard. 17 11X12 wood stalls with bedding and feed @ $15 per night. Includes 5 double stalls. Current health papers required and stallions allowed if reasonably well behaved. Sue Market, the co owner, is quite helpful. Vet lives next door. Farrier nearby. Mechanic on the premises or in Harvard at the Ford dealer. These services available in Harvard.

⌂ *19917 McGuire Road, Harvard, IL 60033*
☎ Day **(815) 568-7225,** or night **943-0022**

Equine Sports Massage Therapy Des Plaines (MT-1)

⌂ *1430 Miner, P.O. Box 141, Des Plaines, IL 60016*
☎ **(312) 320-6036**

Heart of Illinois Arena / Peoria (F-1)

On 9201 N. Galena on Route 29. Call for directions. 200 box stalls with bedding @ $15 per night. Indoor/outdoor arenas and wash racks. Many horse shows here throughout the year and the largest facility of its kind in central Illinois. Pony Express Tack Shop on the premises. Camper/RV hookups available. Vets and farriers available. These services available within 2 blocks.

⌂ *9201 North Galena Road, Peoria, IL 61615*
☎ **(309) 693-1805 or 691-9161**

Huskey's Horse Motel / Wyanet (S-3)
 ≈◎◑☂✕🚐⊱$$

Call for directions and reservations/must be set up IN ADVANCE. 3 miles south of I-80 via Exit 45. ≈ 6 wood stalls ranging from 12X12

to 12X16 with bedding @ $15 per night. Indoor 60X80 arena. Stallions allowed.
✚ 5 vets available- from 3 to 20 miles away/all experienced. ◐ Farrier at ☎ (815) 646-4503.
🚐 Camper/RV hookups available @ $5 per night (free with 2 or more horses). Sewage dumping 4 miles away.
✎ Mechanic on premis-es and another 10 miles away. ⊠✕ These services within 6 miles.
⊱ Located 3 miles from the historic Hennepin Canal Recreation Area-it includes 80 miles of horse trails.
⌂ RR #1/ Box 67, Wyanet, IL 61379
☎ **(309) 895-3181**

Libertyville Saddle Shop / Libertyville (TS-1)
◐

On Peterson Road, Highway 137. Horseman's supplies, saddlery and riding apparel. Have leather repair shop. Accept phone orders.
⌂ 306 Peterson Road, Highway 137, Libertyville, IL 60048
☎ **(708) 362-0570 or FAX (708) 680-3200**

Prairie Hill Barn Bed & Breakfast Princeton (S-4)
 ≈⊱⊨$$$

Less than 2 hours' drive from Chicago. Call for directions. This is the ideal retreat for horse and rider. ≈ No. of stalls unknown at press time but stall/care/feed are @ $20 per stall. ⊨ For the rider, rates from spring to fall run $50 per night for single occupancy or $70 for double occupancy. The rates include full bed & breakfast and the farmhouse is one of the finest, oldest in Illinois. It was built sometime between 1834 and 1850. Have had good feedback from locals about this new facility.
⌂ The Prairie Hill, RR #4/ Box 74, Princeton, IL 61356
☎ **(312) 281-2940 or (815) 447-2487**

Timmerman's Ranch & Saddle Shop / Island Lake (R-1)
═══ ▼ $$

1/2 mile south of Route 176 on Roberts Road. ═══ 44 stalls with bedding @ $15 per night. Call ahead because sometimes they are booked up. Also have good broke horses for sale at all times. ▼ Full line tack shop incl. saddles, hats, belts, western wear, Wrangler Pro Rodeo Shop, and jewelry.

⚐ *Roberts Road, Island Lake, IL 60042*

☎ **(708) 526-8066**

Triple T Cedar Lake Ranch Camping / Vienna Area (R-2)
🚐 ≋ 🐎 ✖ $

10 miles north of Vienna in the heart of the Shawnee National Forest on the River to River Trail. 23 acre lake and sand beach. 🚐 Camper RV hookups (electric and water) @ $9 per night. Dump stations and showers. Cabins available. ≋ Free fishing. 🐎 Many miles of trails. ✖ Grocery store and ice on the premises.

⚐ *RR #3, Vienna, IL 62995*

☎ **(618) 695-2600**

Univ. of Illinois/ College of Veterinary Medicine / Urbana (VS)
⚕

Emergency horse care. Call only for emergencies! May require referral from a vet. NO STALLS FOR TRANSIENT BOARDING. Located at 108 West Hazelwood.

⚐ *2001 South Lincoln, Urbana, IL 61801*

☎ **(217) 333-2000**

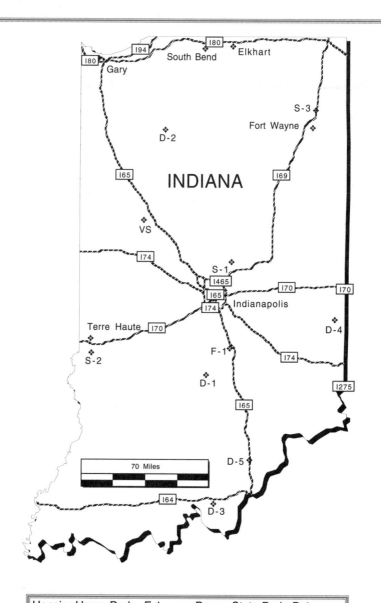

Hoosier Horse Park F-1	Brown State Park D-1
J. Keesling Stables S-1	Tippecanoe D-2
Persimmon Farm S-2	Harrison State Forest D-3
Union Chapel B&B S-3	Whitewater Memorial D-4
Purdue Vet School VS	Clark State Forest D-5

Hoosier Horse Park / Indianapolis Area (F-1)

Go south on I-65 about 30 miles, take Exit 80, then 252W and follow the signs. Then turn right onto Schoolhouse Road, go .7 miles, then take a left (west). Must call for RESERVATIONS! ☎ (812) 526-5929. Park has 256 wood stalls and bedding sold @ $5 per bag. The staff is very friendly and helpful. This large facility was originally built for the Pan American Games in 1987. It is featured as Indiana's most complete equine facility and has 3 dressage arenas, cross country course, and 3 outdoor arenas. Vets and farriers within 5 minutes. The Park is surrounded by 600 acres of the Johnson County Park and a 5200 acre State Fish & Wildlife Area. All these services are nearby.

🏕 *Route 1 / Box 75, Edinburgh, IN 46124*
☎ **(812) 526-5929, 526-8034, or FAX (812) 526-8105**

Janet Keesling Stables & Saddlery Noblesville (S-1)

$$

1/2 mile east of Route 37, call for directions. 30 wood 12X12 stalls with bedding @ $15 per night. Require health papers.

Stallions allowed. ⬧ Vet in Noblesville at Benker Vet Clinic ☎ (317) 773- 5913. 🚐 Electric hookups only for Camper/ RV @ $5 per night. 🔧❌ These services all in Noblesville which is 5 miles away.

🛒 Have tack shop which does custom show saddles, reins, chaps. Have a large selection of used riding clothes-- and can mix sizes while still matching colors.

⚐ *11930 East 211th Street, Noblesville, IN 46060*
☎ **(317) 773-5482**

Persimmon Hollow Farm / Terre Haute (S-2)
〰️⬧♘🚐🔧❌≋$$

From I-70 and US 41, 9/10 mile east of U.S.41 South at Stuckeys Pecan Shop/call for exact directions . ≋ 3 12X12 wood stalls incl. bedding @ $12 per night. Stallions allowed. Require health papers. ⬧ Nearest vet at ☎ (217) 826-5621. ♘ Nearest farrier at ☎ 299-4754. 🚐 Camper/RV hookups 3/4 mile away. Do have electric only hookups @ $5 per night. ≋ Fishing in the area. ⚒ Closest mechanic at Hertz 10 miles away. ☎ (812) 232-0542. ⛽ Nearest fuel 6 miles. ❌ Good food less than a mile away.
⚐ *2966 East Harlan Drive, Terre Haute, IN 47802*
☎ **(812) 299-4754**

Union Chapel Bed & Breakfast /
Fort Wayne (S-3)
〰️⬧♘🚐🛏≋🔧❌$

Exit #116 at Interstate 69 (DuPont Road), go east to Route 427 (Tonkel Road), then north 1 mile, turn right onto Union Chapel-- look for 6336 Union Chapel.≋ 6 10X10 metal stalls w/o bedding @ $8 per night. Health papers required and stallions allowed. 🛏 Bed & breakfast/ prices unknown. 🚐 Camper/RV hookups available @ $10 per night ≋ There is fishing in the area. ⬧ Nearest vet is at Ft. Wayne ☎ 625-6755 .⚒ Mechanic at Fortmeyer Truck Stop which is 6 miles away. ☎ 489- 3511 It's open 24 hours a day. ⛽ Best fuel stop is at Speedway/ Exit 116 and phone is ☎ 484-3713. ❌ Try the DuPont Bar & Grill at ☎ 483-1311.
⚐ *6336 Union Chapel Road, Fort Wayne, IN 46845*
☎ **(219) 627-5663**

Purdue School of Veterinary Medicine / West Lafayette (VS)

♠

For emergencies only! HOURS BY APPOINTMENT ONLY. M-F, 8-6,
SAT 8-12. NO STALLS FOR TRANSIENT HORSES. May require referral
from a vet.

☖ *Lynn Hall, West Lafayette, IN 47907*

☎ **(317) 494-8548 or FAX (317) 496-1166**

Brown County State Park / Nashville (D-1)

🐎$

Call for directions. Largest Indiana State Park-- provides rider with over
75 miles of trails that vary from wide fire roads to narrow single file
trails which meander through hilly forests. Shower house fees $9 and
$4. Plus $1.50 per horse. Horse campgrounds and RV camper hookups.
Wildlife: large deer population and numerous hungry raccoons.

☖ *P.O. Box 608, Nashville, IN 47448*

☎ **(812) 988-6406**

Tippecanoe River/ Winamac (D-2)

🐎

Call for or write for directions. 14 miles of bridle trails, 2761 acres,
and 60 primitive campsites along this beautiful river. Water available at
every 2nd or 3rd campsite. Only one rig at each site. Campsites are
large and offer shade as a rule. The hitch rails are safe and have sand
around them.

☖ *Route 1 / Box 95A, Winamac, IN 46996*

☎ **(219) 946-3213**

Harrison-Crawford State Forest Wyandotte Woods / Corydon (D-3)

🐎

Call or write for directions. This forest is in the central and southern
part of the State bordering the Ohio River. Over 100 miles of trails for
riding. Trails are well marked and good map is available. Many com-
petitive rides in this forest but footing (rocks, mud) can make the footing interesting at different times of the year. Be weatherwise! A picket
line is required and there are few hitch rails. Cannot use trees and
there are no designated campsites-- there are 120 primitive campsites.

☖ *7240 Old Forest Road, Corydon, IN 47112*

☎ **(812) 738- 8232**

Whitewater Memorial / Liberty (D-4)

Call or write for directions. This park borders a reservoir and terrain is hilly and wooded. Very large campsites and quite popular. BOOK AHEAD! Some 15 miles of trails. Make sure to take a picket line-- may be a shortage of hitch rails. ☱ Reservoir has good fishing. Plans to relocate the horse campsite and add electricity and a shower.

⚐ *RR #2 / Box 194, Liberty, IN 47353*

☎ **(317) 458-5565**

Clark State Forest / Henryville (D-5)

Call or write for directions. This forest has over 100 miles of trails for the advanced riders--the hills are steep and trails not well marked--so be a good navigator. Scenic overlooks make some of the trails worth the effort. Parking pads are long so no problem with parking Day riders will find strong hitch rails and picnic tables. 🚐 Good supply of firewood in camp, there is a dump station, and pit toilets. Water is strategically placed to avoid long hauls and there is a system of self-registration.

⚐ *P.O. Box 119, Henryville, IN 47126*

☎ **(812) 294-4306**

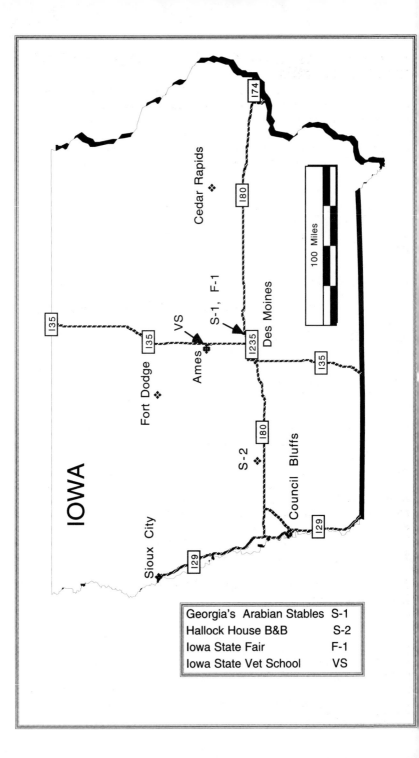

Georgia's Arabian Stables / Altoona (S-1)

≣🚭🖐🕈🚐🔧🗙$$

Off I-80 take Exit 143 (at Union 76 Truck Stop). Call for directions-- at the exit you only have 5 miles to go. ≣ 38 wood stalls with bedding @ $10 per night. Stalls range from 10X10 to 10X12. According to owner "We have been repairing and building and fixing things for a real great place to come. We have a 50--acre farm." 🚭 Nearest vet is in Grimes at ☎ 986- 4530. 🖐 Farrier at Mitchellville(5 miles) at ☎ 967-3879. 🎣🏊 Fishing in the area and have 2 RV camper hookups @ $10 per night. They hope to add showers soon. 🔧 Closest mechanic is at the Union Truck Stop at beginning of listing and number is ☎ 967-4229. They are open 24 hours a day. ⛽ Nearest fuel is Krueger Texaco in Altoona at ☎ 967-3441. 🗙 Good food at Adventureland Inn in Altoona ☎ 265-7321.
✝ *5055 NE 96th Street, Altoona, IA 50009*
☎ **(515) 967-5553**

Hallock House Bed & Breakfast / Brayton (S-2)

≣🛏🚭🖐🕈🏊🔧⛽🗙$$

From I-80 take Exit 60. Go north on Route 71 to Brayton. Turn east at the Town Hall. The Hallock House is the first home on the right hand side of the road--approximately 1 mile. ≣ 2 wood stalls, 10 metal stalls (the metal stalls across the road) with bedding @ $10 per night. Stallions are allowed and health papers are required. Also pasture and holding pens available. 🛏 Two guest rooms with full breakfast @ $40 for double and $32 single. The Barton's House was built in 1882 and has been passed down through the generations. It's a Victorian home with 10' high ceilings and spacious porches for "sitting away the evening." 🚭 Vets in Audubon and Elkhorn. 🖐 Farrier available in Atlantic. 🏊 Fishing ok in the farm ponds.🔧 Closest mechanic is at Hansen Repair 4 miles away. ⛽ Closest fuel is Casey's in Exira. 🗙 Best food is at JR's Lounge in Brayton (check which days open!).
✝ *3265 Jay Ave/ P.O. Box 19, Brayton, IA 50042*
☎ **(800) 945-0663 or (712) 549-2449**

Iowa State Fair / Des Moines (F-1)

≣🚭🚐🔧🗙$

Call for directions and/or look for 3000 East Grand Avenue. Call in advance to confirm stall availability. ≣Over 100 wood stalls in 6 barns. No bedding provided and cost per night is $5 Size varies, stallions welcome. 🚭 There is a vet in the area. 🚐 Campground with camper/RV hookups. 🔧🗙 These services are in the area. There is a good restaurant across the street, according to the Fair Office.
✝ *3000 East Grand Avenue, Des Moines, IA 50317*
☎ **(515) 262-3111**

Iowa State Univ. College of Veterinary Medicine / Ames (VS)

♠

Emergency horse care. Call only for emergencies! May require referral from a vet. NO STALLS FOR TRANSIENT BOARDING. Elwood Drive & 16th Street.

⌂ *2520 Veterinary Administration, Ames, IA 50011*

☎ **(515) 294-1500**

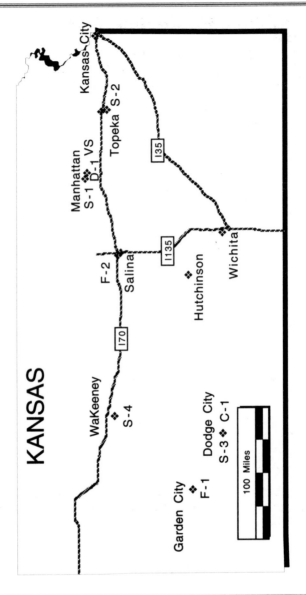

C Bar Stables S-1	Bob Swafford S-3
Circle C Train. Center S-2	Thistle Hill B&B S-4
Finney Fairgrounds F-1	Carnahan Trail D-1
Kansas State Vet School VS	Boothill Museum C-1
Saline Park F-2	

C Bar Stables / Manhattan (S-1)
≋ 🚽🐴✖$$

Call for directions. 2 miles out of Manhattan on Highway 24E. ≋ 4 stalls with bedding @ $10 per night. Current health papers required. 🚽 Nearest vet, Tom Lopp. 🐴 Nearest fuel at APCO--1/2 mile. ✖ Village Inn..

🏇 *9000 Elk Creek Road, Manhattan, KS 66502*
☎ **(913) 776-1287**

Circle C Training Center / Topeka (S-2)
≋🚽♻🐴✖$$

2 miles south of east entrance to turnpike/southeast on Croco Road, call for directions. ≋ 36 wood stalls @ $12 per night. Stallions allowed if advance notice. Have an outdoor arena. Have been in the business for 44 years. Mrs. Chaffee is a horse artist and very hospitable. The Chaffees have put up with everything from Clydesdales to miniature horses. 🚽 Many vets in area. ♻ Farriers available. 🐴 Nearest fuel stop is in Topeka. ✖ Furr's Cafeteria within 10 minutes.

🏇 *3943 Croco Road, Topeka, KS 66609*
☎ **(913) 266-7065**

Finney County Fairgrounds / Garden City (F-1)
≋ 🚐$$

Call for directions, fairgrounds in southwest part of town. Call in advance! ≋ 20 wood stalls with water and w/o bedding @ $10 per night. Electric hookups only w/o sewer or water for $10 per night. Groundskeeper lives on the grounds-- good security. 🐴 Gas station on the corner. ✖ Nearest restaurant on the other side of town.

🏇 *411 South 9th Street, Garden City, KS 67846*
☎ **(316) 272-3640/3641/3642/3643/3644**

Kansas State University / Clinical Sciences Veterinary Medical Hospital / Manhattan (VS)
🏥

Emergency horse care. Call only for emergencies! May require referral from a vet. NO STALLS FOR TRANSIENT BOARDING.

🏇 *Anderson Hall, Manhattan, KS 66506*
☎ **(913) 532-5700**

Saline County Park / Salina (F-2)
≋ 🚐🚽🐾✖$$

From I-135, take Crawford Street exit to east side of town to Ohio. Then a left (north) to Greeley past KPL Building. Then turn left and cross bridge to a T. Take a left at the T, then a right onto gravel road to the Park. From I-70 take Ohio Street exit to Greeley and then take a right, and follow previous directions. Park is in northeast part of Salina. Call in advance! ▰ 271 wood stalls @ $10 per night. Bedding extra @ $2 per bale. Have round outdoor arena and 6 exhibit barns. ⊖ Electric hookups only @ $10 per night. ✛ Vet in the area. ▓✕ All of these services available. Best place to eat is the Ranger Steakhouse.

☝ *Saline County Fair Department, 900 Greeley, Salina, KS 67401*
☎ **(913) 826-6531 or 826-6532**

Bob Swafford / Dodge City (S-3)
▰✛▓✕

1 mile from Dodge House. 2 miles from Silver Spur Lodge. Call ahead for reservations and directions. ▰ 4 wood stalls with wood chips. Neg cog/health papers required. Security lights and gate locked at night. ✛ 2 vets in area, Ripple or Champlin. ▓✕ All services available in Dodge City.

☝ *P.O. Box 1321, Dodge City, KS 67801*
☎ **(316) 225- 7532**

Thistle Hill Bed & Breakfast / WaKeeney (S-4)
▰⊨✛▓✕

Call for directions and reservations. ▰ 2 14X22 metal stalls w/o bedding or larger pens. Stallions allowed. Must have health papers. ⊨ This is traditional country comfort at its best on the Western Kansas prairie! 4 air conditioned 2nd story guest rooms and breakfast includes muffins or hot cakes, eggs, bacon or sausage and plenty of coffee or tea. $50 per room for 2. $40 per room for single occupancy. ✛ Vet in WaKeeney at ☎ 743-5531. ☯ Farrier available at ☎ 743-5531 or 743-2976. ✎ Mechanic available 7 miles away at WaKeeney Travel Plaza (I-70 at US 283) ☎ 743-2157. Open 24 hours a day. ▮ WaKeeney Travel Plaza. ✕ Jade Garden in WaKeeney at ☎ 743-2157.

☝ *Route 1/ Box 93, Wakeeney, KS 67672*
☎ **(913) 743-2644**

Carnahan Creek Trail & Park / Manhattan Area (D-1)
Tuttle Creek Reservoir
🐎

30 miles of good horse trails. For details, contact Dwayne Dailey, local horseman at ☎ (913) 537-7823 (Early evenings only).

☝ *US Army Corps of Engineers, 5020 Tuttle Creek Blvd., Manhattan, KS 66502*
☎ **(913) 539-8511**

Boot Hill Museum / Dodge City (C-1)

© Bruce McAllister

This village museum is located on the original site of Boot Hill Cemetery in downtown Dodge City. You step back into the 1870s as you visit stores, businesses, schools and homes of old Dodge City. Daily medicine shows, gun fights and melodramas. Adults @ $4.50, Senior citizens @ $4, students 7-17 @ $4 and children 6 and under are free. Open 8 a.m.- 8 p.m. summer months. Winter season shorter hours.

Boot Hill Museum, Front Street, Dodge City, KS 67801

☎ **(316) 227-8188**

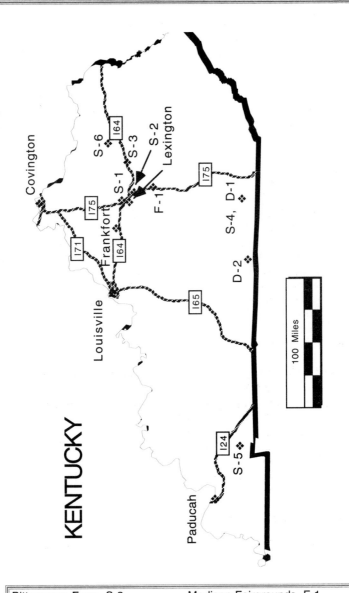

KENTUCKY

Covington

Lexington

Frankfort

Louisville

Paducah

164
S-6 S-3 S-2

175 S-1 F-1

I75

S-4, D-1

175

164

D-2

171

165

124 S-5

100 Miles

Bittergreen Farm S-3
Brook Ledge Farm S-1
D H Western Village S-6
Indian Creek Stables S-4
Land Bet. Lakes Nat Rec S-5

Madison Fairgrounds F-1
Moonridge Farm S-2
Daniel Boone Nat. Forest D-1
Dale Hollow St. Park D-2

Bittergreen Farm / Mt. Sterling (S-3)

3.5 miles off I-64. Require deposit and reservations. First class dressage facility. 24 stalls. Neg cog/health papers required. Indoor arena, FEI stadium course. Bed/breakfast for couples @ $80 per night. Same for singles. In renovated farm house. Cave Run State Park, site of many competitive trail rides, is nearby. Vets available in Mt. Sterling. Haggyerd & McGee Vet Clinic in Lexington is renowned for major equine surgery. Farriers in the area. These facilities available within 3 miles.

1441 Harper's Ridge Road, Mt. Sterling, KY 40353
(606) 498-3068

Brook Ledge Farm / Lexington (S-1)

Call for directions. MUST BOOK AHEAD. Excellent access and have good pull throughs. 20 wood stalls with bedding @ $15 per night. Limited paddock space. Both vet and farrier within 1 mile. Mechanic on premises. Chevron or Shell within 1 mile. Cracker Barrel Restaurant within 1 mile. See Moonridge listing for a seafood restaurant.

2810 Newtown Pike, Lexington, KY 40511
(606) 255-2706

Western Village / Morehead Area (S-6)

12 miles off I-64. Call for directions and reservations. 4 cabins @ $25 per night and 4 stalls for each cabin with a charge of $2 per horse per night. Plenty of wooded trails on property with good access to Daniel Boone National Forest (see separate listing). Vet only 6 miles away--between the Interstate and this facility. Farrier in Morehead--10 miles away. These services available in Morehead, which is also a college town.

Route 1/ Box 219A1, Hillsboro, KY 41049
(800) 737-RIDE or (606) 876-5591

Indian Creek Stables / Cumberland State Park / Whitley City (S-4)

20 miles from I-75 and next to Cumberland State Park. Call for directions. Several stalls with bedding @ $15 per night. Stallions allowed. Main business is trail rides. Many camper/RV hookups at nearby campgrounds. Over 400 miles of trails in Daniel Boone National Forest and Cumberland State Park. Dr. Majors is on call and lives nearby. Nearest farrier is 3 miles away.

Route 1/ Box 473C, Whitley City, KY 42653
(800) 851-9295 or (606) 376-2404

Land Between The Lakes National Recreation Area / Golden Pond (S-5)

25 miles from I-24. Take exit 65 (Cadiz) and then Route 68 to Golden Pond. ▰ This recreation area has a wrangler's campground which has stalls in 2 barns @ $2 per night, first come first served.

▰ The campground also includes some camper/RV hookups, toilet/ shower building, and water.

⚕ *100 Van Morgan Drive, Golden Pond, KY 42211*

☎ **(502) 924-5602**

Madison County Fairgrounds / Richmond (F-1)

Take Exit 90 off I-75 and go through town to the fairgrounds. To stop off first for services take Exit 87. ▰ 40 stalls usually available but call ahead for availability. Usually no charge to put horses up for a night or two. ▰✕ These services within 5--10 minutes. For a good meal, try the Best Western Roadstar Inn on US 25/421 at Junction I-75 ☎ (606) 623-9121. Or for large servings, try Banana's Tavern. From Junction I-75, take exit 87, go 2 blocks north on U.S. 25.

☎ (606) 624-2569.

⚕ *1815 Irvin Road, Richmond, KY 40475*

☎ **(606) 623-3066**

Moonridge Farm / Lexington (S-2)

Call for directions. MUST BOOK AHEAD. Exit 110 off Interstate 75/64. Go left 3/4 mile and it will be on your left. ▰ 62 oak 12X12 stalls with bedding @ $15 per night. Stallions allowed and must have neg cog/health papers. 1 big outside arena, paddocks for stallions, 2 20 acre fields, and 2 40-acre fields. ✚ Dr. James Slaughter within 3 miles. ◗ Farrier 6 miles away. ✕ Plenty of restaurants opposite direction from where you get off Interstate (take a right instead of a left. New Orleans House at 1510 Newtown Pike has excellent seafood. Reservations advised. ☎ (606) 254-3474.

⚕ *2741 Winchester Road, Lexington, KY 40509*

☎ **(606) 299-9816 or FAX (606) 293-5749**

Daniel Boone National Forest / Whitley City (D-1)

Over 50 miles of trails in Stearns area including mountainous terrain, flat ridge tops, and 3 wild rivers. Forest service has horse trail informa- tion packets which they can mail to you. USFS trails expert is Bill Brumm. ⚕ *P.O. Box 429, Whitley City, KY 42653*

☎ **(606) 376-5323**

Dale Hollow Lake State Park / Bow (D-2)

Courtesy of Kentucky Parks

This 28,000 acre park straddles the border between Kentucky and Tennessee. Campsites with hitching posts and plenty of riding trails. Lake winds through mountains and valleys of the Cumberland foothills. From Cave City, take KY 90 east then south on KY 449 and KY 1206.

6371 State Park Road, Bow, KY 42714-9728

☎ **(502) 433-7431**

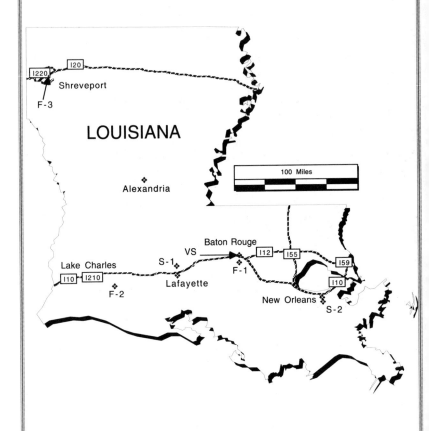

100 Miles

LOUISIANA

Shreveport
F-3
I20
I220

Alexandria

Baton Rouge
VS
S-1
F-1
I12
I55
I59
Lafayette
Lake Charles
I10
I210
F-2
New Orleans
S-2
I10

BRRC Center F-1
Burton Coliseum F-2
Louisiana St. Fair F-3
LSU Vet School VS
Plaisance Stables S-2
Trader's Rest Farms S-1

BRRC / Farr Park / Horse Activities Center/ Baton Rouge (F-1)

Take College Drive exit off Interstate, take first left, go 5.5 miles then take a left at the levee and go 1/2 a mile. Then one more left. Recommend confirming these directions. ⇒ 200 wood stalls w/o bedding (it can be bought at extra charge). Stalls @ $10 per night. ✚ Close to LSU Vet Center and plenty of resident vets available. 🚐 300 Camper/ RV hookups @ $10 per night. These facilities include laundry and showers. 🅙 Plenty of these services close to the park. ✖ Dajonel's at 7327 Jefferson Highway, 4 miles from College Drive and I-10 intersection ☎ 924-7537.
⌂ *6400 River Road, Baton Rouge, LA 70820*
☎ **(504) 769-7805**

Burton Coliseum / Lake Charles (F-2)

Going east on I-210 take Coliseum/Airport Exit. Going west take Highway 14/Cameron Exit. ⇒ 86 stalls w/o bedding @ $3 per night 🚐 Camper/RV hookups. ✚🅤🅙 These services available. ✖ Piccadilly Cafeteria in Prien Lake Mall. ☎ 477-7010
⌂ *7001 Gulf Highway, Lake Charles, LA 70605*
☎ **(318) 478-9010**

Louisiana State Fair / Shreveport (F-3)

Off I-20 4 miles west of Shreveport. Call number below and ask for Livestock Dept. to insure gates will be open. Normally they are open only 7a.m.-4p.m. during the week unless you have made special arrangements. ⇒ 197 stalls w/o shavings ($5/bag extra) @ $10 per night. Security guard on call @ $6 per hour. 🚐 Over 100 Camper/RV hookups @ $10 per night. ✚🅤🅙 These services available. ✖ Try Mike Anderson's Seafood. From I-20 go south .7 miles on Line Ave. ☎ 868-9568. If you have $$$$ the ultimate is Monsieur Patou 3 miles south of I-20 on Fairfield, then 1.5 blocks east on Pierremont Road. Dress code. Reservations required ☎ 868-9822.
⌂ *P.O. Box 38327, Shreveport, LA 71133*
☎ **(318) 635-1361**

Louisiana State Univ. College of Veterinary Medicine / Baton Rouge (VS)

Emergency horse care. Call only for emergencies! May require referral from a vet. NO STALLS FOR TRANSIENT BOARDING. On south Stadium Drive. ⌂ *South Stadium Drive, Baton Rouge, LA 70803-8402*
☎ **(504) 346-3131**

Plaisance Stables / New Orleans / Gretna Area (S-2)
▰➕⚲♞✕$

Near Terrytown-- off Behrman Highway. Call for directions and reservations. ▰ 40 stalls. Price per night negotiable. ➕⚲ Vet and farrier available. ♞✕ These services nearby.

⚑ *2600 Peter Street, Gretna, LA 70053*

☎ **(504) 394-8360**

Trader's Rest Farm / Lafayette Area (S-1)
▰➕⚲♞🛠✕$$

I-10 take exit 100 and go north 1/2 mile/ its north of Lafayette. ▰ 108 10X10 stalls with bedding @ $15 per night. Stallions allowed. ➕ Vet in Lafayette at ☎ 235-9945. ⚲ Farrier in Lafayette at ☎ 233-0635. 🛠 Closest mechanic 1 mile away at 76 truck stop at ☎ 237-7676 (open 7 days a week/ 24 hours a day). ✕ Don's Seafood at ☎ 235-3551 or for local dishes Chez Pastor and Maugie's at ☎ 234-5189. For steak & seafood, try Blair House Restaurant at ☎ 234-0357.

⚑ *P.O. Box 156, Carencro, LA 70520*

☎ **(800) 544-6773 or (318) 234-2382**

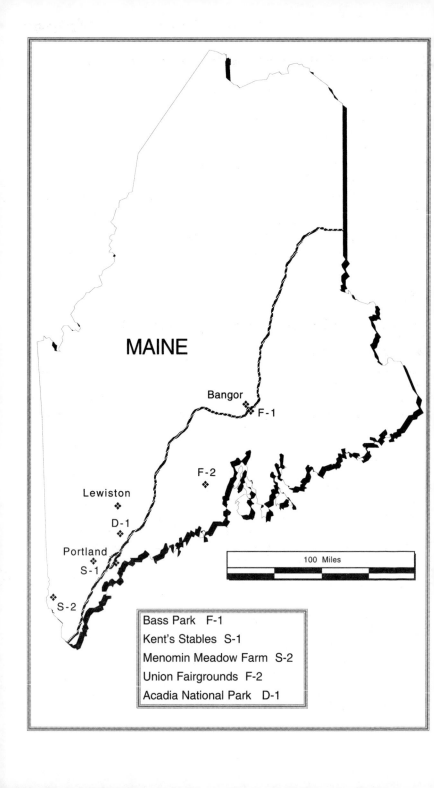

MAINE

Bangor
F-1

F-2

Lewiston

D-1

Portland
S-1

S-2

100 Miles

Bass Park F-1
Kent's Stables S-1
Menomin Meadow Farm S-2
Union Fairgrounds F-2
Acadia National Park D-1

Bass Park / Bangor Raceway / Bangor (F-1)

Off Route 95. CALL AHEAD. May 29--July 25 no stalls available. 200 stalls w/o bedding @ $5 per night.

100 Dutton Street, Bangor, ME 04401

☎ **(207) 942-9000**

Kent's Stables / Gorham (S-1)

On Route 114/Gorham. Call for final directions and reservations. 9 wood stalls with bedding @ $10 per night. 32 acres, grass turnouts, and new indoor arena. Electric hookup available. Nearby trails available. Vets and farriers available in town of Gray. These services available in Windham. For dinner try the Barn House Tavern in Windham.

762 Fort Hill Road, Gorham, ME 04038

☎ **(207) 839-5351**

Menomin Meadow Farm / East Lebanon (S-2)

On outskirts of Rochester, New Hampshire. Call for specific directions. About 6 miles from Spaulding Turnpike in New Hampshire. 15 wood stalls, varying from 10X12 to 12X16, incl. bedding. Current health papers required and stallions must have reservations/ok. Board horses @ $15 per night and $25 per night for stallions. Built a new barn in 1991 and there is easy trailer parking and turnaround. According to owner, "My farm is a good overnight stop on the way to Acadia (it's 6 hours from the farm). I've had several overnighters from New York and New Jersey. Good vet in Rochester at ☎ (603) 332- 6482. Rooms for rent and electric hookups. See Acadia National Park listing. Good mechanic only 4 miles away at MR Truck Repairs. Located on Route 202 and can be reached at ☎ (207) 339-2123. Two gas stations are located between farm and highway. One open all night on Route 202 in Rochester, NH.

RR #1/ Box 1319D (Columbus Circle), East Lebanon, ME 04027

☎ **(207) 457-1774**

Union Fairgrounds /Union (F-2)

Off Route 17. 50 wood stalls w/o bedding. CALL IN ADVANCE for Howard Hawes at ☎ (207) 785-3557. Vet in area. RV hookups available. Many lakes and ponds with bass, trout, and salmon. Good restaurant within 1/4 mile from fairground.

☎ **(207) 785-3281** (or try number above)

Acadia National Park / Bar Harbor (D-1)

From 95N go to 1A south-- then take Route 3 to Ellsworth. Over 50 miles of carriage roads, 7 of which are on Rockefeller land. Ed Winterburg has the concession at Wildwood Stables for the Park and can be reached at ☎ (207) 276-3622. He might have some box/ standing stalls available but don't count on it. ⊨ There is also the Otter Creek Bed & Breakfast near Seal Harbor and it's close to the stables and the harbor ☎ (800) 845-5852.

☩ *P.O. Box 177, Bar Harbor, ME 04609*
☎ **(207) 288-3338**

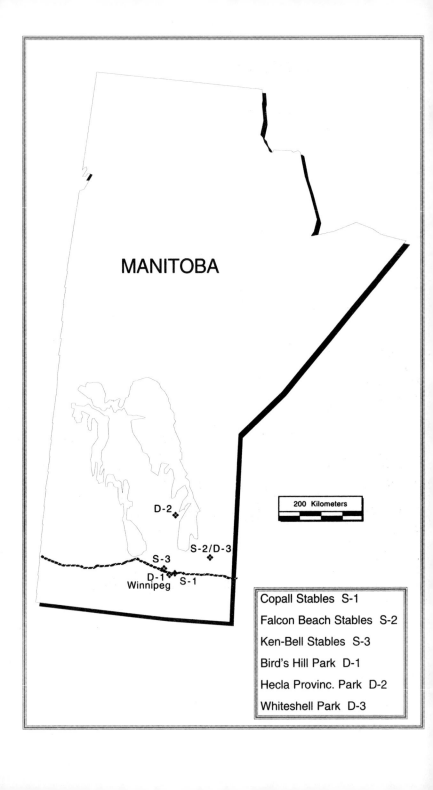

MANITOBA

200 Kilometers

D-2

S-2/D-3

S-3

D-1
Winnipeg
S-1

Copall Stables S-1

Falcon Beach Stables S-2

Ken-Bell Stables S-3

Bird's Hill Park D-1

Hecla Provinc. Park D-2

Whiteshell Park D-3

Copall Stables / Lorette (S-1)

▬ ▼ 🔳🔳🔳🔳 $$

12 miles east of the Mint. Call for directions. ▬ 30 large box stalls @ $10 per night. Security camera, indoor arena, heated barn and lounge. ▼ Tack shop on the premises. 🔳🔳🔳🔳 These services available in Winnipeg.

⌐ *Box 425, Lorette, MB R0A 0Y0 CANADA*

☎ **(204) 878- 2061**

Falcon Beach Stables / Falcon Lake (S-2)

▬ 🐎🔳🔳🔳🔳 $$

90 miles(150 km) east of Winnipeg on Trans Canada Highway #1. ▬ 20 stalls with bedding @ $10 per night. 🐎 See Whiteshell Provincial Park listing. 🔳 On premises. 🔳 Nearest vet 70 miles away. 🔳🔳 All of these services available in Falcon Lake

Ken-Bell Stables / Winnipeg (S-3)

▬🔳🔳🔳🔳🔳 $$

1 mile north of Winnipeg on Highway #59. ▬ 8 12X12 stalls @ $10 per night. Indoor arena. If you have stallions, call ahead for their approval. Contact: Ken Patterson. 🔳🔳🔳🔳 These services available in Winnipeg.

⌐ *2820 Speering Avenue, Winnipeg, MB CANADA*

☎ **(204) 668-8055**

Bird's Hill Provincial Park / Winnipeg Area (D-1)

🐎

24 km northeast of Winnipeg on Provincial Trunk Highway 59. You can go in main entrance, although there is a horse gate about 3 km further northeast on #59. Manitoba provides excellent summer and winter trail maps which show where horses are allowed. There is a concession stable at ☎ 222-1137.

☎ **(204) 222-9151**

Hecla Provincial Park / Winnipeg Region (D-2)

🐎

2.5 hour drive from Winnipeg on Highway 8. A heavily wooded archipelago named for Icelandic volcano that pushed the original settlers to Canada. This area is a major flyway and over 50,000 waterfowl spend their summers here. Many moose and other wildlife can be seen here early and late in the day. 🔳🔳 Fuel and food available at Gull Harbor. Maps available. Open May through September.

☎ **(204) 378-2945**

Whiteshell Provincial Park / Falcon Lake (D-3)

90 miles east of Winnipeg on Trans Canada Highway #1. No designated riding trails, but the Falcon Beach Riding Stables have developed some in the south end of the Park. They also have breakfast rides, overnight pack trips and privately guided rides. ✝ For more information and a brochure, contact: Falcon Beach Riding Stables, Falcon Lake, Manitoba R0E 0N0 CANADA or call them at ☎ (204) 349-2410 (for boarding see separate listing).

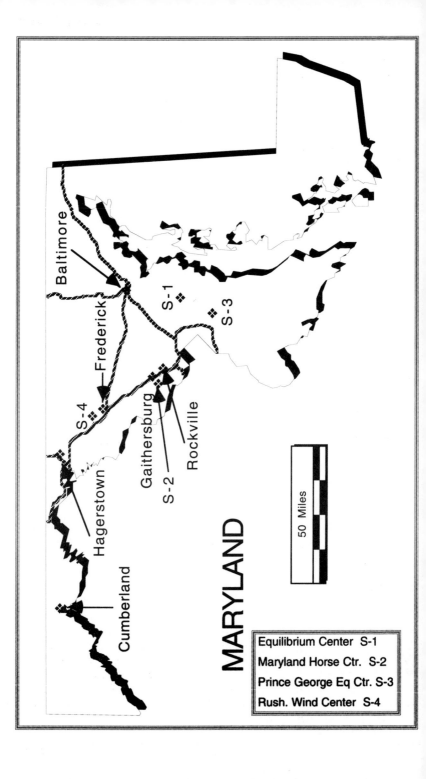

MARYLAND

Baltimore

Frederick

S-1

S-3

S-4

Hagerstown

Gaithersburg

S-2

Rockville

Cumberland

50 Miles

Equilibrium Center   S-1
Maryland Horse Ctr.   S-2
Prince George Eq Ctr. S-3
Rush. Wind Center   S-4

Equilibrium Horse Center / Annapolis (S-1)

2.5 miles from Route 50/301. From Route 50, go north on 424 then right on Underwood. It's near Annapolis. ▰ 53 12X12 metal stalls with sawdust @ $20 per night. Health papers required. Dressage, eventing and hunter shows. Summer programs, instruction at all levels. Indoor arena, ➤ Wooded trails and open fields. ▰ Electric hookups @ $10 per night. ✚ Dr. Stott is nearby at Lothian, MD at ☎ (301) 627-8668. ◑ John Crandell is nearest farrier. His office is in West River. ✎ Nearest mechanic is Leo's RV Service 3 miles away. ▮ Crofton, 3 miles away, is closest fuel. ✖ Good place to eat is Jasper's, 3 miles away, in Crofton.

⌖ *1685 Underwood Road, Gambrills, MD 21054*

☎ **(410) 721-0885**

Maryland Horse Center/Gaithersburg(S-2)

Near I-95 and #270. Call for directions. ▰ 100 metal stalls with bedding @ $20 per night. Require current health papers and stallions are allowed. ▰ camper/RV hookups with showers, electricity @ $20 per night. ✚ Fishing in the area. ✚ Nearest vet is in Damascus ☎ (301) 253-3992. ◑ Several farriers available. ✎ Nearest mechanic is Darnestown Texaco (6 miles away). ▮✖ These services available.

⌖ *14211 Quince Orchard Road, Gaithersburg, MD 20878*

☎ **(301) 948-8585**

Prince George's Equestrian Center / Upper Marlboro (S-3)

7 miles from Interstate 95/Capital Beltway to Exit 11A Pennsylvania

Ave.--7 miles to PGEC exit. ▰ 200 10X10 stalls(72 are wood) w/o bedding @ $10. Bedding can be arranged. Current health papers are required.

✚ Dr. Stott in Lothian at ☎ (301) 627-8668. ▰ Camper/RV hookups available @ $10 per night.

✎ ▮ Closest mechanic/fuel at Marlboro Texaco ☎ 627-3353. ✖ Wayson's Restaurant at Lothian ☎ 627-2383.

⌖ *14955 Pennsylvania Ave., Upper Marlboro, MD 20772*

☎ **(301) 952-4740**

Rushing Winds Stables / Frederick (S-4)

Within an hour's drive of Washington, Gettysburg, and Baltimore. Near Route 15, I-70, and I-270. Currently 6 stalls available @ $15 per night and have arena, wash stall with hot/cold water. Current neg cog/ health papers required. 1 full-service RV hookup and additional electric only hookups. Can put up people who cannot find another place to stay if space is available. Very good vet nearby. Farrier close by and responds quickly to calls. Mechanics available in Frederick. Fuel within 2 miles. Good restaurants within 8 miles.

9912 Masser, Frederick, MD 21702

☎ **(301) 898-9133**

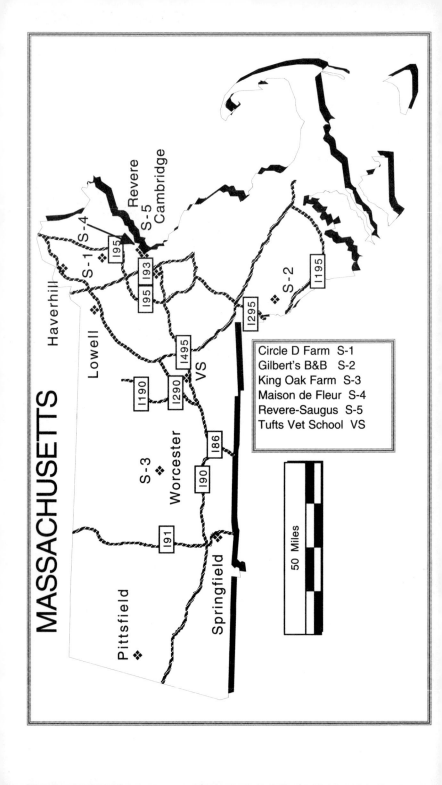

MASSACHUSETTS

Haverhill

Lowell

Revere
S-5
Cambridge

Pittsfield

Worcester

Springfield

VS

S-1
S-4
S-3
S-2

I95
I93
I95
I195
I295
I495
I290
I190
I86
I90
I91

Circle D Farm   S-1
Gilbert's B&B   S-2
King Oak Farm   S-3
Maison de Fleur   S-4
Revere-Saugus   S-5
Tufts Vet School   VS

50 Miles

Circle D Farm / Middleton (S-1)

Call for directions. 15 stalls and outdoor ring. 6 miles of beautiful trails and open all year.

61 Essex, Middleton, MA 01949

☎ **(508) 777-5300**

Gilbert's Bed & Breakfast / Rehobeth (S-2)

Take Exit 3 from I-195 in Mass. from Providence on Route 195. Bear right onto Route 6 to first traffic light. Take Route 118N. Spring Street is first right once in Rehobeth. Gilbert's B&B is 1 mile on the left. 2 10X10 wood stalls with bedding @ $15 per night. Neg cog/health papers required. Stallions not allowed. 150 year

old farmhouse which has had visitors from all over the World. Country breakfast includes juice, coffee, tea, milk, fresh fruit, eggs, sausage, and homemade muffins. 3 bedrooms with full bathroom shared by guests. Double occupancy @ $50 per night. Single occupancy @ $32 per night. ✚ Nearest vet is Amy Hurd in Seekonk at ☎ (508) 336-3381. ☽ Nearest farrier is Sal Lopez in Rehobeth at ☎ (508) 252-4701. ✎ Closest mechanic is 3.5 miles away at Sears ☎ (508) 324-6500 or Firestone at ☎ (508) 678-6380. ▌ Charter Food Store 3.5 miles away at ☎ (508) 674-9250. ✖ Best food at Marti's Family Bistro in Swansea at ☎ (508) 673-8898.

30 Spring Street, Rehobeth, MA 02769

☎ **(508) 252-6416**

King Oak Farm / Southampton (S-3)

Take Exit 3 off the Massachusetts Turnpike and go 6 miles north on Route 10. Farm is on the right. MUST CALL AHEAD & CHECK FOR AVAILABILITY. Sometimes all the stalls are booked up. 37 wood stalls with bedding. No stallions allowed. ▼ Tack shop on the premises. ✚ Vet 8 miles away.

P.O. Box 12, Southampton, MA 01037

☎ **(413) 527-4454**

Maison de Fleur Arabian / Dunstable (S-4)

≡◑◓♜✖

5 miles from Route 3. Call for directions. ≡ 17 new wood stalls with
bedding and rubber mats. TV surveillance cameras. Hot/cold water for
wash area. Stallions allowed. Contact: Rae. ◑◓ Vet and farrier in the
area. ♜✖ Available in Lowell or Nashua, NH.

⚐ *407 Forest Hill Road, Dunstable, MA 01820*

☎(508) 649-9138

Revere-Saugus Riding Academy / Revere (S-5)

≡◑

Located off Route 1 north of Saugus, right over the Revere line. Take
Route 1 north over the Tobin Bridge. Continue on past Route 60 and
Kappy's Liquor Store on your right. After the "Entering Saugus" sign,
turn right on Robin Road just past the Comfort Inn. Follow the road up
the hill and to the left. ≡ Stalls by the night/rates unknown. Horses
fed at least three times a day. Stalls constantly cleaned and looked
after. Staff on hand 24 hours a day, ready to deal with any emergency.
Full-sized indoor arena, indoor and outdoor rings. ◑ Equine dentistry.

⚐ *122 Morris Street, Revere, MA 02151*

☎ **(617) 322-7788 or FAX (617) 397-8260**

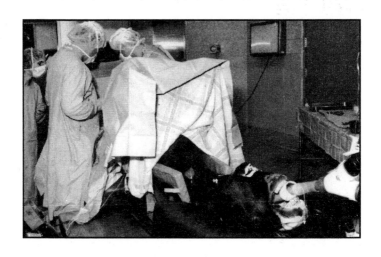

Tufts New England Veterinary Center / North Grafton (VS-1)
⌂

Some of the finest care in the nation for large animals. Advanced equipment and procedures to handle complex diagnoses and treatments. Emergency service, 7 days a week, 24 hours a day (Please call ahead so that we may prepare for your arrival). NO STALLS FOR TRANSIENT HORSES. Call only for emergencies! May require referral from a vet (Photo by David Willman for Tufts USVM).

⌖ *200 Westboro Road, North Grafton, MA 01536*
☎ **(508) 839-5395**

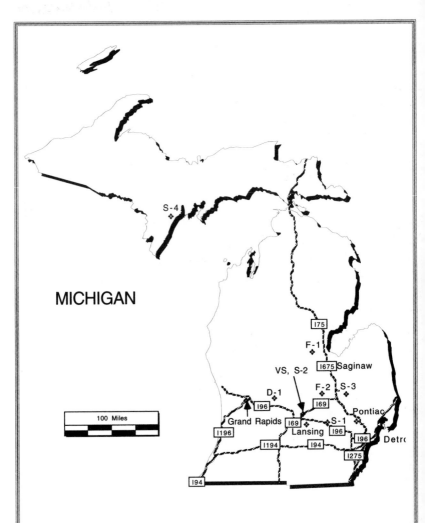

MICHIGAN

100 Miles

Cozy Cole Farm S-1	Roland Kammer S-3
MSU Vet School VS	Shiawassie Fairgrd. F-2
Midland Fairground F-1	Stoney Acres Farm S-4
Nottingham Eq Ctr S-2	Ionia State Rec Area D-1

Cozy Cole Farm / Howell (S-1)
▰▰⊕▮▨

Off Route 23/59. Call for directions. ▰▰ 31 stalls with bedding.
2 barns, paddocks and 40 acres. Indoor arena and plenty of room for
semis to turn around. Contact: Duci Cole
⚲ *7342 Clyde Road, Howell, MI 48843*
☎ **(517) 548-5053**

Michigan State Univ. College of Veterinary Medicine / East Lansing (VS)
⌂

Emergency horse care. Call only for emergencies! May require referral
from a vet. NO STALLS FOR TRANSIENT BOARDING.
⚲ *A-120E Fee Hall, East Lansing, MI 48824-1316*
☎ **(517) 353-9710**

Midland County Fairgrounds / Midland (F-1)
▰▰⊕⊍🚐▮▨$

Off Route 75 go to U.S. 10 and take Eastman Road Exit. MUST CALL IN
ADVANCE. ▰▰ 200 wood stalls with water and w/o bedding @ $6
per night. Current health papers required. camper/RV hookups available @ $5 partial service, $10 full service. ⊕ Nearest vet is 20 miles
away. ⊍ Farrier on the grounds. ▮▨ These services within 1/2 mile.
⚲ *6905 Eastman Road, Midland, MI 48640*
☎ **(517) 835-7901**

Nottingham Equestrian Center East Lansing (S-2)
▰▰⊕⊍

Off U.S. #27 take Lake Lansing Exit east--10 minutes drive--call for
exact directions. Must call in advance and make reservations.
▰▰ 30 wood stalls with bedding. Stallions not allowed.
⊕⊍ Vet and farrier in the area.
⚲ *16848 East Towar Avenue, East Lansing, MI 48823*
☎ **(517) 351-7304**

Roland Kammer / Flint Area (S-3)
▰▰ 🚐⊕⊍▨$$

Near the Canadian border (60 miles). Good layover spot when crossing
the border. 1.5 miles east of M-15. ▰▰ 43 wood stalls with bedding
@ $10 per night. 🚐 1 Camper/RV hookup available.
⊕⊍ Vet and farrier in the area. ▨ Closest good restaurants- in
Davison (2 miles) and Flint (10 miles).
⚲ *11291 Richfield Road, Davison, MI 48423*
☎ **(313) 653-0273**

Shiawassie County Fairgrounds / Corunna (F-2)

On Route 69, follow the signs. MUST HAVE ADVANCE NOTICE. Caretaker Bob and his wife very helpful. They do have an answering machine at ☎ (517) 288-3291 (home number). 100 stalls/ grounds normally locked. Camper/RV hookups. These services available in Corunna.

☎ (517) 288-3291

Stoney Acres Farm / Escanaba Area (S-4)

13 miles south of Escanaba on Highway M-35. 4 10X12 stalls with bedding @ $20 per night. Current health papers are required and stallions are allowed. Electric hookups available. Vet 3 miles away ☎ (906) 789-9603. Closest mechanic is 10 miles away in Lake Forest on South M-35. Closest fuel at Escanaba. Try the Bay Side Resort on South M-35.

1865 M-35, Bark River, MI 49807

☎ (906) 786-3500

Ionia State Recreation Area / Ionia (D-1)

Off I-96. This is a horseman's campground with a beautiful manmade lake and horse trails. Maps available. A good place to stay overnight if you want to rough it and don't need a stall. Overnight fee is $10. Showers and bathrooms available. Excellent fishing in the lake and plenty of trails.

2880 West David Highway, Ionia, MI 48846

☎ (616) 527-3750

MINNESOTA

R-1

I535 Duluth

I94

I35

Bloomington   Minneapolis / St. Paul
F-1   I494   VS

101 Miles

I35

Rochester   Winona

S-2

S-1   I90

Maul Ranch R-1
McLeod Fairgrounds F-1
Paint. Prairie Farm S-1
Gaylen/Margaret Schewe S-2
Univ. of Minnesota Vet Sch. VS

Maul Ranch / Moorhead (R-1)

3.5 miles from Route 29. Off I-29 (at Harwood, ND), 3.5 miles east, and then 1/2 mile south. It will be 2nd farm. 20 8X11 wood stalls with sawdust @ $15 per night. Stallions not allowed. Health papers required. No hookups but parking available on premises with advance notice. Nearest vet at Fargo at ☎ 232-3391. Farrier in the area. Closest mechanic at Jay's Repair 2 miles away. Both of these services 3.5 miles away at Harwood, ND.

Route 1/ Box 124, Moorhead, MN 56560
☎ **(218) 233-4476**

McLeod County Fairgrounds Hutchinson (F-1)

Highway 15 to south end of Hutchinson. 100 stalls. Brand new facility--probably complete by press time. Will be Camper/RV hookups in the near future. Nearest vet Virgil Voigt. Nearest farrier Daryl MacKeanz. Fuel within 2 miles. Prairie House has good food.

Highway 15, Hutchinson, MN 55350
☎ **(612) 587-4377** or Eric Smith at **(612) 587-8434**

Painted Prairie Farm / Prairie House on Round Lake / Round Lake (S-1)

4.5 miles off Interstate 90. South off I-90 then go 4.5 miles on State Highway 264. 24 stalls (16 wood) with shavings @ $7.50 per night (paddock) or @ $15 per night small stall with turnout). Stalls range from 10X12 to 14X14. Stallions allowed and health papers are required.

3 Camper/RV hookups available @ $5 per night. 4 rooms available for B&B. Fishing in the area. Vet in Sibley, IA at ☎ (712) 754- 2549. 7 miles--closest mechanic and fuel at Bob's Truck Stop in Worthington at ☎ (507) 376-4422. They are open 24 hours a day. Windmill Cafe at Worthington at ☎ (507) 376-5223.

RR #1 / Box 105, Round Lake, MN 56167
☎ **(507) 945-8934**

Gaylen & Margaret Schewe Stables
Glenville (S-2)
≋ ▬☎⚡♞⚒✗$$

1.5 miles south of 35W. Exit # 2 on County Road 18--go to County Road 83 and take a right and stable 1 mile. Stable is about 2.5 miles from 35W. ≋ 2 wood stalls with straw ON REQUEST @ $10 per night. One stall 8X12, the other 40X60. Stallions ok if they behave. Must have current neg cog/ health papers. ✚ Call ahead for appointment/ Albert Lea, MN or Northwood, IA ☎ (515) 592-3101. ⚒ Nearest farrier is Lynn Nelson in Albert Lea, MN ☎ (507) 373-6196. ▬ Camper/RV hookup available and showers in their home. Donations accepted. ✶ Fishing 4 miles south. ✎ Nearest mechanic, Kermit Bronson, is only 1/4 mile away. ▮ Albert Lea-- 12 miles north. ✗ Nearest good food in Albert Lea at Day's Inn ☎ (507) 373-6471.
☦ *Route 2/ Box 103, Glenville, MN 56036*
☎ **(507) 448-3786**

University of Minnesota College of
Veterinary Medicine / St. Paul (VS)
⌂

Emergency horse care 24 hours a day, 7 days a week. Call only for emergencies! May require referral from a vet. NO STALLS FOR TRANSIENT BOARDING. Opposite the fairgrounds.
☦ *1365 Gortner Avenue, St. Paul, MN 55108*
☎ **(612) 625-6700** or after hours **(612) 625-9711**

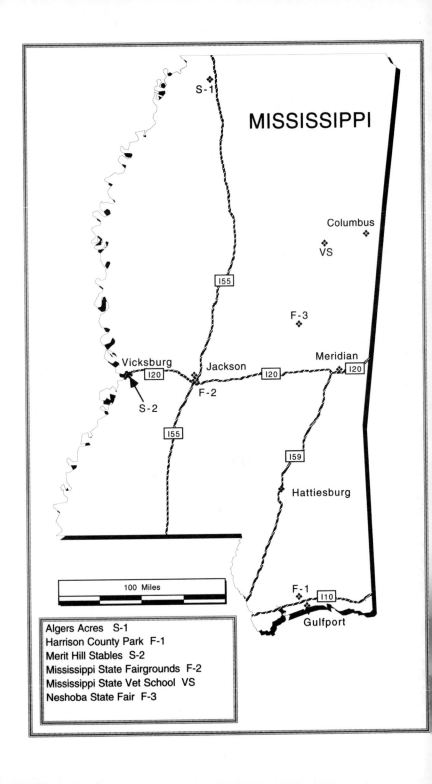

MISSISSIPPI

S-1

Columbus
VS

I55

F-3

Vicksburg | I20 | Jackson | I20 | Meridian | I20

F-2

S-2

I55

I59

Hattiesburg

100 Miles

F-1 | I10
Gulfport

Algers Acres S-1
Harrison County Park F-1
Merit Hill Stables S-2
Mississippi State Fairgrounds F-2
Mississippi State Vet School VS
Neshoba State Fair F-3

Algers Acres / Memphis Area (S-1)

4 miles off Highway 55/14 miles south of Memphis. 134 wood stalls @ $10 per night with bedding (@ $5 per night w/o bedding). Stallions allowed in special stalls. Camper/RV hookups. Next to park and near Arkabutla Lake. Vet and farrier in the area. Nearest mechanic 3 miles away at Chevy/ Ford dealers. Nearest food at Love's Cafe or Church's Chicken.

3611 Highway 304 West, Hernando, MS 38632
☎ **(601) 429-5284**

Harrison County Park / Gulfport (F-1)

On Route 49 South, link up with 53W--go 5 miles and take a left on County Farm Road. Go 1 mile and its on your right. Contact: Mike McMillen. 96 wood stalls with bedding @ $10 (or $5 w/o bedding). Camper/RV hookups available with electricity and water @ $25 per night. Quite a few vets in the area. These services available within 13 miles.

15147 Community Road, Gulfport, MS 39503
☎ **(601) 831-3350**

Merit Hill Stables / Vicksburg (S-2)

From west Bovina Exit, turn north 1.5 miles to golf course, turn right on Clear Creek Drive, go 1.3 miles to front gate. From east: Flowers Exit, turn south across I-20 to gravel frontage road. Turn right on frontage road and go 2.5 miles--gate will be on your left. 13 10X12 wood stalls with bedding @ $15 per night per horse. Stallions are allowed with advance reservations and neg cog/ health papers are required. Camper/RV hookups available in Bovina. Nearest vet in Vicksburg at ☎ (601) 636-9410. Farrier in the area. Closest truck mechanic 6 miles at Steven's Service Center/24 hours on call at ☎ (601) 636-7634. Closest fuel in Bovina/ gas and diesel. For lunch try Bovina Cafe in Bovina. For dinner try restaurants in Vicksburg.

732 Brabston Road, Vicksburg, MS 39180
☎ **(601) 634-1345**

Mississippi State Fairgrounds / Jackson (F-2)

≋ 🚐➕🔌🚰⬛$

Take the High Street Exit off I-55. ≋ 300 stalls w/o bedding. MUST MAKE RESERVATIONS! Stalls @ $5 per night. Contact: Tom Strickland. ➕🔌🚰⬛ All these services nearby. Several restaurants within walking distance.

⌖ *P.O. Box 892, Jackson, MS 39205*
☎ **(601) 961-4000**

Mississippi State College of Veterinary Medicine / Columbus Area (VS)

⌂

Emergency horse care. Call only for emergencies! May require referral from a vet. NO STALLS FOR TRANSIENT BOARDING. Facility at Wise Center in the town of Starkville.

⌖ *P.O. Drawer V, Mississippi State, MS 39762*
☎ **(601) 325-3432**

Neshoba State Fair / Philadelphia (F-3)

≋ 🚐➕

Off Highway I-20 at Newton, then take #15 north to Philadelphia #21 South. Fair has horse and cattle shows throughout the year. Race Track. Wagon trains from several points in the State come here every February. Contact : Dwight Barrett. ≋ 100 wood stalls, ranging in size from 8X10 to 10X10. Free for 1 or 2 nights. 🚐 3-4 Camper/RV hookups available. ➕ Several vets in the Philadelphia area.

⌖ *Highway 21 South, Philadelphia, MS 39350*
☎ **(601) 656-8480**

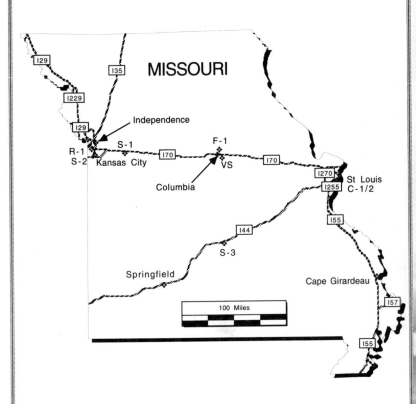

Benjamin Ranch R-1	Midway Expo Center F-1
40 Mile Farm S-1	Univ. of Missouri Vet Sch. VS
Knaus Equestrian Ctr. S-2	Anheuser Busch Brewery C-1
Laurie Quarter Horses S-3	Grant's Farm C-2

Benjamin Ranch / Kansas City (R-1)
≋ 🚐➕♘🔧✕$$

1 block east of I-435. I-70 coming east or west turn south to 87th Street. This facility features hay rides, rodeos, chuck wagon dinners, country western, sleigh rides and private parties. ≋ 45 10X12 wood stalls with bedding @ $15 per night. Stallions are allowed and must have health papers. 🚐 Electric hookups only. ➕ Vet in Lees Summit, MO ☎ (816) 5524-0464. ♘ Farrier on premises. 🔧 Closest mechanic 1 mile away at Fleetwood Chevy. 🔧✕ Plenty of services in Kansas City.
⚕ *6401 East 87th Street, Kansas City, MO 64138*
☎ **(816) 761-5055**

40 Mile Farm / Odessa (S-1)
≋ 🚐➕♘🔧✕$$

On I-70 2 miles east of Odessa. ≋ 4 wood stalls with bedding

@ $10 per night. Only well behaved stallions allowed. Require neg cog/health papers. 🚐 Electric hookups only. ➕ Dr. Peddicord in Odessa at ☎ 633-5712. ♘ Nearest farrier is Scott Nadler in Independence at ☎ 373-2794. 🔧 Closest mechanic in Oak Grove at Truck Stop ☎ 625-4116 (open 24 hours a day). ✕ Good places to eat: Whistle Stop in Odessa at ☎ 633-7949, Truck Stop in Oak Grove at ☎ 625-4115, or another truck stop at ☎ 633-7811.
⚕ *Route 2 / Box 183, Odessa, MO 64076*
☎ **(816) 633-4940**

Knaus Equestrian Center / Kansas City (S-2)
≋➕✕

CALL AHEAD. In south part of Kansas City. ≋ 200 wood/metal stalls with bedding. ➕ Vet nearby. ✕ Jess & Jim's Steakhouse nearby. The

Woodlands, 2 blocks east from Junction I-435 on Leavenworth Road (9900 Leavenworth). ☎ (913) 299-3434.
⚕ *800 East 147th Street, Kansas City, MO 64146*
☎ **(816) 942-1224**

Laurie Quarter Horses / Waynesville (S-3)

I-44 to Highway 17-- to T Highway-- 2.5 miles to gravel, .3 miles off T Highway. Call for exact directions if not familiar with the area.

≋ 23 wood stalls, ranging from 10X12 to 12X15 with bedding @ $25 per night. Indoor and outdoor arenas. Stallions allowed and current health papers required. 🚐 Electric hookups only @ $ 10 per night. ✚ Vet in Lebanon(25 miles away) at ☎ (417) 532-9147. ⚒ Farrier available. ⛽ Nearest fuel and mechanic/ 5 miles. ✕ In Buckhorn try the Ted Williams Restaurant.

✝ *Route 1/ Box 374, Waynesville, MO 65583*
☎ **(314) 774-6512**

Midway Expo Center / Columbia (F-1)

Take Exit 21 at I-70/Highway 40. ≋ 237 wood stalls w/o bedding (available at extra cost). 🚐 Camper/RV hookups available. 90 room motel and 24 hour restaurant on the premises. Contact: C W Adams.

✝ *Columbia, MO 65202*
☎ **(314) 445-8338**

University of Missouri College of Veterinary Medicine / Columbia (VS)

⬥

Emergency horse care. Call only for emergencies! May require referral from a vet. NO STALLS FOR TRANSIENT BOARDING. Located at 379 Campus Drive.

✝ *W203 Veterinary Medicine Building, Columbia, MO 65211*
☎ **(314) 882-3513**

Anheuser-Busch Brewery / St. Louis (C-1)

I-55 to Arsenal Street Exit. Tour this famous brewery and see their Clydesdales. Traditional home of the "Gentle Giants".

1127 Pestalozzi Street, St. Louis, MO 63118

☎ **(314) 577-9755**

Grant's Farm / St. Louis / (C-2)

From downtown, I-55 south, then turn right on Reavis Barracks and then a left on Gravois. Ancestral home of the Busch family on 281 acres Clydesdales can be seen here as well as at the brewery in St. Louis.

10501 Gravois Road, St. Louis, MO 63123

☎ **(314) 843-1700**

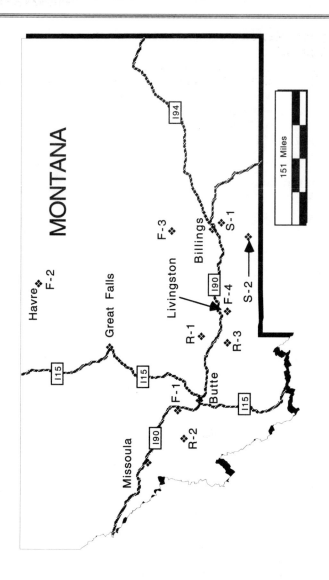

MONTANA

151 Miles

Add Reese Stables S-1	Park County Fairgrounds F-4
Bob's Arena F-1	Roundup Fairgrounds F-3
Circle of Friends B&B S-2	Great Northern Fairgrds F-2
D J Bar Ranch R-1	320 Ranch R-3
Rocking Ranch R-2	

Add Reese Stables / Billings (S-1)

Call for exact directions. Stable faces I-90. Easy access from either east or west. 20 12X14 stalls with sawdust @ $12 . Stallions allowed. Camper/RV hookups within two blocks. Vet and farrier in the area. Mechanic 1/2 mile away at West Parkway Truck stop. These services available within 1/2 mile.

1007 Mullowney Lane, Billings, MT 59101

☎ (406) 259-6248

Bob's Arena / Deer Lodge (F-1)

From I-90 take Exit 184. You can see u.s. from the freeway (within 300 yards). 25 12X12 wood stalls with shavings @ $10 per horse per night. Stallions allowed. Vet in Deer Lodge at ☎ 846- 3627. Farrier in Clinton at ☎ 544- 2158. Closest mechanic is at John's Tuneup at ☎ 846- 2075 and they are open 12 hours a day. Nearest fuel in Deer Lodge at ☎ 846-3969 (1/8 mile). Good food in Deer Lodge at ☎ 846-2620 (1/8 mile).

167 BLD Road, Deer Lodge, MT 59722

☎ (406) 846-1989

Circle of Friends Bed & Breakfast / Bridger (S-2)

25 miles south of I-90 on State Highway 310 across from the state rest area/turnout. 2 12X12 loafing sheds with straw or chips @ $10 per night. Stallions allowed and health papers required. 3 bedrooms available. $45 per night for double with bathroom. For single $30 per night (shared bathroom) and double @ $35 per night (shared bathroom). Full breakfast served and dinner available @ $5 for adults and $3 for children. Hostess, Dorothy Sue Phillips, is a transplanted Alaska teacher/ innkeeper. According to her brochure, " Bridger is a small town of less than a thousand people who work hard, smile often, and offer a handshake to outsiders".

2 vets in Bridger. ☎ 662-3330. Farrier available from Fromberg (4 miles) at ☎ 668- 7492. Fishing in the area. Closest mechanic is at CONOCO in Bridger (3 miles) at ☎ 662-3633 and their hours are 8-6.

North American Horse Travel Guide

◼ Closest good fuel is at Maverick in Bridger. ☒ Stringtown Buckeye in Bridger at ☎ 662-3230.
☦ *Route 1/ Box 1250, Bridger, MT 59014*
☎ **(406) 662-3264**

DJ Bar Ranch / Belgrade (R-1)
≣ ⛺☰⛽♘☒$

8 miles from Interstate 90--take Manhattan or Belgrade exit and call for directions. ≣ 3 12X12 stalls with bedding, auto H2O @ $8 per night. Stallions allowed and current health papers are required.
⛺ Electric hookups only. ☰ Excellent fishing in the area. ✚ Vet in Belgrade at ☎ 388-VETS. ♘ Farrier in Belgrade. ✎ Nearest mechanic 8 miles away at Albertson's Auto, 105 North Broadway ☎ 284-3731, Mon-Sat 8-5, Sun 8-12. ◼ Fuel in Belgrade at ☎ 388-4008.
☒ Good food in Manhattan 8 miles away at ☎ 284-6443.
☦ *5155 Round Mt. Road, Belgrade, MT 59714*
☎ **(406) 388-7463**

Rocking Ranch / Philipsburg (R-2)
≣ ⛺☰✚♘☒$

West of Highway 1--across from the airport. ≣ 10 15X15 stalls with wood shavings and auto H2O. Stallions allowed. Have indoor and outdoor arenas. Contact: Bill & Carolynn Victor. ⛺ Full Camper/RV hookups @ $5 per night.☰ Fishing in the area. ✚ Vet available in Philipsburg at ☎ 859-3838. ✎ Nearest mechanic at Winninghoff Motors in Philipsburg at ☎ 859-3657. Open daily.
◼☒ These services available nearby.
☦ *P.O. Box 247, Philipsburg, MT 59858*
☎ **(406) 859-3845**

Park County Fairgrounds / Livingston (F-4)
≣✚♘☒$

Go down main street toward the river and take a left at the "Y". Go 1/2 mile on Vista View Drive and it's on your right. ≣ 52 stalls (30 inside) @ $5 per night w/o bedding. ✚♘ Vet and farrier in the area.
◼☒ These services available nearby.
☦ *P.O. Box 146, Livingston, MT 59047*
☎ **(406) 222-8677**

Roundup Fairgrounds / Roundup (F-3)
≣ ⛺☰✚♘$

In Roundup, turn east off Main and follow 2nd Avenue/ fairground is 2 miles from Highway 87. ≣ 20/30 wood stalls w/o bedding @ $5 per night contribution. Stallions allowed. Contact: Gay Holliday.
⛺ Campground and RV park @ $5 per night contribution. ☰ Fishing in the area. ✚ Vet in town at ☎ 323-2287. ♘ Farrier in town is Dave

Tomlin at ☎ 323-2222. ✎ Closest mechanic is at A &A Implement
☎ 323- 1702, open Mon.-Fri. 8-5 and Sat. 8-12. 🏮 Main Street Conoco
in Roundup at ☎ 323-3646 . ❌ Stella's at ☎ 323-1166.
☎ **(406) 323-2588**

The Great Northern Fairgrounds / Havre (F-2)
🚂🏠🍴🐎✚🏮✎❌$

On Highway 2 West. Call if problem finding. 🚂 34 metal stalls with
bedding @ $5 per night. Stallions allowed. Have 140X200 indoor arena
and 180X300 outdoor arena. 🚐 30 Camper/RV hookups available @
$10.40 per night. 🍴🐎 Bear Paw mountains 1/2 mile drive. ✚ Vet 3
miles away at ☎ (406) 265-8901. ✎ Mechanic 3 miles away at Williams
Field Service ☎ (406) 265-8484. Trailer repair at Norman's (4 miles)
at☎ (406) 265-4523. 🏮 At Town Pump ☎ (406) 265-9577. ❌ Several
places to eat in Havre.
✉ *1676 Highway 2 West, Havre, MT 59501- 6104*
☎ **(406) 265-7121 or FAX (406) 265-5487**

320 Ranch / Gallatin Gateway (R-3)
🚂🏠🍴✚✎🏮❌$$

1/2 mile off Highway
191. 🚂 16 stalls with
bedding @ $10 per night.
Stallions allowed.
🚐 No RV but we do
rent cabins. 🍴 Fishing in
the area. ✚ Vet in
Bozeman.
✎ Nearest mechanic 6
miles away. 🏮 Nearest
fuel in Big Sky (6 miles). ❌ at the ranch--320 Steakhouse.
✉ *205 Buffalo Horn Creek, Gallatin Gateway, MT 59730*
☎ **(406) 995-4283**

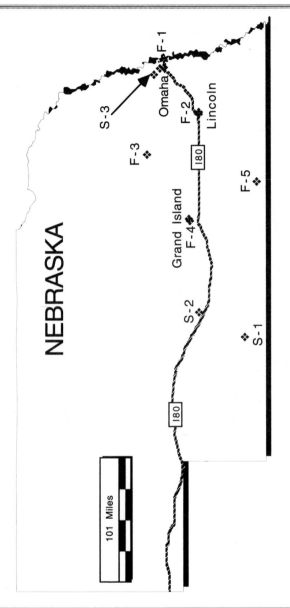

NEBRASKA

101 Miles

Aksarben County Fair F-1	Platte Ag Society F-3
Fonner Park F-4	Plum Creek Vet Clinic S-2
Mueller's Stable S-1	Thayer Fairgrounds F-5
Nebraska State Park F-2	TLC Ranch B&B S-3

Aksarben-Douglas County Fair / Omaha (F-1)

Off I-80 take 72nd Street and go 1 mile. 800 stalls w/o bedding @ $10 per night. Vet and farrier on the premises. Camper/RV hookups available @ $10 per night. These services within 1-2 blocks.

P.O. Box 6069, Omaha, NE 68106

☎ (402) 444-4031

Fonner Park / Grand Island (F-4)

From I-80, take the first Grand Island Exit and go to the southeast part of Grand Island. Stalls available on a space available basis. There is no charge for stalls but you must provide bedding, feed, and cleanup.. They do have several horse shows through the year, so you might want to call ahead. There is a vet in Grand Island. These services available in Grand Island.

P.O. Box 490, Grand Island, NE 68802

☎ (308) 382-4515

Mueller's Training Stable / Cambridge (S-1)

Alongside Highway 6/34 1 mile east of town. 16 metal inside 12X12 stalls with bedding and 16 outside 20X20 stalls with bedding @ $10 per night. Auto H20. Stallions allowed. 2 Camper/RV hookups available @ $10 per night. Fishing in the area.

Nearest vet in Curtis at ☎ 367-8688. Nearest farrier at Cambridge at ☎ 697-4307. Mechanic 1 mile away at GMC dealer and Hansen Repair. Fuel at Cambridge COOP.

Route 3/ Box 220, Cambridge, NE 69022

☎ (308) 697-4307

Nebraska State Park / Lincoln (F-2)

Take I-82 to 180 to Cornhusker Highway (#6) and follow signs. 1280 stalls w/o bedding @ $10 per night. Additional nights @ $7. Camper/RV hookups @ $12 per night. Contact: Sharon. Vet and farrier available. These services available within 2 miles.

P.O. Box 81223, Lincoln, NE 68501

☎ (402) 474-5371

Platte County Agricultural Society / Columbus (F-3)

75 miles west of Omaha on Highway 30 at U.S. 81 Junction. 940 stalls @ under $5 per night. Can negotiate on price. Full time caretaker

on the grounds. ⛽🔧🍴 Days Inn within 1 mile and for dinner try Johnnie's Steakhouse at East Highway 30 and 3rd Ave. ☎ 563-3434
P.O. Box 1335, Columbus, NE 68601
☎ (402) 564-0133

Plum Creek Veterinary Clinic / Lexington (S-2)

$$$

Located 1.5 miles south of I-80 on Highway 283. 8 12X12 padded cement stalls with bedding @ $17 per night. Stallions allowed. Several Camper/RV hookups available @ $7 per night. Vet on premises. Several farriers in Lexington. Mechanic and fuel 1.5 miles at Nebraska Land at ☎ 324-6374. Open 24 hours a day. In Lexington.
Route 2 / Box 88, Lexington, NE 68850
☎ (308) 324-2016

Thayer County Fairgrounds / Hebron Area (F-5)

On south end of town of Deshler, a small town of 1000 population. Only tough time to get stalls usually the 2nd or 3rd weekend of August. Portable ring. Water available from hydrant. Contact Larry Lueders at address or phone number below. 40 stalls. Vet in Hebron. These services available in Hebron and there is a mechanic in Deshler.
P.O. Box 389, Deshler, NE 68340
☎ (402) 365-7662

TLC Ranch/ Bed & Breakfast / Omaha (S-3)

$$

5 miles off I-680 on Highway 133 North. 1/4 mile off I-33. Call for complete directions. 8 metal stalls with bedding (10X12 to 10X10) @ $ 10 per night. Stallions allowed. Electric only @ $10 per night. 2 people @ $45. Have 2 bedrooms and also queen sofa sleeper

in walkout rec room with 1/2 bath. ➕ Vet in Omaha at ☎ (402) 493-3393. ♀ Farriers in Omaha at ☎ 492-8875 and 571-8078,✎ Closest mechanic 12 miles away at Woodhouse Ford ☎ 341-9786 (at I-680 Exit). ⛽ Wheelers in Omaha.
☎ 571-3401 ❌ Perkins Restaurant in Omaha.
⚐ *11329 Pawnee Road, Omaha, NE 68142*
☎ **(402) 572-6033**

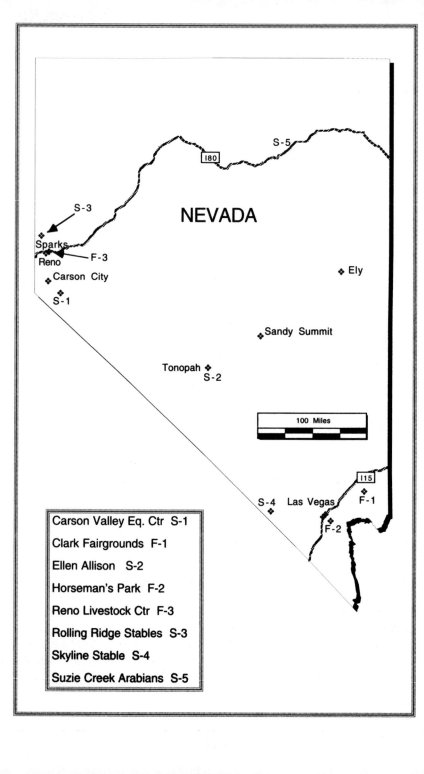

Carson Valley Equestrian Center / Carson City Area (S-1)
≡≡◼▢❶◍▮◾$$

On main route 5 miles south of Carson City(Highway 395).
≡≡ 20 insulated wood stalls with bedding @ $10 per night. Corrals with shelters @ $7 per night. Indoor arena, hunter jumper arena, and 100 acre layout. ▤ Within 1/4 mile there is a campground with complete facilities. ❶◍ On call. ▮◾ These services in Carson City.
⌖ *3060 Highway 395, Minden, NV 89423*
☎ **(702) 267-3118**

Clark County Fairground / East Las Vegas(F-1)
≡≡❶◍ ▤▢▮◾$$

50 minutes out of Las Vegas toward St. George on I-15, take Logandale--Overton exit south on Route 169, go 6 miles south and take a left at Wally's convenience store to end of Whipple Road.
≡≡ 10 outside pens, ranging in size from 20X20 to 20X50 with water @ $15 per day. 5 different arena areas. Grounds enclosed with 6' chain link fence. 5 acres of landscaped turf and trees. ▤ Electric only at $10 per night. Try Fun & Sun for Camper/RV hookups in Valley of Fire State Park, if you don't mind the 15 mile drive ☎ 397-8894. ▣ Only 15 miles to Lake Mead Recreational Area or Valley of Fire State Park.
❶ Nearest vet Dr. Kristin Peterson 1 mile away in Logandale.
◍ Nearest farrier David May ☎ 397-2534. ◈ Nearest truck mechanic B&D Service 10 miles away at ☎ 397-8300. ▮ Fuel at Wally's ☎ 398-3400. ◾ Sugar's Home Plate 6 miles away at ☎ 397-8084.
⌖ *P.O. Box 615, Overton, NV 89040*
☎ **(702) 397-8088 or FAX (702) 397-2321**

Ellen Allison / Tonopah (S-2)
≡≡❶▮◈◾$$

Outside Tonopah on Highway 6, towards Ely on left side 2 miles out. 24 wood/metal stalls with bedding @ $10 per night. Good security--big guard dogs. ❶ 120 miles away in Bishop, CA. ▮◾ These services available in Tonopah.
⌖ *P.O. Box 241, Tonopah, NV 89049*
☎ **(702) 482-3626**

Horseman's Park / Las Vegas (F-2)
≡≡❶◍▮◾$$

1 mile away Sam's Town Casino on 5800 East Flamingo. ≡≡ 320 covered stalls w/o bedding @ $10 per night. And 20 pens @ $3 per night. Big horse shows during the year and have 3 big arenas plus 2 for practice. ❶◍ Vets and farriers available. ▮◾ These services available nearby. ⌖ *5800 East Flamingo, Las Vegas, NV 89122*
☎ **(702) 455- 7548**

Reno Livestock Event Center / Reno (F-3)

From I-80 take Wells Avenue Exit north-- also close to #395.
24 10X10 stalls with rubber mats available for transient horses w/o
bedding @ $17 per night. Shavings available @ $5.75 per bag. Indoor
and outdoor arenas. Vet and farrier available.
☞ *1350 North Wells Avenue, Reno, NV 89512*
☎ **(702) 688-5751**

Rolling Ridge Stables / Reno (S-3)

Call for directions. 10 stalls plus outside pens with shelters.
Stallions must have reservations. Require neg cog/health papers.
Vet and farrier available. Within 2 miles. Pizza Parlor 1.5
miles away.
☞ *3440 Rolling Ridge Court, Reno, NV 89506*
☎ **(702) 972-0309**

Skyline Stable / Pahrump / West of Las Vegas (S-4)

Take Calvada Blvd. off Route 160 to Blagg Road and turn south-- stable on left (4 miles from 160). 12 metal covered stalls @ $6 per
night. Stallions allowed. Current health papers required. 20 acres of

pasture.
Camper/RV hookups @
$5 per night. Vet in
Pahrump at ☎ 727-
6086. All ser-
vices available in
Pahrump.
☞ *HC 73/ Box 15045,
2901 South Blagg,
Pahrump, NV 89041*
☎ **(702) 727-7227**

Suzie Creek Arabians / Elko (S-5)

Off I-80 take Exit 292 and stable is about 3 miles. Call for directions.
12 indoor stalls with shavings @ $20 per night and 5 outside
runs @ $15 per night. Stallions allowed and must have health papers.
Vet in Elko at ☎ (702) 738-1155. Farrier in Elko at (702) 753-
6602. Fishing in the area. These services available in Elko 8
miles away. ☞ *P.O. Box 1360, Elko, NV 89803*
☎ **(702) 738- 8631**

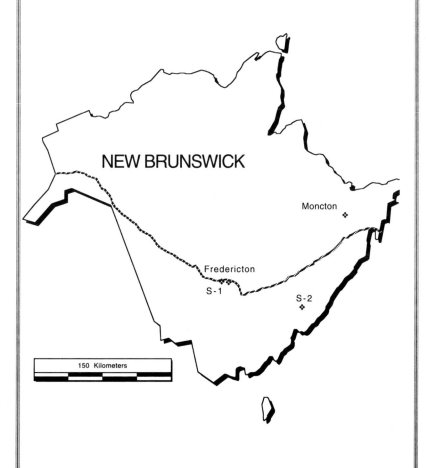

NEW BRUNSWICK

Moncton

Fredericton

S-1

S-2

150 Kilometers

Royal Road Riding Stables S-1
Butternut Stables S-2

Royal Road Riding Stables / Fredericton(S-1)

Off Highway 105 (Ring Road) on Royal Road. In northwest Fredricton. Must call ahead for reservations. 32 box stalls and 36 standing stalls. Indoor and outdoor arenas. Box stalls @ $10 per night. Lessons in English and Western riding. Weekend clinics and supervised trail rides. One of the larger facilities in New Brunswick. Sales of show and pleasure horses. Trails nearby. Tack shop on the premises. Overnight accomodation at the stable or motels within 5 miles (8 km). Vets and farriers available. These services available within 5 miles.

RR #7, Fredericton, NB E3B 4X8 CANADA

☎ **(506) 450-3059 or 452-0040**

Butternut Stables / Hampton (S-2)

On Highway #1, go opposite direction from Hampton at the Hampton Exit. Go 800 yards south on Hall Road, turning on to Robertson Road/ stable will be on your right. 40 wood stalls @ $15 per night. Current health papers required and stallions are allowed. Indoor and outdoor arenas. Tack shop on the premises and also sell horse trailers. Access to trails. Vet and farrier available. These services available in nearby St. John. Two good places to eat are Grannan's on Market Street ☎ (506) 634-1555 and Incredible Edibles on Princess Street ☎ (506) 633-7554.

RR # 4, Hampton, NB E0G 1Z0 CANADA

☎ **(506) 832-3219**

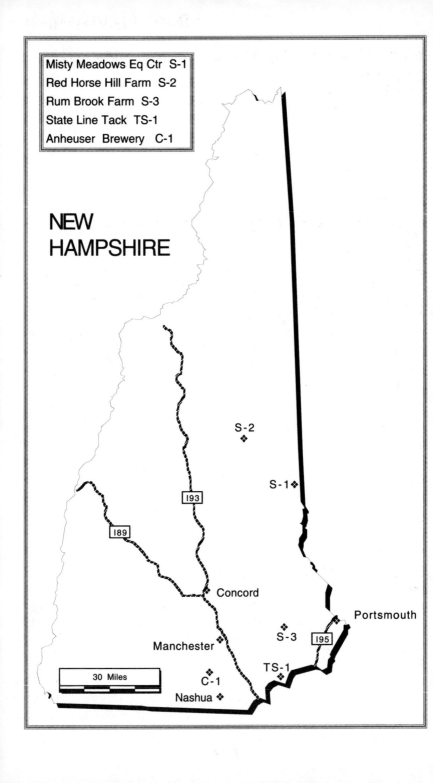

Misty Meadows Equestrian Center / Ossipee Area (S-1)
≈ ⊁ ⊡Ů⊠⊠$$

3 miles off Route 16 south of Ossipee. Call for directions. ≈ 20 stalls with bedding @ $10 per night. Indoor arena, jumping field, and 1/4 mile track. Contact Krista or William Houston. ⊁ Access to trails. ⊡Ů Vet and farrier available. ⊠⊠ These services available in East Wakefield and Ossipee.

⊕ *Ballard's Ridge Road, East Wakefield, NH 03830*
☎ **(603) 522-8893**

Red Horse Hill Farm / South Tamworth (S-2)
≈ ⊁ ⊨⊠⊠$$

Off I-93 to #104 to Route 25 and follow signs to facility. Or Route 25 to 113 North Sandwich, turn on #113 over Bearcamp River, take next right on Bunker Hill Road, and facility will be 1 mile on your right. ≈ 13 stalls with bedding @ $15 per night. New barn built in 1990 with hot/ cold water wash stall, 11X11 box stalls with rubber mats, and grated windows. Dressage ring, cross country course, grass pasture and wood fencing. Require neg cog and current health papers. ⊁ Over 20 miles of trails. ⊨ Bed and breakfast. Great views of pastures, pond in wooded country. For couples, rate ranges from $65 to $75 and $45 per night for singles. Have tennis court. Contact Diana Louis.

⊕ *Bunker Hill Road, South Tamworth, NH 03883*
☎ **(603) 323-7275**

Rum Brook Morgan Farm / Epping (S-3)
≈

Call for directions and reservations! Take Route 87 off Route 125. ≈ 28 wood stalls and have indoor/outdoor arenas.

⊕ *44 Hedding Road, Epping, NH 03042-2526*
☎ **(603) 679-5982**

State Line Tack, Inc. / Plaistow (TS-1)
♥

From Route 495 North, exit 51B onto Route 125 North. Straight through 3 sets of lights to Route 121. Store is 1/4 mile on the left. Discount tack store. Riding equipment, apparel, stable equipment, and vet supplies.

⊕ *Route 121, Plaistow, NH 03865*
☎ **(800) 228-9208**

North American Horse Travel Guide

Anheuser-Busch Brewery / Merrimack (C-1)

Take Route 3 (Everett Turnpike) to Exit 10 (Industrial Drive) located between Nashua and Manchester. This brewery has Clydesdales which you can see when you go on your tour.

⚐ *221 Daniel Webster Highway, Merrimack, NH 03054*

☎ **(603) 595-1202**

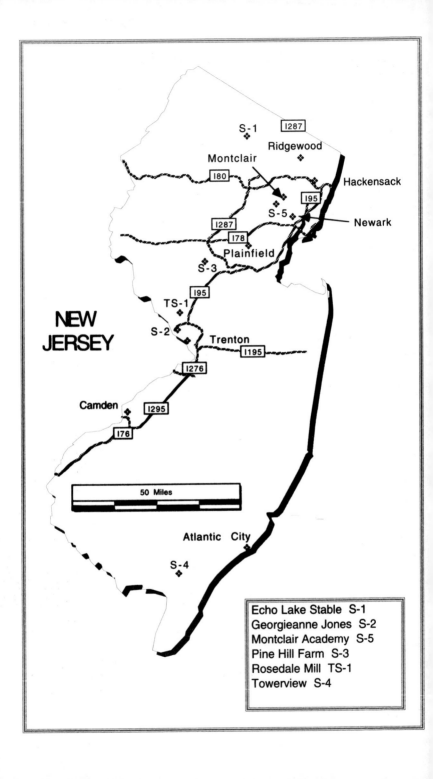

Echo Lake Stable / Newfoundland (S-1)
▤ ⬛⬛⬛⬛

Take I-80 to 23N Exit, 15 miles to Echo Lake Road. Call for exact directions. ▤ 100 cinder block stalls with bedding. Stallions allowed. Specialize in quarter horses. ⬛ Electric hookups. ⬛ Vet within 15 minutes. ⬛ Farrier on the premises. ⬛⬛ These services within 1 mile.
⬛ *55 Blakely Lane, Newfoundland, NJ 07435*
☎ **(201) 697-1257**

Georgieanne Jones / Trenton Area (S-2)
▤⬛⬛⬛⬛

From I-95, 1.2 miles off Exit 3, 1.4 miles from Route 31. Call for exact directions. ▤ 4 stalls with bedding, ranging in size from 10X10 to 10X14. Price depends on size and number of stalls required. Stallions allowed if booked in advance. Current health papers required. ⬛ Can provide equine massage for the travel weary/competition weary equine traveler to help them get to their destination in the best mental and physical condition. ⬛ Hopewell Vet Group, Hopewell, NJ ☎ (609) 466-0131 or Mid-Atlantic Equine Medical Center at ☎ (609) 397-0078. ⬛ Kevin McMinn at Cream Ridge at ☎ (609) 259-2528. ⬛ Hub Leasing at 2836 Brunswick Pike (U.S.1) at ☎ 883-4400, Skip's Sunoco at Route 31 & Ewingville Road ☎ 882-9787 or Dave Burkett at 1483 Prospect Street ☎ 883-7531. ⬛ Picerno's at Ewing ☎ (609) 882-1098. ⬛ Ground Round, Ewing ☎ 771-9509, Stage Depot at Pennington ☎ 466-2000, Wildflowers, Pennington ☎ 737-2392, and Angela's, Ewing ☎ 882-9404.
⬛ *146 Scotch Road, Ewing, NJ 08628*
☎ **(609) 882-1098**

Montclair Riding Academy / West Orange (S-5)
▤⬛⬛⬛$$$+

On Woodland Avenue off Route 280. Call for directions and availability. ▤ 100 stalls with bedding and feed @ $35 per night. ⬛ Good trails in the area. ⬛⬛ These services nearby. ⬛ For dress code and atmosphere, try The Manor at ☎ (201) 731-2360. Reservations required. They have a big and varied menu and have lobster buffets Tuesdays through Fridays. For a more casual meal, try Pals Cabin 1/8 mile north of I-280/Exit 8B. ☎ (201) 731-4000.
⬛ *Route 280/ Woodland Avenue, West Orange, NJ 07052*
☎ **(201) 731-4182**

Pine Hill Farm / Somerville (S-3)

≣≢⚡🐎⚕♞✕$$$

Near Routes 78, 287, 2. Off Route 22/Reddington. Call for directions.
≣≢ 50 10X12 wood stalls with sawdust bedding @ $25 per night.
Stallions NOT allowed. 🐎 Trails on 100 acres, cross country course,
dressage barn, heated lounges, and owner operated since 1971. Indoor
arena and 3 outdoor rings. Contact: Linda Loss.
⚑ *104 Harlan School Road, Somerville, NJ 08876*
☎ **(908) 722-7087**

Rosedale Mill / Pennington (TS-1)

♈

Feed & supply store on Route 31. 4 miles away from previous listing
(S-2). ☎ **(609) 737- 2008**

Towerview / Belleplain (S-4)

≣≢ 🚐🎣🐎⚡⚕♞✕$

Call for directions. **≣≢** 3 10X10 stalls with bedding and auto H2O.
Prefer no stallions. Current health papers required. 🚐 1 Camper/RV
hookup @ $5 per night. Showers also available. 🎣 Fishing in the
ocean and bay. 🐎 Located near beaches and Belleplain Park. The
park is about 11,000 acres and crisscrossed by many dirt roads. Ideal
for trail riding or driving horses. Lake at the park for swimming and

canoeing. Has camping facilities. ✚ Vet available in Vineland, NJ at
☎ 691-3131. �׫ Several farriers in the area. ▮✎✖ All of these facilities
nearby. Ocean City and Sea Isle City for food and 8 miles away in
Seaville recommend the Seaville Tavern at ☎ (609) 624-3136.

⚐ *395 Head of the River Road, Belleplain, NJ 08270*

☎ **(609) 861-5851** (evenings) or **926-4083** (days)

Farmington

NEW MEXICO

I25

S-2

Santa Fe

I40

S-1

I25

Albuquerque

F-4

I40

S-4

D-2

Carlsbad

I25

F-1, D-1

F-3

Hobbs

Las Cruces

I10

S-3

101 Miles

Eastern NM State Fair F-1   Bottomless St. Park D-1
Galisteo Inn S-1   Quebradas Road D-2
Jake McClure Arena F-3
New Mexico St. Fairgrds F-4
Red Rock Stables S-2
Southwest Stables S-3
Western Stables S-4

Eastern New Mexico State Fair / Roswell (F-1)

≈⊞☉♞⌷☒$

At 2500 Southeast Main Street. **≈** 40 outdoor stalls with auto H20 @ $5 per night. Contact Joanne Prince. **⇝** Bottomless Lakes State Park is 18-20 miles away. See listing for Park in this section. **⊞** Dr. Leonard Blach is 3 miles away and his number is **☎** 623-9119. **☯** Nearest farrier is Dan Johnson at **☎** 623-3855. **⚒** Nearest mechanic at Callaway & Sons Garage 1.5 miles away **☎** 623-1988. **⛽** Fuel available in Roswell area. **☒** Recommend Mario's which is 2 miles away **☎** 623-1740.

⌂ *P.O. Box 824, Roswell, NM 88201*
☎ (505) 623-9411

The Galisteo Inn / Santa Fe (S-1)

≈⊨⇝☒$$$

23 miles south of Santa Fe on Highway 41. **≈** Over 10 stalls @ $12 per night w/o feed or $17 per night with feed. 2 horse limit and you must be guests at the Inn. Most of the stalls occupied, so make reservations! They also have an arena hot walker **⇝** Nearby trails. **⊨** This historic hacienda comes with swimming pool and hot tub. Rooms run between $90 and $160 per night. Breakfasts are continental plus which includes bread, fruits, cereals and coffee or tea. This is definitely for the vacation minded equestrian! **☒** If you want to splurge on

dinner in nearby Santa Fe, try the Coyote Cafe
☎ (505) 983-1615 or the Pink Adobe ☎ (505) 983-7712. Both are quite
popular so book as far in advance as possible.
⚐   HC- 75 / Box 4, Galisteo, NM 87540
☎ (505) 982-1506

Jake McClure Arena / Lea County Fairgrounds / Lovington (F-3)
�̸ 🚐 ⚡🔌♒♞✖$

1/2 mile off State Highways 18, 83/82 at Commercial Avenue and
Washington. Call ahead. Many horse functions every year.
�̸ 78 wood/metal stalls w/o bedding. Metal stalls are 10X10 @ $5
per night. Wood stalls are 12X12 @ $7.50 per night. Water available
and bedding available @ $2 a bale. Stallions allowed. Warm up ring,
arena, and cement wash rack. 🚐 36 Camper/RV hookups @ $5 per
night. Showers available. ≋ Fishing in the area. ✚ Vet in Lovington at
☎ 396- 5841. ♨ Ron Berry in Lovington at ☎ 396-4356.♒ Knapp's
Auto Service 2 miles away at ☎ 396-7309. Open 24 hours a day.
🛢 Fuel nearby. ✖ Lovington Inn ☎ 396-5346, Ribeye Steakhouse
☎ 396-8553, and Pioneer Steakhouse ☎ 396-2348.
⚐   101 Commercial Avenue, Lovington, NM 88260
☎ (505) 396-5344

New Mexico State Fairgrounds Albuquerque (F-4)
�̸🔌✖$$

On San Pedro between Central and Lomas. �̸ Many stalls available
@ $10 per night. 24 hour security on premises. Office closes at 5 p.m.
so make arrangements before then for feed. 🔌✖ All of these services
close by and across the freeway. Many good restaurants in the
Winrock Mall-- from Mexican to American food.
⚐   300 San Pedro, Albuquerque, NM 87108
☎ (505) 265-1791

Red Rock Stables / Gallup Area (S-2)
🚌 🚐 ♞✚♒♒✖$$

Off I-40 in Red Rock State Park which is 6 miles east of Gallup.
🚌 50 10X12 wood and metal stalls with bedding @ $10 per
night. Very large outdoor arena (Capacity-8000). Stallions allowed.
Mary Ellen describe her operation as "safe, serviceable, secure, and
scenic." 🚐 Camper/RV hookups available all year @ $8 for electric
only and @ $12 for full hookups. Riding trails in Red Rock State Park
or 10 miles to unlimited riding in National Forest-- Zuni Mountains.
✚ Experienced vet 8 miles away @ ☎ (505) 722-2251. ♨ Farrier @
(505) 778-5536. Closest mechanic at Amigo Chevy at ☎ (505) 722-
7701 or at Ford dealer at ☎ (505) 863-5522. Trailer repair at Navajo
Tractor & Trailer Sales at ☎ (505) 863-3806. 🛢 Fuel at Giant Travel

Center at ☎ 722-6655. ☒ Pedro's at ☎ (505) 863-9755 or Earl's at ☎ (505) 863-4201.

⌘ *P.O. Box 396, Church Rock, NM 87311*

☎ **(505) 722-3145**

Southwest Stables / Deming (S-3)

⊞ ⊕ ❚ ▚ ☒ $$

2 miles west of Deming on the old Lordsburg Highway. ⊞ 8 stalls ranging in size from 12X12 to 12X24 w/o bedding. Stalls priced @ $15 for the first stall, $10 for additional stalls. Stallions allowed. ⊞ Electric hookups and water free. ❚ Vet in Deming at ☎ 546-2621. ▚ ☒ These services available in Deming.

⌘ *Star Route 1 / Box 183, Deming, NM 88031*

☎ **(505) 546-7816**

Western Stables / Tucumcari (S-4)

⊞ ⊕ ❚ Ü ▚ ☒ $$

1 mile from Exit 331 off I-40. Call for directions- also close to old Route 66. ⊞ 8 12X16 stalls with bedding @ $10.50 to 12.50, depending on size. 12X16 stalls come with runs. Stallions allowed and health papers are required.
⊞ 2 Camper/RV

hookups available. ❚ Vet in Tucumcari at ☎ 461-3900. Ü Farrier at Tucumcari at ☎ 461-4311 (advance appointment required). ▚ Closest mechanic 1/4 mile at John's Truck Service, Tucumcari at ☎ 461-2085. On call 24 hours a day. ❚ Fuel at TTT . ☒ Good food at Golden Corral in Tucumcari (1/2 mile away).

⌘ *P.O. Box 1072, Tucumcari, NM 88401*

☎ **(505) 461-0274**

North American Horse Travel Guide

Bottomless Lakes State Park / Roswell (D-1)

10 miles east of Roswell on U.S. 380, then 6 miles south on NM 409. Several lakes surrounded by red bluffs. Lea Lake has a concession building with cafe. Pecos Valley Horse Club does a trail ride in this park every Spring. Park is 1400 acres.

⚐ *Auto Route E, Box 1200, Roswell, NM 88201*

☎ **(505) 624- 6058 or 622-1177**

Quebradas Road / Escondida Area (D-2)

This BLM-- managed road traverses 24 miles of rugged Chihuahuan desert land east of Socorro. Great scenery-- a blend of mountains and desert with multi-- colored cliffs. From I-25 take Escondida Exit(#152) and after 1/2 mile east take County A-135, passing Escondida Lake (on your left), then the Rio Grande, ending up in Pueblito. Trail begins .6 miles south and runs east and then southeast, ending up 24 miles later at County Road A-129 Junction. Several arroyo crossings on this rough road can flood after storms. At mile 9.9 there is the Presilla Wilderness Study Area. At mile 17.2 you come close to the restricted White Sands Missile Range.

⚐ *BLM Socorro Resource Area, 198 Neel Avenue NW, Socorro, NM 87801*

☎ **(505) 835-0412**

Four Corners

© Bruce McAllister

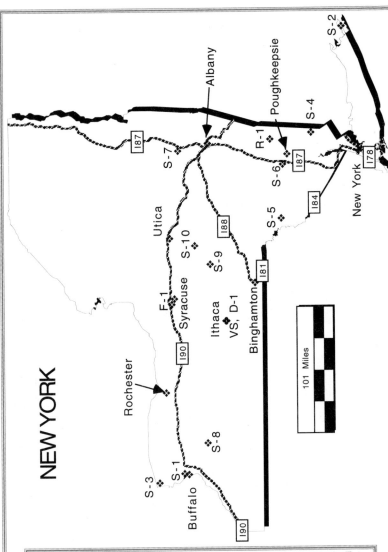

NEW YORK

Buffalo Equestrian Center S-1
Cornell Vet School   VS
Deep Hollow Ranch Stable S-2
Farm at the Fork S-3
Heather Hill Equestrian Ctr S-4
Indigo Stables   S-5
Mohonk House   S-6
Rolling Meadow Farm   S-7
Jensen Stable   S-8

New York St. Fairgrounds F-1
Roseland Ranch   R-1
Spindletop Farm   S-9
West Wind Ranch   S-10
Finger Lakes Nat. Forest D-1

Buffalo Equestrian Center / Buffalo (S-1)

Take 90 East to 33W Buffalo to 198 to Delaware Exit. Turn right. Call for directions if coming from a different way. 100 stalls with bedding @ $25 per night. Stallions allowed. Vets and farriers in the area. These services available/Equestrian Center is centrally located. Lord Chumley's 1/2 mile north on SR 384 (Delaware) at 481 Delaware. (716) 886-2220.

950 Amherst Street, Buffalo, NY 14216

(716) 877-9295

Cornell College of Veterinary Medicine Large Animal Clinic / Ithaca (VS)

Emergency horse care. Call only for emergencies! May require referral from a vet. NO STALLS FOR TRANSIENT BOARDING. From Route 13, take 366W.

Ithaca, NY 14850

(607) 253-3100 or 255-7753

Deep Hollow Ranch Stables / Long Island (S-2)

Last town on Long Island--off Route 27E. Call for directions. 70 wood stalls. Stallions allowed. 4000 acres of trails. Vet 20 minutes away. Farrier 10 miles away. Contact: Diane.

P.O. Box 835, Montauk, NY 11954

(516) 668-2744 or FAX (516) 668-3902

Farm at the Fork / Youngstown (S-3)

About 14 miles north of U.S. vet inspection station at U.S./Canadian border crossing in Lewistown, NY. From Lewistown, take NY #18 east to NY #93E. Farm is about 1 mile from NY #93 in Youngstown, NY. Call for final directions. 16 wood stalls with shavings @ $15 per night. Stalls range from 10X10 to 10X11, to 12X12. Stallions allowed and require current health papers. 65X65 indoor lighted arena and barn has indoor wash area with each stall lighted.  Four Mile Creek Campsite nearby with dump sites, laundries, comfort stations, and water. Electric hookups @ $12 per night and $10 per night for non-- electric. This facility is 1.5 miles from Farm at the Fork. ✚ Vet in Batavia at ☎ 343-0112. ☴ Fishing at Lake Ontario (1.5 miles). ⛟ Fuel at Riverview Service Station in Youngstown ☎ 745-7150. ☒ Good food at Old Fort Inn in Youngstown at ☎ 745-7144.

⚐ *1530 Braley Road, Youngstown, NY 14174*

☎ **(716) 745-3173**

Heather Hill Equestrian Center / Brewster (S-4)

1/2 mile on Route 22 off #684. Call for final directions. ▰ 51 stalls with bedding. 3 outdoor arenas, 1 indoor arena. ⚘ Trail system is being redone at this time. ✚ Plenty of vets in the area. ⛟ At Good Old Days in Brewster. ☒ The Arch in Brewster.

⚐ *RD # 6 / Big Elm Road, Brewster, NY 10509*

☎ **(914) 279-6736**

Indigo Stables / Jeffersonville (S-5)

Off #17 to 17B West, go 12 miles and follow signs. Call for final directions.

▰ 10 wood stalls with bedding @ $30 per night. Have paddocks. Allow well--behaved stallions. ⚘ 150 acres of wooded trails and streams. Dinner rides to local restaurants and overnight rides (incl. tents and meals).

✚ Vet 2 miles away. ♘ Farrier 4 miles away. ⛟☒ These services 2 miles away.

⚐ *Swiss Hill Road, Jeffersonville, NY 12748*

☎ **(914) 482-3158**

Mohonk House / New Platz (S-6)
$$

Get off the
New York
Thruway at
Exit 18 and go
up the hill- its
tower can eas-
ily be seen.
High in the
Catskills this is
a five star get-
away for you
and your
horse.

Rooms
with all meals
range from
about $200 per day to over $350 during high season. In the Fall and
Spring you might get lower rates. Your horse will have a more
economical rate @ $15 per day which includes his/her room and board
(in a box stall). Call ahead for reservations.

Lake Mohonk, New Paltz, NY 12561

☎ (914) 255-4500

Rolling Meadow Farm / Ballston Spa (S-7)
$$$

From the south, take Exit 12 and then Route 67 west to White Road.
Call for final directions. 27 12X12 stalls with bedding @ $20 per
night. No hookups but do have showers. Vet at ☎ (518) 692-
2227 Tom Costello in Schuylerville. These services within 3
miles.

161 White Road, Ballston Spa, NY 12020

☎ (518) 885-3248

Jensen Stable / LeRoy (S-8)
$$$

Take LeRoy Exit from Route 90, go south on #19 to LeRoy. At light
(Route 5) turn right-- 1 mile from light. Call for final directions.
Require advance notice. 2 12X14 wood stalls with shavings @
$18 per night. Stallions allowed and health papers required. Hay
grain/mash available. Both vet and farrier 20 minutes away.
These services nearby, but this facility has special rate at nearby
Day's Inn and will help with lodging.

7077 West Main Street, LeRoy, NY 14082

☎ (716) 768-8452

New York State Fairgrounds / Syracuse (F-1)
≋ ⏚⊕Ů⊗®⊠$$

Off Route 690. Take Fairgrounds Exit. It's west of downtown Syracuse. ≋ 500 wood stalls w/o bedding @ $12 per stall per night. Fairgrounds can arrange for bedding at extra charge. ⏚ Camper/RV hookups available @ $12 per night. ⊕Ů Vets and farriers on call. ⊗® These services close by. ⊠ For an atmospheric dinner in a restored feed mill near a stream, try Glen Loch Restaurant, 7.5 miles southeast on I-690 & 481 to Jamesville exit. Then go 1 mile east to 4626 North Street ☎ (315) 469-6969.
⁺ *State Fair Blvd., Syracuse, NY 13209*
☎ **(315) 487-7711**

Roseland Ranch / Stanfordville (R-1)
≋ ⤳

Call for directions. ≋ 75 stalls. Large indoor arena. ⤳ 800 acres of trails. Close to area wineries. Special rates for horse if you stay at the Ranch.
⁺ *P.O. Box 41, Stanfordville, NY 12581*
☎ **(914) 868-1350**

Spindletop Farm, Inc. / Norwich (S-9)
≋ ⏚⊰▼⊕Ů®⊗⊠$$$

Route 23 W to County Road 16--2 miles take a right on Morley Road. Call for final directions. ≋ 20 12X12 stalls with bedding @ $20 per night. Stallions not allowed. Current health papers required.
⏚ Camper/RV hookups at $50 per night (don't know if that includes the horse). Camper available. ▼ Tack shop at facility. ⊕ Vet in Norwich at ☎ (607) 336-4335. Ů Farrier in Sherburne at ☎ (607) 674-4728. ® Mechanic 8 miles away at Benedict's on East River Road. ☎ (607) 674-4728. ⊰ Fishing in the area. ⛽ Fuel at Blue Ox in Norwich ☎ (607) 334-8328. ⊠ Good food at Hands Inn in Norwich ☎(607) 334- 8224.
⁺ *P.O.Box 91/ Morley Road, Plymouth, NY 13832*
☎ **(607) 336-1942**

West Wind Ranch / Brookfield (S-10)
≋ ⏚⊨⤳⊕Ů⊠$$

Near Route 20 and Route 8. Call for directions. ⤳ This is the site of the well-known New York 100 Mile Trail Ride every 4th of July week-end. Accommodations very tight then but this is a great place to go riding--plenty of trails! ⏚ Brookfield offers roofed tie stalls and camp-sites for those who want to rough it and not stay at West Wind Ranch. Josie La More can put you up at West Wind for B&B as well as your horse and she is across from the fairgrounds. ≋ 7 wood box stalls

with bedding @ $10 per night. Well behaved stallions are allowed.
⊨⊣ For bed & breakfast, a double will run $40 per night and a single,
$30 per night. Josie will serve a continental breakfast as part of the
package. If you want to go somewhere nice for dinner she recommends the home cooking at the Beaver Den on Academy in
Brookfield.

⌖ *Fairground Road, Brookfield, NY 13314*
☎ **(315) 899-6203**

Finger Lakes National Forest / Ithaca (D-1)

© Photo courtesy of USFS

Between Seneca Lake
and Cayuga Lake just
north of Ithaca. 25 miles
of trails around the
mountain with great
views of the lakes!
Camp sites can be
easily located once you
get a map from the
District Ranger. Or you
can get a room or have a
meal nearby at the Red House Country Inn ☎ (607) 546-8566. Their
rooms range from over $50 to $75 per night for a double and that
includes breakfast.

☎ **(607) 594-2750** (USFS)

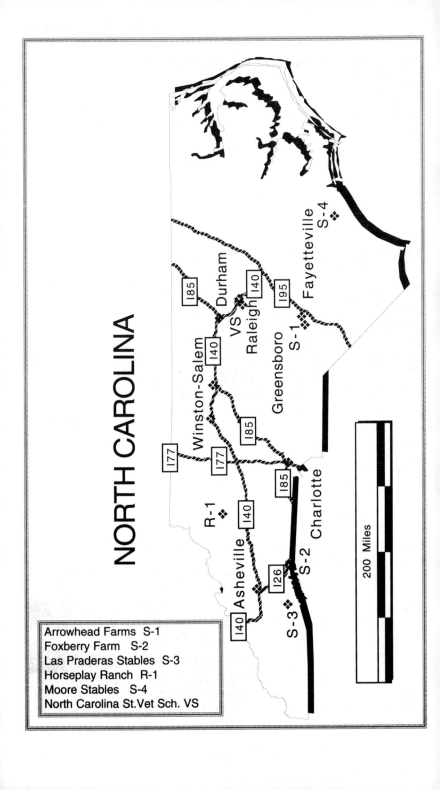

NORTH CAROLINA

Durham
Raleigh
VS
Fayetteville
S-4
S-1
185
140
195
Greensboro
Winston-Salem
140
185
177
177
185
R-1
140
Charlotte
S-2
Asheville
126
S-3
140

200 Miles

Arrowhead Farms S-1
Foxberry Farm   S-2
Las Praderas Stables S-3
Horseplay Ranch R-1
Moore Stables S-4
North Carolina St.Vet Sch. VS

Arrowhead Farms / Fayetteville (S-1)

About 10 miles from Route 95. From north, Exit 56, from South Exit 40 to Owen. Left on Raeford Road to Strickland Bridge. Call for final directions if in doubt! 20 12X12 wood stalls with bedding @ $15 per stall per night. Electric hookups only @ $5 per night. Vet in Fayetteville at ☎ 864-1535. Farrier in Fayetteville at ☎ 483-6878. Mechanic 3 miles away at Tire Sales & Service on Raeford Road ☎ 425- 8155. Hours Mon.-Fri. 8-5:30, Sat. 8-1. These services in Fayetteville.

Route 8/ Box 934, Fayetteville, NC 28304

☎ **(919) 425-3631**

Foxberry Farm / Tryon (S-2)

From Highway 26 take Exit 1, go east 8.5 miles. 6 10X13 stalls (5 wood) with bedding @ $15 per night. $55 per person for bed & breakfast. Stallions allowed and require neg cog/ health papers. Vet in Columbus at ☎ 859-3193. Farrier in Rutherford at ☎ (704) 245-7675. Closest mechanic 6 miles at Larry Stott's Garage in Columbus ☎ (704) 894-3291, open Mon.-Fri., 8-5. Fuel at BP Interstate in Landrum at ☎ 457-2334 or 457-4372. Brannon's in Landrum at ☎ 457-3827.

Route 1/ Box 222, Tryon, NC 28782

☎ **(704) 863-2753**

Las Praderas Stables / Brevard (S-3)

From Route 276S, go 1.7 miles. Call for directions. 22 12X12 wood/metal stalls @ $15 per night. Stallions allowed and health papers required. Nice rooms, rec room-- good place to take a breather! Prices based on 2 night stays and cottages run from $60 per night to $115 per night depending on season-- all cottages sleep from 4 to 6 people.

Contact for details on meals. Beautiful location and there are 4 separate cottages. ✚ Vet in Horseshoe at ☎ (704) 891-9685. ♃ Farrier in Etowah at ☎ (704) 891-3850. ✎ Mechanics available 9 miles away. ▓ Several in Brevard.

✖ Good food at the Raintree in Brevard at ☎ (704) 862-5832.

☖ *See Off Mt. Road, Route 1/ Box 12A, Brevard, NC 28712*

☎ **(704) 883-3375**

Horseplay Ranch / Lenoir (R-1)

I-40 to Highway 64-90- 6 miles east of Lenoir. Call in advance please!

═ 4 10X10 wood stalls with bedding @ $5 per night. Stallions allowed and require neg cog/health papers.

🚐 Limited Camper/RV hookups @ $10 per night- primitive camping but electric available. ≋ Pond on my property. ▼ Tack shop in the area. 🐎 Many trails nearby--24 acre ranch. ✚ Vet in Lenoir. ♃ Farrier in Hudson. ✎ Mechanic Boyd Hollar lives within 4 miles. ▓ Oakhill Superette 2 miles away in Lenoir.

✖ Grinders Switch in Lenoir.

☖ *Route 2/ Box 727, Lenoir, NC 28645*

☎ **(704) 757-9114**

Trail ride at Horseplay Ranch

Moore Stables & Riding Academy / Jacksonville (S-4)

Route 40E to Exit 373 and go east 4 miles. Turn left go 2.5 miles, turn right on #24, go 28 miles and take a left-- and follow the signs. 34 concrete stalls with bedding. Stallions not allowed and require neg cog/health papers. Electric hookups only. Cross country course. Have had horse trials here. 1 acre lighted ring. Vet on premises. 2 farriers nearby. Mechanic at stables. Closest fuel 1 mile away in Keensville. Good food at Bud-Johnny's in Jacksonville. Contact: Sam Moore.

138 Trudi Lane, Jacksonville, NC 28540

☎ **(919) 324-2555**

North Carolina State College of Veterinary Medicine / Raleigh (VS)

Emergency horse care. Call only for emergencies! May require referral from a vet. NO STALLS FOR TRANSIENT BOARDING.

4700 Hillsborough Street, Raleigh, NC 27606

☎ **(919) 821-9500**

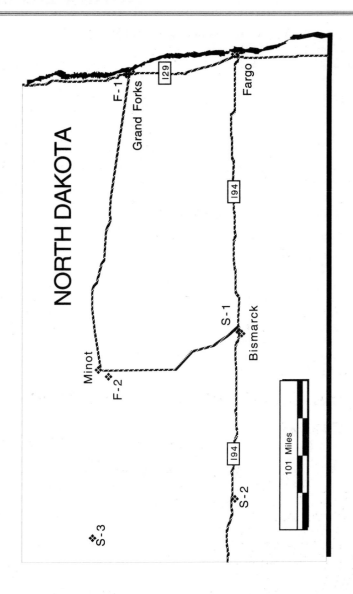

NORTH DAKOTA

129
Grand Forks
F-1
Fargo

194

Minot
F-2

S-1
Bismarck

194

S-2

S-3

101 Miles

Gateway Arena S-1   Bob Roles Stables S-3
Grand Forks Fair F-1
North Dakota State Fair F-2
Rainbow Black Arabians S-2

Gateway Arena / Bismarck (S-1)

From I-94, use Exit 36 and take Highway 83N-- just north of intersection-- within 2 miles. Contact: Les Mahin . Ron Hendrickson, the owner, is a vet in Bismarck. 75 wood/metal stalls with bedding @ $10 per night. Range in size from 10X10 to 12X36. Have auto H2O. Stallions allowed and require health papers. 112 Camper/RV hookups at KOA @ $17.50 for full hookup. ☎ 222-2662. They also have camping cabins @ $17.50. Fishing in the nearby Missouri River. Vet in Bismarck at ☎ 258-9841. Farrier in Bismarck at ☎ 255-0162. Closest mechanic is at Stan Paklich Chevy on Highway 83N at ☎ 223-5800 and they are on call 6 days a week. Fuel 1/2 mile away at Conoco ☎ 255-2744. Red Lobster in Bismarck at ☎ 222-2063.

RR # 1/ Box 3, Bismarck, ND 58501- 9702
☎ **(701) 224-1216**

Greater Grand Forks Fair / Grand Forks (F-1)

From Interstate I-29, take Gateway Drive 1/2 mile east. 10 stalls with bedding and auto H2O. Price negotiable. Camper/RV hookups available. Vet within 1 mile. These services available within 1 mile and there is a restaurant across the street.

2300 Gateway Drive, Grand Forks, ND 58203
☎ **(701) 772-3421**

North Dakota State Fair / Minot (F-2)

On Burdick Expressway east. Call for more details weekdays 8-5. 100 wood stalls w/o bedding @ $12 per night. Camper/RV hookups available @ $5 per night. Vet and farrier in Minot area. All of these services close by. Sheraton across the street.

P.O. Box 1796, Minot, ND 58702
☎ **(701) 857-7620**

Rainbow Black Arabians / Belfield (S-2)

2 miles east of Belfield at I-94 and Highway 85. 6 stalls with bedding @ $10 per night and have corrals. Stalls range in size from 15X15 to 15X20. Stallions allowed. Have an outdoor arena. Space for campers but no hookups. There is a motel 2miles away called the Bel-Vu ☎ (701) 575-4245. Badlands 16 miles west. Teddy Roosevelt Memorial Park has nightly musicals during the summer months. Nearest vet is Dr. Brummond at ☎ (701) 225-0240 and there is a farrier in the area. These services available in Belfield.. For food, try Trapper's at ☎ (701) 575-8585. It's 2 miles from the stables.

🕆   *P.O. Box 825, Belfield, ND 58622*

☎ **(701) 575-4064**

Bob Roles Stables / Williston (S-3)

5 miles north of Highway 2 and 85N, go 1 mile west. 10 indoor/ 10 outdoor stalls with bedding. 60X120 arena and walker.

Camper/RV hookups available 4 miles away at KOA Campground. Vet and farrier in the area. These services available 6 miles away in Williston.

🕆   *P.O. Box 1154, Williston, ND 58801*

☎ **(701) 572-2905**

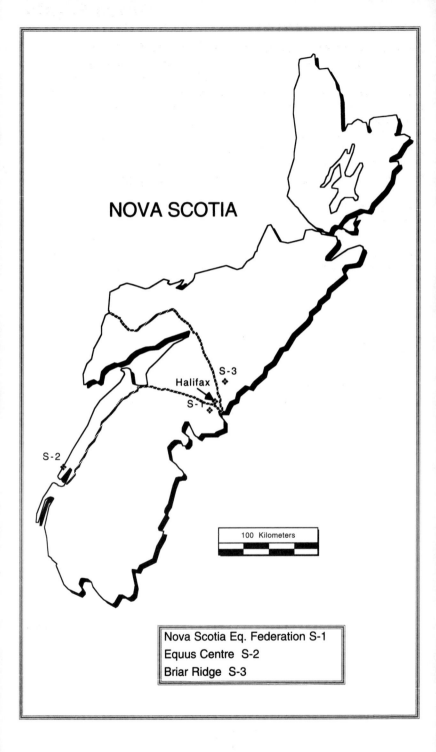

NOVA SCOTIA

S-3

Halifax

S-1

S-2

100 Kilometers

Nova Scotia Eq. Federation S-1
Equus Centre S-2
Briar Ridge S-3

Nova Scotia Equestrian Federation (S-1)

No current list of stables available, but this organization could help if you need information on events, trail rides, vets or a specific area in Nova Scotia. We have shown some facilities below which are printed in the current Nova Scotia Travel Guide Book which can be obtained from Nova Scotia Dept. of Tourism and Culture, Box 456, Halifax NS B3J 2R5 or 1-800-341-6096(USA) or 1-800-565-0000 (Canada). Federation address and telephone number follow.

✆ *Box 3010, South Halifax, NS B3J 3G6 CANADA*

☎ **(902) 425-5450/ EXT 333 or FAX (902) 425-5606**

Equus Centre / Granville Ferry (S-2)

Near ferry to mainland. Contact: Jennifer Gale. She is very helpful and knows of other facilities around Nova Scotia. Though her facility does have a children's riding camp, it also has equestrian training. On space available basis. Call ahead! Vet and farrier nearby.

✆ *RR# 1, Granville Ferry, Digby County B0S 1K0 CANADA*

☎ **(902) 532-2460**

Briar Ridge / Mt. Uniacke (S-3)

New facility which could be an excellent jumping off point. Located in central Nova Scotia. Unknown if they can board transient horses. By press time could not find a telephone number. Equus Centre might be of some help in locating this facility.

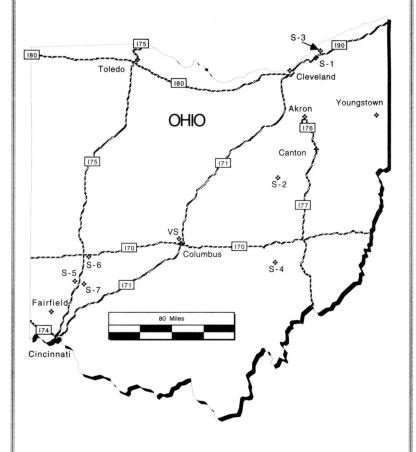

Dorchester Farms S-1   Ohio State Vet School VS
Kricket Hill Farm S-2   Red Cardinal Barn S-6
Lake Erie College Eq Ctr S-3   Wildwood Stables S-7
McNutt Farm/ Lodge S-4
Menker's Circle 6 Farm S-5

Dorchester Farms / Kirtland (S-1)

Up the street from I-90. Exit at 306 South. ⚡ 50 wood stalls with bedding @ $10 per night. Stallions allowed and current health papers required. Have 1 indoor/2 outdoor arenas. 🐎 Access to nearby trails. ➕⚕ Vet and farrier in the area. 🔧✖ Services available in Kirtland.
📮 *8560 Billings, Kirtland, OH 44094*
☎ **(216) 256-9254**

Kricket Hill Farm / Millersburg (S-2)

4 miles north of Millersburg on Route 83, turn left on TR 346 and it will be the 4th place on your right. ⚡ 4 12X12 wood stalls with bedding @ $7.50 per horse per night. Stallions allowed and current health papers required.
⊨ Bed & breakfast available.

🚐Camper/RV hookups available. ➕ Vet in Berlin at ☎ 893-2057. ⚕ Farrier available in Mt. Hope. 🔧 Nearest mechanic at Barnhart's BP on 799 S. Washington in Millersburg. ☎ 674-4836. Open 7 a.m.-p.m. 7 days a week. ✖🔧 Nearest fuel at Red Head in Millersburg at ☎ 674-5827. ✖ Horse & Harness in Fredericksburg at ☎ 695-3431.
📮 *6825 TR 346, Millersburg, OH 44654*
☎ **(216) 674-2430**

Lake Erie College Equestrian Center / Concord Township (S-3)

Call for directions. On space available basis. ⚡ 100 wood stalls with bedding @ $10 a night. Stallions allowed and current health papers are required. Lake

Erie College offers one of the best dressage training/stable management programs in the U.S.

⚐ *8031 Morley Road, Concord Township, OH 44060*

☎ **(216) 352-3393**

McNutt Farm & Outdoorsman Lodge Zanesville Area (S-4)

≋ ⊨ 🐎 ⚒ 🔌 ❌ $$

Off I-70, take Exit 155 S/SR 60 south. 35 miles southwest of I-77 Cambridge Exit. All good all weather roads. Call for directions.

≋ Indoor stalls with bedding @ $10 per horse per night. Wash rack, outdoor arena and 🐎 trails. Stallions allowed and must have current health papers. ⊨ Bed & breakfast available @ $30 per night.

≋ Fishing in the area.

⚐ *6120 Cutler Lake Road, Blue Rock, OH 43720*

☎ **(614) 674-4555**

Menker's Circle 6 Farm / Miamisburg (S-5)

≋ 🚐 ⚒ 🔌 ❌ $$$

In Washington Township off Interstate 75/675. Call for directions. Contact: Bob Menker. ≋ 6 out of 80 wood stalls available for transient horses @ $20 per night. Stallions allowed and current health papers required. 🚐 Some Camper/RV hookups available nearby.

✚ Vet available in Waynesville. ⚒ Farrier available. ❌ These services available in Miamisburg.

⚐ *11090 Yankee Road, Miamisburg OH 45342*

☎ **(513) 885-3911**

Ohio State College of Veterinary Medicine Columbus (VS)

⌂

Emergency horse care. Call only for emergencies! May require referral from a vet. NO STALLS FOR TRANSIENT BOARDING.

⚐ *1935 Coffey Road, Columbus, OH 43210*

☎ **(614) 292-6661**

Red Cardinal Barn / Dayton (S-6)

≋ 🚐 ⚒ 🔌 ❌ $$

5 miles from I-70. 6 miles from I-75. Call for directions. ≋ 9 12X12 stalls with straw bedding @ $15 per night. Stallions not allowed and require current health papers. 🚐 Campground 2 miles away. ✚ On request-- lives in Dayton. ⚒ In Dayton--on request. ❌ These services all within 3 miles.

⚐ *4470 Union Schoolhouse Road, Dayton, OH 45424*

☎ **(513) 233-7658**

Wildwood Stables / Centerville (S-7)

Call for directions. 35 wood stalls with bedding. 2-3 available for transient horses. Only well- behaved stallions allowed and must cleared in advance with Debbie. Indoor and outdoor lighted dressage arenas. Close to parks and trails. Vet in Centerville. Farrier available. Close to these services, including hotels.

11205 Gephart Road, Centerville, OH 45458

☎ **(513) 885-9941** (stable) **or 885-7532** (home)

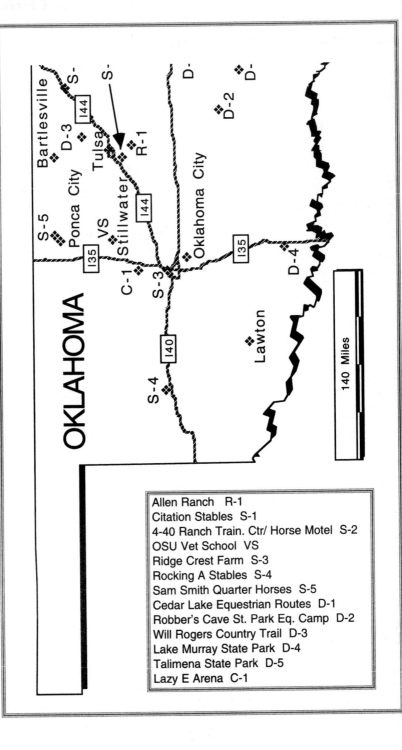

OKLAHOMA

Bartlesville
144
S-
S-
D-
D- D-
D-2
D-3
Tulsa
R-1
Ponca City
S-5
VS
Stillwater
144
Oklahoma City
135
S-4
140
C-1
S-3
135
D-4
Lawton

140 Miles

Allen Ranch   R-1
Citation Stables   S-1
4-40 Ranch Train. Ctr/ Horse Motel   S-2
OSU Vet School   VS
Ridge Crest Farm   S-3
Rocking A Stables   S-4
Sam Smith Quarter Horses   S-5
Cedar Lake Equestrian Routes   D-1
Robber's Cave St. Park Eq. Camp   D-2
Will Rogers Country Trail   D-3
Lake Murray State Park   D-4
Talimena State Park   D-5
Lazy E Arena   C-1

Allen Ranch / Tulsa Area (R-1)

🦓🚐🐂🐎➕🔌🔧❎$$

15 miles south of Tulsa. 6 miles off I-75. Call for directions. 🦓 30 stalls with bedding @ $10 per night and we feed. Stallions allowed. 🚐 Camper/RV hookups available. 🐂 Tack shop on premises. 🐎 Have longhorn cattle drives and about 200 miles of trails available. ➕ Clem Cotlom 4 miles away in Bixby. ☎ (918) 366-3330. 🔌🔧 These services available in the Tulsa area. ❎ We have dinner available on certain nights.

⌖ *19600 South Memorial, Bixby, OK 74008*

☎ **(918) 366-3010**

Citation Stables & Show Barn / Jenks (S-1)

🦓🚐≈➕🔌🔧❎$$

2.5 miles east of Highway 75. 🦓 58 concrete/steel 12X12 stalls with shavings @ $10 per night. Require neg cog/health papers within past 6 months. Stallions allowed. 1 acre under roof/indoor riding arena. On site management. This facility quite popular with people taking their horses through Oklahoma because of its proximity to the Interstate and because it usually has some vacant stalls. 🚐 2-3 electric hookups. ≷ Fishing in the area. ✚ Vet in Anderson ☎ 252-7407. ♨ 3 farriers available. Call ☎ 366-2893. ✎ Closest mechanic 2 miles away at Texaco in Jenks. ◼◼ These services available in Jenks.

⊹   *302 West 111th Street South, Jenks, OK 74037*

☎ **(918) 298-3700**

4-40 Ranch Training Center & Horse Motel Vinita (S-2)

≥≥≥ 🏇✚♨▨◼◼

From I-44, exit at Vinita (#289), go 7 miles east on Highway 66-60. Or at Afton Exit (#302) go 10 miles west on Highway 66-60. ≥≥≥ 40 stalls with bedding. Require neg cog/health papers. Indoor/outdoor arenas, wash stall, and training track. 🐎 Great trail rides on county section lines. ✚♨ Vet and farrier on call. ▨◼◼ These services available in Vinita.

⊹   *Route 2/ Box 88, Vinita, OK 74301*

☎ **(918) 256-2660**

Oklahoma State Boren Vet Medical Teaching Hospital / Stillwater (VS)

⌂

Emergency horse care. Call only for emergencies! May require referral from a vet. NO STALLS FOR TRANSIENT BOARDING.

⊹   *Stillwater, OK 74078-0205*

☎ **(405) 744-6656**

Ridge Crest Farm / Oklahoma City (S-3)

≥≥≥ 🚐✚♨▨◼◼$$

Off I-44/35. 5 minutes from Remington Park, within 1.5 miles of the Cowboy Hall of Fame, 15 minutes from the fairgrounds, and 15 minutes from downtown. ≥≥≥ 65 metal stalls with bedding @ $10 per night. Stallions allowed. Indoor and outdoor lighted arenas. 2 hot walkers. 🚐 Only parking space for Camper/RVs. ✚♨ Vet and farrier available. ▨◼◼ All of these services nearby.

⊹   *6800 North Miramar, Oklahoma City, OK 73111*

☎ **(405) 478-1166**

Rocking A Stables / Clinton (S-4)

≥≥≥ 🚐≷✚♨▨◼◼$

Take Exit 62 off I-40 and go to Cork's Conoco. ≥≥≥ 12 10X12 wood stalls with bedding and water @ $6 per night. Stallions allowed. 🚐 Electric hookups available @ $4 per night. ≷ Fishing in the area. ✚♨ Vet

and farrier in Clinton. At Cork's Conoco. Food 3 miles away in Clinton.

🏠 *Route 2/ Box 40, Clinton, OK 73601*
☎ **(405) 323-1550**

Sam Smith Quarter Horses / Ponca City (S-5)
$$

1.5 miles east of the Arkansas River on Highway 60. 10 wood stalls with bedding @ $10 per night. Sam is a friendly sort and can put up horses on a space available basis. He can also put up stallions. Current health papers are required. 2 vets on call. Farrier available. These services available in Ponca City.

🏠 *Route 3/ Box 716, Ponca City, OK 74604*
☎ **(405) 762-6014**

Cedar Lake Equestrian Routes / Heavener (D-1)

Explore Ouachita National Forest and old logging roads.

🏠 *Ouachita Nat. Forest, USFS, Federal Building, Hot Springs AR 71902*
☎ **(501) 321-5202,** Mon.-Fri., 8 a.m.-4 p.m.

Robbers Cave State Park Equestrian Camp Wilburton (D-2)

3.5 hours southeast of Oklahoma City. 8600 acres of rolling hills and 3 small lakes. 2 trails average 25 miles in length. The equestrian campground offers a comfort station with showers, electrical and water hookups for RVs. One of the trails starts there and follows old forest roads, pipeline right of ways, and creeks

Photo courtesy of Fred Marvel/ State of Oklahoma

as it winds its way through the pine and oak-- hickory forest.
Fishing good for catfish and bass. Small grocery store and cafe.

🏠 *P.O. Box 9, Wilburton, OK 74578*
☎ **(918) 465-2565**

Will Rogers Country Centennial Trail Oologah (D-3)

🐎

On the shores of scenic Oologah Lake. This 18-mile trail has an abundance of wildlife and follows the shoreline with a cutoff and interior trails around Kite Hill. It crosses public hunting areas and is closed during deer season. Camping allowed only in designated areas.

🕆 *Oologah Resident Office, P.O. Box 700, Oologah, OK 74053*

☎ **(918) 443-2250**

Lake Murray State Park / Ardmore (D-4)

🐎

This park includes a scenic field trial area--part of it bordering on Lake Murray. If there are no activities going on at the time, people can ride in this area. No support facilities.

🕆 *P.O. Box 1649, Ardmore, OK 73402*

☎ **(405) 223-4044**

Photo courtesy of Fred Marvel
State of Oklahoma

Talimena State Park / Talihina (D-5)

🐎

First come first serve on RV camper hookups- no reservations!

🕆 *P.O. Box 318, Talihina, OK 74571*

☎ **(918) 567-2052**

Lazy E Arena / Guthrie (C-1)

Top bull riders from all over North America compete here yearly for big purse. Arena outfitters. Many major events throughout the year and worth a stopover if something going on. Unfortunately no stalls available for transient horses but they might refer you to somebody nearby.

✝ *Route 5/ Box 393, Guthrie, OK 73044*
☎ **(405) 282- 3004**

ONTARIO

Sudbury

Ottawa

Sault Ste. Marie

Peterborough

400 Kilometers

Guelph
VS
S-1/2

S-3

Toronto

High Fields Polo & Equestrian Farm S-3
Twitmarsh Farm S-1
Travis Hall Arabians S-2
University of Guelph Vet School   VS

High Fields Polo & Equestrian Farm / Zephyr (S-3)

🏇📧🐎➕♘🅧$$$

45 minutes northeast of downtown Toronto, this facility offers 175 acres of groomed trails with many nearby facilities for swimming, skiing, golfing and tennis. Directions: 404 north to Davis Drive, 16.5 km east on Davis Drive. 7.5 km north on 3rd Concession of Uxbridge. 🏇 Box stalls with shavings, feed and private turnout @ $25 per night. Require neg cog/health papers. 📧 Bed & breakfast @ $45 per night single, $60 double. Deposit for one night's lodging required. Additional meals can be arranged, incl. gourmet dinner with wine @ $25 per person (3 bedrooms available incl. 1 with jacuzzi). 🐎 175 acres of trails. Escorted trail rides @ $25 per hour for guests only. ➕♘ Vet and farrier available. ⛽ Fuel available within 2 miles. 🔧 Mechanic 5 miles away. 🅧 Good food available 10 miles away.

✝ *RR #1 Zephr, ON   L0E 1T0 CANADA*
☎ **(416) 479-6132** (Phone or FAX) or Stable **(416) 473-6356**

Twitmarsh Farm Ltd. / Campbellville (S-1)

≋ ⊟ 🚐 ❤ ∪ ⚞ 🔧 ✖ $$

1 hour's drive west of Toronto. From #401 take Exit 312 (Guelph Line) and go 4 miles. Call for detailed directions.

≋ 13 wood 11X12 stalls with bedding @ $15 per night. 1 large loafing barn, paddocks with loafing sheds @ $10 per night.

🚐 Self contained apartment sleeps 4, has fully equipped kitchen, and 4 piece bathroom. Guests can cater for themselves @ $ 35 per night for first person and @ $20 per night for additional guests. 🎣 Good fishing in the area. ❤ Vet in Campbellville. ∪ Farrier in Rockwood. 🔧 Closest mechanic at Sunoco station 2 miles away. ⛽ Fuel available within 1 km. ✖ Restaurant within 3 km.(in Campbellville).

✉ *RR #1, Campbellville, ON L0P 1B0 CANADA*

☎ (416) 854-9833

Travis Hall Arabians / Rockwood (S-2)

≋ 🚐 ❤ ⚞ 🔧 ✖ $$$

In Mennonite country. ≋ 28 stalls with bedding @ $35 per night. Spacious indoor arenas on 92 acres of private land near quiet country roads. No smoking. 🚐 Water and hydro hook ups. ❤∪ Vets and farriers in the area. 🔧✖ These services all nearby.

✉ *RR #3, Rockwood, ON N0B 2K0 CANADA*

☎ (519) 843-4293

University of Guelph / Ontario Vet College (VS-1)

✚

Emergency vet care for horses. Horse must be recommended by a vet. Located in Guelph which is about an hour's drive west of Toronto.

☎ (519) 824-4120

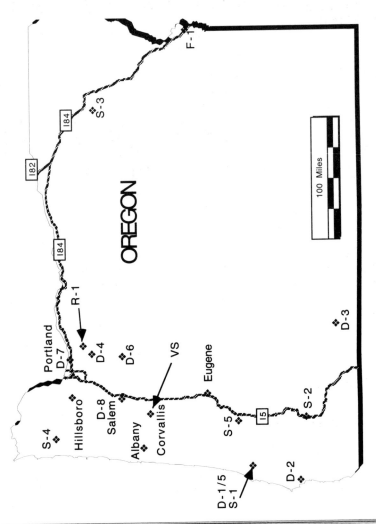

OREGON

100 Miles

| 182 |
| 184 |
| 184 |
| 15 |

F-1

S-3

R-1

D-7 Portland
D-4
D-6
Hillsboro
S-4
D-8
Salem
Albany
Corvallis
VS
Eugene
S-5
S-2
D-3

D-1/5
S-1
D-2

Burnt Spur Equine B&B R-1	Bullard's Beach St. Park D-1
Family Four Stables S-1	Cape Blanco State Park D-2
Malheur County Fairground F-1	Collier State Park D-3
Mountainside Stables S-3	Milo McIver St. Park D-4
Oregon State Vet School VS	Nehalem Bay St. Park D-5
Pearl Creek Stables S-4	Silver Falls St. Park D-6
Ride & Rest Horse Motel S-5	Tryon Creek State Park D-7
Sunny Valley KOA S-2	Willamette Mission St Park D-8

Burnt Spur Equine Bed & Breakfast / Sandy (R-1)

2 miles from Highway 26, 20 miles from Highway 84, 24 miles from Highway 205. 2 miles east of Sandy, turn south on Firwood go 2 miles and turn left onto Locksmith.

6 12X12 wood stalls with bedding and w/o feed @ $10 per horse per night. Stalls range from 12X12 to 24X24 and they have 6 pens. Current health papers are required. According to owner "We have 2 small pastures for turnout and sand outdoor arena. We also have hot walker and wash rack. We are located at the base of Mt. Hood, less than an hour from fishing and trails for horses. There are 2 great horse campgrounds." 4 Camper/RV hookups w/o septic @ $5 per night. Fishing in the area. Vet in Gresham at ☎ 666-1500. Farrier in Colton at ☎ 824-5978. Closest mechanic is 2 miles away at Deane's Auto on Highway 26 at ☎ 668-4563, open Mon.-Fri. 7:30 a.m. to 6:00 p.m. Closest fuel at Shorty's Corner in Sandy. Toll Gate in Sandy.

 42100 SE Locksmith Lane, Sandy, OR 97055
☎ **(503) 668-9716**

Family Four Stables / Coos Bay (S-1)

On Highway 101. 60 miles from I-5 via Highway 42. Call for detailed directions. 42 wood 12X12 stalls with cedar shavings and auto H20 @ $10 per night. Current health papers are required and stallions are allowed. Camper/RV hookups available @ $10 per night. Fishing in the area. Vets and farriers in Coos Bay. These services available in Coos Bay.

 662 Family Four Drive, Coos Bay, OR 97420
☎ **(503) 267-5301 or 267-5859**

Malheur County Fairgrounds / Ontario (F-1)

In northwest part of Ontario on NW 9th Street. 40 stalls with bedding @ $ 6 per night. Arena, race track, and 2 horse barns. 40 Camper/RV hookups available @ $5 per night. Fishing in the area. Vet in Ontario at ☎ 889-7776. Farrier available. Closest

mechanic is at Ontario Diesel (2 miles away) at 588 SE 1st Avenue
☎ 889-8681. Open weekdays, 8-5.
⚑ 795 NW 9th Street, Ontario, OR 97914
☎ (503) 889- 3431

Mountainside Stables / LaGrande (S-3)
〓〓ᗕ❶Ɂ❒✖$$
7 miles off I-84. From I-84 take Exit 261. Go north on #82 towards
Wallowa Lake/Island City. Turn left at flash. yellow light- follow #82
over RR tracks and bridge, immediately get into left turn lane at curve
and turn onto Hunter Road. Go 4 miles to Standley Lane, turning left,
go 3/4 mile to Orchard Road and take a right. Mountainside is 1st and
only driveway on your right. 〓〓 10 10X12 wood stalls with bedding
@ $10 per night. For pasture @ $5 per night. Current health papers are
required and stallions are not allowed. ᗕ Fishing in the area. ❶ Vet in
LaGrande at ☎ 963-2748. Ɂ Farrier in LaGrande at ☎ 962-7189.
❧ Closest mechanic is 7 miles at Eagle Truck & Machine, 26th and
Highway 82 at ☎ 963-8551. On call 24 hours a day. ❏ Fuel at Flying J
Truck Stop in LaGrande at ☎ 963-3432. ✖ Good places to eat in
LaGrande.
⚑ 64635 Orchard Road, LaGrande, OR 97850
☎ (503) 963-7035

Oregon State University College of Veterinary Medicine / Corvallis (VS)
⌂
Emergency horse care 24 hours a day, 7 days a week. Call only for
emergencies! May require referral from a vet. NO STALLS FOR TRAN-
SIENT BOARDING. Located at Magruder Hall 158 on the campus.
⚑ Magruder Hall 158, Corvallis, OR 97331-4801
☎ (503) 737-2858

Pearl Creek Stables / Nehalem (S-4)
〓〓
On Route 53, 3.5 miles east of Highway 101. 〓〓 8 rubber matted
stalls with bedding and water. On the coast. Ride 7 miles of Manzanita
coast and many miles of Nehalem Bay State Park trails (see Park listing
this section).
⚑ 17150 Camp Four Road, Nehalem, OR 97131
☎ (503) 368-5267

Ride & Rest Horse Motel / Oakland (S-5)
〓〓ᗕ❶Ɂ❒✖$$
 Off I-5, take Exit 142 and go west 1/4 mile. Entrance will be on your
left. 16 12X12 box stalls with shavings and auto H20 @ $10 per night.
Include outside corral. Indoor 75X85 arena. ᗕ Fishing in the area.
❶ Vet in Oakland at ☎ 459- 1854. Ɂ Farrier available daylight hours

from Roseburg ☎ 673-1049. ⚒ Closest mechanic is at Smalley's in Sutherland at ☎ 459-4838. On call 24 hours a day, 7 days a week. ⛽ Closest fuel 6 miles away in Sutherland. ☎ 459- 4838. ✖ Closest good food at Oakland's ☎ 459-3796.
⌂ *500 Metz Hill Road, Oakland, OR 97462*
☎ **(503) 459-9220**

Sunny Valley KOA / Grants Pass (S-2)

⚏🚐≈☐◑⚒🔪✖📷$$

From I-5 take Exit 71 and follow the signs.
⚏ 10 14X14 wood stalls with bedding and auto H20 @ $12.50 per night. Current health papers are required.
🚐 Camper/RV hookups, including showers available @ $19 per night. Also have Kamping Kabins @ $26 per night.

≈ Fishing in the area. ✚ Vet in Grants Pass at ☎ 479-2221.
☾ Farrier available in Grant's Pass. ⚒ Closest mechanic is Ken Pettijohn at Wolf Creek (4 miles away) at ☎ 866-2518. He is on call 24 hours a day. ⛽ In Grants Pass. ✖ Aunt Mary's Tavern in Sunny Valley at ☎ 474-1130. 📷 If you want to cool off, go to the Riverside Inn and take a jet boat excursion on the exciting Rogue River. They also have rooms overlooking the Rogue River ☎ (800) 334-4567.
⌂ *140 Old Stage Road, Sunny Valley, OR 97497*
☎ **(503) 479-0209**

NOTE- Following State Park listings all allow horses and some have horse campsites available @ $9 per night. There is also a $1 fee per horse per day. According to latest information, horses are free to run on the beaches at the beach state parks. But if any question it is best to call ahead.

Bullard's Beach State Park / South of Coos Bay (D-1)

🐎🚐$$

On Highway 101, 25 miles south of Coos Bay. 2 miles north of Bandon. Almost 4 miles of equestrian trails and horse camps. Lighthouse is open in the summer. Campground with showers. 92 full hookups.
☎ **(503) 347-2209**

Cape Blanco State Park (D-2)

11 miles northwest of Port Orford and 5.5 miles off Highway 101.
3.5 miles of equestrian trails
and has a lighthouse dating
back to 1870. Watch for sea
lions.

☙ *P.O. Box 1345, Port
Orford, OR 97465*
☎ **(503) 332-6774**

Courtesy Oregon Parks/Recreation

Collier State Park / Klamath Falls Area (D-3)

30 miles north of Klamath Falls on U.S. # 97. Good rest area for
horses. Water available. No horse camps, can go riding on
adjacent/nearby USFS lands. Call for further details.
☎ **(503) 783- 2471**

Milo McIver State Park / Estacada (D-4)

5 miles west of Estacada on Oregon #211 on the Clackamas River.
Campground with showers and 45 electric hookups. 4.5 miles of
equestrian trails.
☎ **(503) 222- 2223**

Nehalem Bay State Park / Coos Bay Area (D-5)

On Highway
101, 25 miles
south of Coos
Bay. Near
Dandon.
☎ **(503)
347-2209**

Courtesy Oregon
Parks/Recreation

Silver Falls State Park / Salem Area (D-6)
🐎🚐$$

26 miles east of Salem off Oregon #22 on Oregon #214. This park has 14 waterfalls and is Oregon's largest state park. 12 miles of equestrian trails and a horse camp.
☎ **(503) 873-8681**

Tryon Creek State Park / Portland Area (D-7)
🐎

6 miles southwest of Portland off I-5 on Terwilliger Blvd. Day riding on 3.5 miles of equestrian trails.
☎ **(503) 653-3166**

Willamette Mission State Park / Salem Area (D-8)
🐎

8 miles north of Salem on Wheatland Ferry Road/Oregon # 99W. Day riding on 2 miles of equestrian trails. Park is on the Willamette River.
☎ **(503) 581-4325**

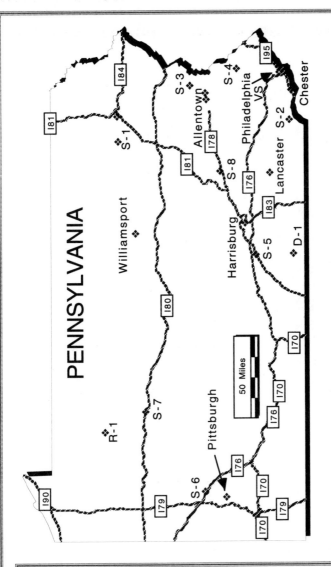

PENNSYLVANIA

Borrowdale Acres S-1
Flying W Ranch R-1
Gateway Stables S-2
Half Halt Training Center S-3
Mill Creek B&B S-4
Rocking L Stables S-5
Sun & Cricket B&B S-6

Univ. of PA Vet School VS
Valley View Stables S-7
Windy Ridge Farm S-8
Gettysburg Nat. Military Park D-1

Borrowdale Acres / Wilkes-Barre Scranton Area (S-1)
🚫➕❌$$$

Call for directions. 42 wood stalls with bedding @ $20 per night. Contact: Carol Malig. ➕ Dallas Vet Clinic within 1 mile ☎ (717) 675-0313. ❌ For dinner try Pickett's Charge ☎ (717) 675-4511.
🏇 *1050 Ryman Road, Dallas, PA 18612*
☎ **(717) 675-5612**

Flying W Ranch / Tionesta (R-1)
🚫🚚🐎🕎

Call for directions. 🚫 40 stalls with bedding. This is a working ranch, surrounded by half a million acres of the Allegheny National Forest and has plenty of hay fields and hilly terrain. Horse camping for those who want to get away from it all. Have championship rodeo every year which attracts up to 15,000 visitors, so call ahead and make reservations. 🚐 50 Camper/RV hookups. 🕎 Farrier available.
🏇 *Star Route 2/ Box 150K, Tionesta, PA 16353*
Winter Address: 312 Penn Bank Bldg., Warren, PA 16365
☎ **(814) 463- 7663** ☎ Winter**: (814) 726-2437**

Gateway Stables / Kennett Square (S-2)
🚫➕🕎🔧❌$$

On Route 1 south at Longwood, turn east on Bayard Road--2 miles to dead end, right 1/4 mile to Merrybell Lane, follow signs to stables. 🚫 22 10X12 wood stalls with bedding and auto H20 @ $15 per night. Stallions allowed only with prior permission and current health papers required. ➕ Vet in New Bolton at University of Pennsylvania at ☎ (215) 444-5800. 🕎 Farrier Doug Nielsen nearby. 🔧 Mechanic is 5 miles away at Sunoco in Mendenhall on Route 52. ⛽ Closest fuel at Longwood Sunoco in Kennett Square. ❌ Longwood Inn at Kennett Square at ☎ (215) 444-3515.
🏇 *RR# 3 / Merrybell Lane, Kennett Square, PA 19348*
☎ **(215) 444-9928 or 444-1255**

Half Halt Training Centre / Nazareth (S-3)
🚫➕🕎🔧❌$$$

6 miles from Route 33. From Route 191, exit at Stockertown, take a left-- 3 miles on your right, take Rose Inn Avenue--2 miles on Rose Inn to stop sign- farm on your right. 🚫 2 12X12 stalls with bedding @ $25 per night. No stallions allowed and require current neg cog/health papers. ➕ Vet in Northampton at ☎ (215) 262-3203.🕎 Farrier Jim Fritz at ☎ (717) 992-4550. 🔧 Mechanic within 2 miles.❌ Food at the Galley Restaurant at Wind Gap at ☎ (215) 863-7585.
🏇 *547A Jacobsburg Road, Nazareth, PA 18064*
☎ **(215) 759-4926**

Mill Creek Farm Bed & Breakfast Buckingham (S-4)

From Pennsylvania Turnpike go north on 611--at Exit 27 go to Route 202 to Quarry Road (2348 Quarry Road). 13 stalls with bedding, ranging from 12X12 to 12X14.

Stallions not allowed and current health papers are required. Rates per room vary from $90 to $135 and include full country breakfast. Beautiful mountain backdrop, farm pond, and plenty of pastures.

5 guest rooms. Fishing in the area. Many horse parks nearby as well as the Bucks County Horse Park which is a 1000 acre facility with jumps. Also 2 state parks nearby. Vet 1/4 mile away in Buckingham. Farrier in Buckingham. Mechanic within 5 miles. Fuel in Doylestown. In Buckingham.

P.O. Box 816, Buckingham, PA 18912
☎ **(215) 794-0776 or (800) 562-1776**

Rocking L Stables / Carlisle (S-5)

Route 76 off I-81. Call for directions. 20 wood stalls with bedding. Stallions allowed. Plenty of trails on 2500 acres. Contact: Glen Lightner. Vet and farrier within 5 miles.

201 Pleasant Hall Road, Carlisle, PA 17013
☎ **(717) 243-3174**

Sun & Cricket Bed & Breakfast / Gibsonia (S-6)

Take Route 8 to Bakerstown--then east 2.5 miles on Red Belt Sun & Cricket is 2.5 miles from Route 8 and 5 miles from U.S. #76 (PA Turnpike).

6 10X12 wood stalls with bedding and auto H20 @ $15 per night. Mini suite with a porch of its own in a new carriage house next to the barn. Snack tray awaits your arrival and there's a stereo and TV. For two people @

$50 per night. ✚ Dr. Frank on call in Mars at ☎ (412) 625-9433. ☖
Farrier Robert Jamison on call in Evans City at ☎ 538- 5136.
⚒ Mechanic 1/2 mile away at Best Tire at ☎ 443-7520. Mon.- Sat.,
9a.m- 7p.m. ⛽ Fuel 3 miles away in Gibsonia at Amoco ☎ 443-6458.
❌ Pines Tavern in Gibsonia at ☎ 625-3252.
⌂ *R. D. #7/ Box 135, Gibsonia, PA 15044*
☎ **(412) 443-8558**

University of Pennsylvania School of Vet Medicine / Philadelphia (VS)
⌂

Emergency horse care 24 hours a day, 7 days a week. Call only for
emergencies! May require referral from a vet. NO STALLS FOR TRAN-
SIENT BOARDING. Must make appointment over telephone first.
Located at 926 Kennett Square.
⌂ *3800 Spruce Street, Philadelphia, PA 19104-6044*
☎ **(215) 382-0791**

Valley View Stables / Brookville (S-7)
⊟ ⛺ ≋ ☖ ⚒ ❌ $$

From I-80 take Exit 13 (TruckStop of America) and call for directions.
Only 4 miles from I-80. ⊟ 16 10X10 stalls with sawdust @ $15 per
night. No stallions allowed and current health papers are required.
⛺ Camper/RV hookups provided free unless using AC. ≋ Fishing in
the area. ✚ Vet in Brookville at ☎ 849-2211.☖ Farrier available in
Brookville. ⚒ Mechanic at Truck Stop of America exit. Open 24 hours
a day. ⛽❌ These services available in Brookville.
⌂ *RD#4/ Box 345A, Brookville, PA 15825*
☎ **(814) 849-2407**

Windy Ridge Farm / Bethel (S-8)
⊟ ⛺ ≋ ☖ ⚒ ❌ $$

Off I-78, take Exit #2. Go north from exit 1 mile, right on Bashore
Road, left on Bennett Street. Call for final directions. ⊟ 5 wood
stalls with bedding @ $15 per night. Range in size from 12X15 to
10X12. Stallions allowed and current health papers required.
⛺ Electric hookups available. ≋ Fishing in the area. ✚ Vet in
Manheim at ☎ (800) 845-6532. ☖ Farrier at ☎ (717) 775-3564.
⚒ Closest mechanic 2 miles away at Frystown on Route 645.
⛽❌ These services 2 miles away in Frystown. Restaurant at ☎ 933-
5008.
⌂ *401 Swope Road, Bethel, PA 19507*
☎ **(717) 933-5888**

Gettysburg National Military Park / Gettysburg Area (D-1)

Horse trails around the park boundaries. You will pass the Union and Confederate cannons and sense what happened on this great battlefield. Its a good day's ride and historical sites are well marked. For lodging call the Gettysburg Travel Council at ☎ (717) 334-6274.
☎ **(717) 334-1124**

Windy Ridge Farm, Bethel

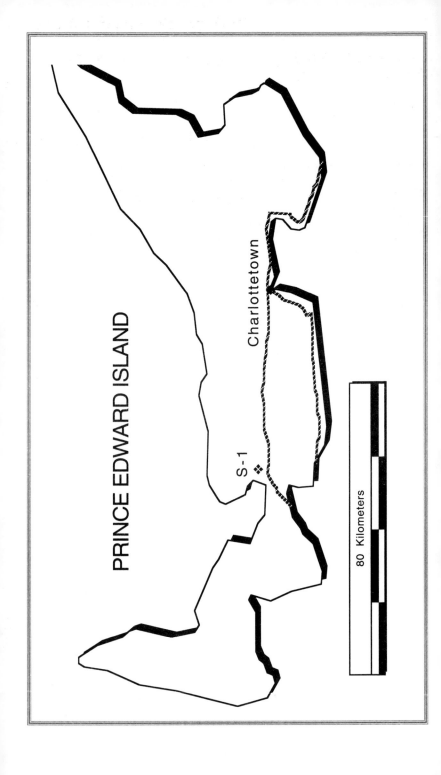

Handibear Hills / South Granville (S-1)

⌁🚐⊨‡✪♘⚒✕$$

On Route 231--3 miles from Route #2. From Highway #2, turn north on Highway #230, then turn left on Highway 231. ⌁ 16 wood stalls with bedding @ $10 per night (standing/can convert to box). 🚐 Electric hookups @ $15-20 per night. Camper/RV hookups at nearby national park. ⊨ There is a bed and breakfast just down the road in South Granville @ $25 per night. Name is Riata Roch. ‡ Fishing in the area. ♘ Mechanic 3 miles away at Weeks Garage (Fredericton) at ☎ 964-2045. Open 6 days a week/12 hours a day. 🛢 Fuel at Fredericton at ☎ 964-2045. ✕ Good dinner at New Glasgow Lobster Suppers in New Glasgow.

✝ *RR# 2, Breadalbane, South Granville, PEI   C0A 1E0 CANADA*
☎ **(902) 964-3220**

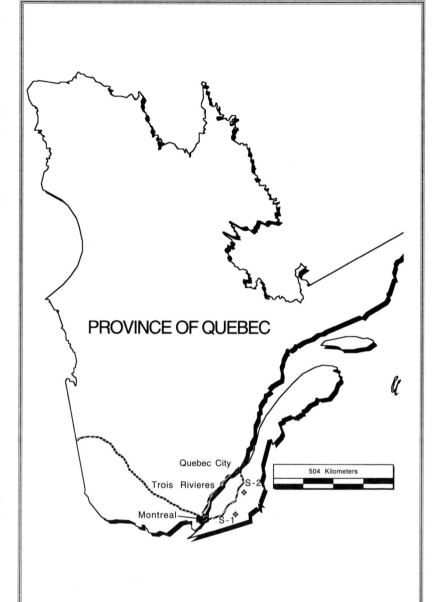

PROVINCE OF QUEBEC

Quebec City

Trois Rivieres

504 Kilometers

S-2

Montreal

S-1

S-1 Ferme L'Oiseau Bleu
S-2 Vue D'En O

Ferme L'Oiseau Bleu / Kingsbury (S-1)

Bed & breakfast facility. English spoken.
⚐ *415, Oak Hill, R.R. 1, Kingsbury, (QC) J0B 1X0, Canada*
☎ **(819) 826-2114**

Vue D'En O / St-Ferdinand (S-2)
$$$

Located in the mountains this bed and breakfast facility supplies guides and even horses if you don't have yours along. All meals are available--lunch and dinner extra. Bed & breakfast and guided ride @ $65-70 or @ $125 if they also supply the horse. Parties limited to 6 people. 10 stalls available. English spoken.
⚐ *Case postale 53, St-Ferdinand, (QC) G0N 1N0, Canada*
☎ **(819) 382-2828**

Québec à cheval / Montréal

This federation has lists of various equestrian clubs, ranches, and supplied us with the two bed and breakfasts listed above. They are an

Copyright Ministry of Tourism of Quebec   Iles-de-la-Madeleine

excellent source for information. They recommend the equestrian clubs as the best source of help for visiting equestrians. There are over 30 equestrian clubs in this province and their telephone numbers are shown after this listing.

✝ *4545 av. Pierre-De Coubertin C.P. 1000, Succursale M, Montreal, (Québec) H1V 3R2, Canada*

☎ **(514) 252-3002 or FAX (514) 251-8038**

Club Equestre Les 4 As	(418) 426-2781
Club Des 4 Fers Inc.	(418) 533-5518
Assoc. Equestre Regionale Abitibi-Temiscamingue	(819) 728-2207
Assoc. des Amateurs de Ranch de la Region de L' Amiante	(418) 475-6741
Les Amis des Chevaux de Maskinonge	(819) 344-2816
Les Amis du Ranch Inc.	(819) 344-2816
Appaloosa-Huron Inc.	(418) 843-4385
Assoc. Equestre Regional Western du Golf	(418) 269-5347
Assoc. Equestre des Collines de la Gatineau	(819) 647-3651
Assoc. Chevaline de la Lievre	(819) 587-3653
Assoc. Equestre de L'or Blanc	(819) 879-4471
Les Balladeurs Equestres Laurentides-Lanaudiere	(514) 431-3999
Club Equestre des Bois-Francs	(819) 353-2745
La Cavalcade du Canton d'Auclair	(418) 853-3061
Club Cavaleros de St-Narcisse	(418) 889-9055
Les Cavaliers de la Frontiere Sud-Ouest	(514) 826-3379
Club des Cavaliers du Nord	(418) 279-3335
Les Cavaliers du Pays de L'Erable	(418) 774-3726
Charlevoix a Cheval Inc.	(418) 435-5601
Les Coureurs des Bois, Selle et Voiture	(819) 449-6407
Club Equitation de Rouyn-Noranda	(819) 797-8239
Estrie a Cheval	(819) 843-9553
La Grande Foulee	(418) 329-3608
Le Groupe Equitami	(418) 672-2800
Club Equestre La Licorne	(819) 427-5295

Club Equestre les Forestiers	(514) 694-3532
Club Equestre de Mirabel	(514) 258-4132
Club Randonnee Equestre Du Mont-Rigaud	(514) 458-5586
Le Nord a Cheval	(819) 326-5789
Club de Randonnees a Cheval de la Mauricie	(819) 535-1502
Club des Randonnees des Festivities Western	(418) 588-6171
Club des Randonnees Hippiques du Quebec	(514) 375-2284
Assoc. des Randonneurs Equestres du Quebec	(514) 742-5248
La Releve du Sport Equestre	(418) 338-2089
Club Equestre Saint-Gregoire	(514) 358-1618

Fédération Équestre Du Québec / Montréal

This federation publishes complete lists of western and classic horse facilities in the Province of Québec, showing what services each can offer. All of the listings in this province were supplied by Fédération Équestre Du Québec

⌖ *4545, Ave. Pierre-de-Coubertin, C.P. 1000, Succ. M, Montréal, QC H1V 3R2*

☎ **(514) 252-3053 or FAX (514) 252-3165**

REGION RIVE- NORD

Centre Équestre Des Mille îles Inc.

⌖ *646, Boul. des Mille-îles, Laval, H7L 1K5*

☎ **(514) 622-3033**

Centre Équestre Val Morin

⌖ *1573, 7e Avenue, Val Morin, J7Z 5T4*

☎ **(819) 322-2137**

Sonsational Farms / Centre Équestre De Joliette

⌖ *460, rang Rivière Nord, St. Liguori, J0K 2X0*

☎ **(514) 754-2091**

OUTAOUAIS

Centre Équestre Petite Nation

⌷ *B.P.#7, Route 321 Nord, St-André Avellin, J0V 1W0*
☎ **(819) 983-6570**

CENTRE DU QUÉBEC

Ferme Franchère

Contact: Anne Bélanger
⌷ *115, Route 263, Ste-Hélène-de-Chester, G0P 1H0*
☎ **(819) 382-2307**

Ferme Poirier

⌷ *211, chemin Ste-Marguerite, Pointe-du-Lac, G0X 1Z0*
☎ **(819) 377-1718**

QUÉBEC

Club D'Équitation Radisson

⌷ *418, rang du Petit Capsa, St-Augustin-de- Demaures, G1K 3W8*
☎ **(418) 878-4459**

Club Équestre de Québec

⌷ *51, boul. St-Sacrement, St-Gabriel-de- Valcartier, G0A 4S0*
☎ **(418) 844-2713**

Domaine La Voltige

⌷ *2140, rang St-Ange, Ste Foy, G2E 3L9*
☎ **(418) 871-7418**

Écurie Hélène Coulombe

⌷ *1122, route Gravel, Pont-Roge, G0A 2X0*
☎ **(418) 876-3165**

EST DU QUÉBEC
Académie Équestre de Rimouski

⌷ *1035-A, St. Germain Ouest, Rimouski, G5L 7B5*
☎ **(418) 722-5156**

SAGUENAY LAC-SAINT-JEAN

Centre Équestre Norcel

⚞ 2759, rang St-Eusèbe, St-Félicien, G8K 2N9

☎ **(418) 679-3701**

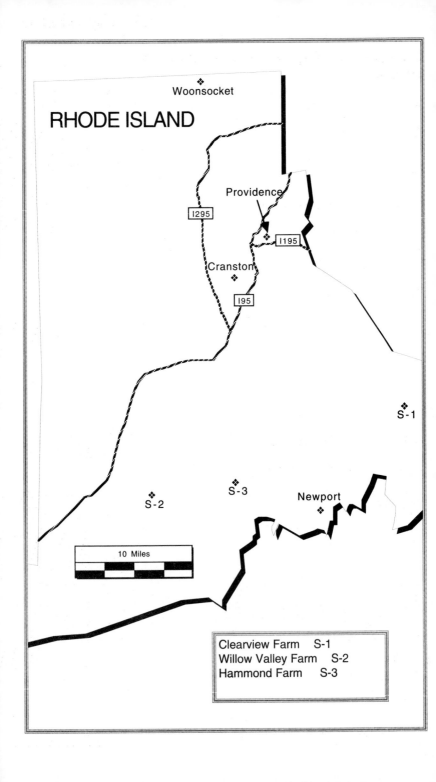

Clearview Farm / Tiverton (S-1)

From Providence, 95N take eastbound exit to 24E. Go to Tiverton exit and take a left, going through Stonebridge-- another 2 miles and it will be on your left. Directions complicated and call ahead if any questions! 30 wood stalls with bedding. This facility is a hunter farm and has show riding. Try the Coachman Restaurant.

5630 Main Road, Tiverton, RI 02878

☎ (401) 625-1458

Willow Valley Farm / West Kingston (S-2)

$$

Off Route 95. Call for directions. 13 wood stalls @ $11 per day. Health papers required. This is a hunter/jumper facility. Contact: Allison Ward.

360 Hillsdale Road, West Kingston, RI 02892

☎ (401) 539-2742

Hammond Farm / Saunderstown (S-3)

$$

Take I-95 to Route 1, go north (close to University of Rhode Island). Require advance notice and recommend that you call for directions. 20 wood stalls with bedding @ $15 per night. Near the ocean, this 4 year old facility boasts that horses get A-1 care. Facility has 70X140 indoor arena, grass paddocks, and outdoor arena. Hunter/

jumper/equitation facility with training, instruction, and sales.
▚✎☒ This is a resort area, so plenty of quality services available.
Except during the summer, lodging could be hard to find. But
Hammond Farm would be happy to assist in finding accommodations.
Contact: Cyd Edgerley Fraser
⌖ *2124 Tower Hill Road, Saunderstown, RI 02874*
☎ **(401) 295-5588**

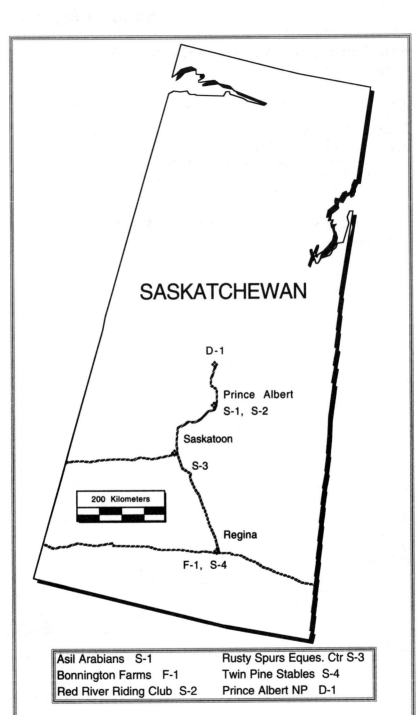

SASKATCHEWAN

D-1

Prince Albert
S-1, S-2

Saskatoon

S-3

200 Kilometers

Regina

F-1, S-4

Asil Arabians S-1	Rusty Spurs Eques. Ctr S-3
Bonnington Farms F-1	Twin Pine Stables S-4
Red River Riding Club S-2	Prince Albert NP D-1

Asil Arabians / Prince Albert (S-1)
�🔵💧🔦📷✂️$

8 miles southeast of Prince Albert. Call for directions and reservations. � 8 wood stalls with metal bars and rubber mats @ $5 per night. Have heating, air exchanger, and a new facility with outdoor arena. 🔵💧 Vet and farrier on call in Prince Albert. 🔦📷✂️ These services available in Prince Albert. For Greek food, try the Venice House at 15th and Central Avenue. Try Greek ribs. ☎ (306) 764-6555.
†   *Box 275, Prince Albert, SK S6V 5R5 CANADA*
☎ **(306) 764-7900**

Bonnington Farms / Regina (F-1)
🚶side🔦📷✂️

From Regina 6 miles north of Husky Station on East #1. 🚶side 4 stalls and 3 big outside pens with wire fencing. This facility breeds American paints. 🔦📷✂️ These services available in Regina. For food, recommend either Golf's Steak House at ☎ (306) 525-5808 or The Harvest Eating House at ☎ (306) 545-3777.
†   *RR #1, Regina, SK S4P 2Z1 CANADA*
☎ **(306) 545-0973**

Red River Riding Club / Prince Albert (S-2)
🚶side🔵💧🔦📷✂️$$

4 miles north of Prince Albert on Highway #2. 🚶side 26 box stalls @ $15 per night and 18 tie stalls @ $10 per night. Outdoor paddocks and have indoor arena. Manager is Ken Murray. 🔵 💧 3 vets and a farrier in Prince Albert area. 🔦 📷 ✂️ These services available in Prince Albert. See first SK listing for Greek food..
☎ **(306) 763-3434**

Rusty Spurs Equestrian Centre / Saskatoon (S-3)
🚶side🔦📷✂️

Near exhibition grounds. Call for directions. 🚶side 96 stalls on space available basis--price unknown.. 🔦📷✂️ These services available in Saskatoon. For good atmosphere and food, try R. J. Willoughby's at the Holiday Inn.
†   *RR #5, Saskatoon, SK S7K 3J8 CANADA*
☎ **(306) 373-4317**

North American Horse Travel Guide

Twin Pine Stables / Regina (S-4)

▰ ❦▮✕ $$

2 miles west of Lewvan Drive on 13th Avenue (near Regina Airport)
▰ 20 wood stalls with mats @ $15 per night. Health papers
required. Indoor and outdoor arenas. Clinics and shows.
❦▮✕These services available in Regina and for a nice meal try the
Red Ox Restaurant which is within 2 miles of the stables.

✝ *Box 405, Regina, SK S4P 3A2*
☎ **(306) 757-4882**

NOTE- All of these listings were developed with the help of SHOW
TRAIL, the official magazine of the Saskatchewan Horse Federation.

✝ *2205 Victoria Avenue, Regina, SK S4P OS4.*
☎ **(306) 780-9449 or FAX 525-4009**

Prince Albert National Park / Waskesiu Lake Region (D-1)

🐎🐟🚐

The park is in central Saskatchewan, 90 km. north of Prince Albert.
includes some 3875 sq. km. of wilderness and more than seven major
lakes. 🚐 Waskesiu Lake has RV hookups, campgrounds and luxu
hotels. 🐎 Permit trail riding in south part of park. Access through
south gate. Get map from park first--otherwise it might be hard to
find this entrance. 🐟 Lakes have good fishing. Open year round. $
per car per day or $6 per car for 4 days.

✝ *Superintendent, Prince Albert National Park, Box 100, Waskesiu
Lake, SK S0J 2Y0 CANADA*
☎ **(306) 663-5322**

SASKATCHEWAN

PRINCE ALBERT NATIONAL PARK
PARC NATIONAL PRINCE-ALBERT

From CANADA PARKS

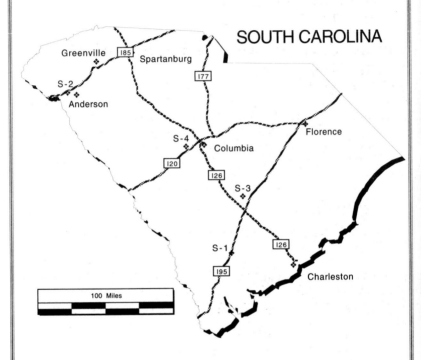

SOUTH CAROLINA

Greenville [I85] Spartanburg

S-2 [I77]

Anderson

S-4 [I20] Columbia Florence

[I26] S-3

S-1 [I26]

[I95] Charleston

100 Miles

Cramberry Stables	S-4
Mount Carmel Farm B&B	S-1
Penn's Wood Stables	S-2
RV Shirer Thoroughbreds	S-3

Cramberry Stables / Lexington (S-4)

Close to I-20, I-26. Call for directions. If you bring own feed/bucket for water Stalls @ $10 per night. For full service stalls @ $ 20 per night. 100 X200 indoor arena, wash rack, full size lounge, locker room. This is a full service facility, except no Camper/RV hookups. These services all within 3 miles. Places to eat include the Lexington Arms and Cinnamon Hill.

⌐ *P.O. Box 100, Lexington, SC 29071*
☎ **(803) 359-1033**

Mount Carmel Farm Bed & Breakfast / Walterboro (S-1)

Call for directions. 3.5 miles from I-95. 8 stalls @ $15 per night. Call for details, health paper requirements. Contact : M. MacKnee. 2 rooms with private bath @ $ 50 per night. Includes breakfast. These services available in Walterboro. Sassafras Cafe. From I-95 take Exit 53 3.5 miles east to 125 East Washington Street. ☎ (803) 549-6397.

⌐ *Route 2 / Box 58A, Walterboro, SC 29488*
☎ **(803) 538-5970**

Penn's Wood Stables / Anderson (S-2)

2 miles from Clemson Exit of I-85. Take your first left and then 3rd right. Call for directions and landmarks. Advance reservations required! Unknown number of stalls with bedding. Vet available. Farrier on premises. These services available in Anderson. Decent food at Morrison's Cafeteria, 3 miles south of Junction I-85, U.S. 76 and SR 28, Exit 19A.

⌐ *1930 Denver Road, Anderson, SC 29625*
☎ **(803) 261-8476**

RV Shirer Thoroughbreds Elloree (S-3)

From I-95 take Exit 98 and go west on Route 6/60. 7 miles to Harlin Street. Turn right and go 1 mile. 10 very large wood stalls with bedding and auto H20 @ $10 per night. Stallions allowed and require current neg cog/health papers. 🚐 Electric only for Camper/RV @ $5 per night. 🎣 Fishing in the area. ✚ Vet in St. Matthew's at ☎ 874-1006. ♘ Farrier in Bamberg at ☎ 245-2848. ✎ Mechanic 1 mile away at Fogle Texaco on main street in Elloree at ☎ 897-2543, open 9-6. ⛽ Fuel at Elloree Truck Stop at ☎ 897-3460. ✘ Try Duke's BarBQue in Elloree at ☎ 897-2962.

⌖ *P.O. Box 640, Elloree, SC 29047*

☎ **(803) 897-3376**

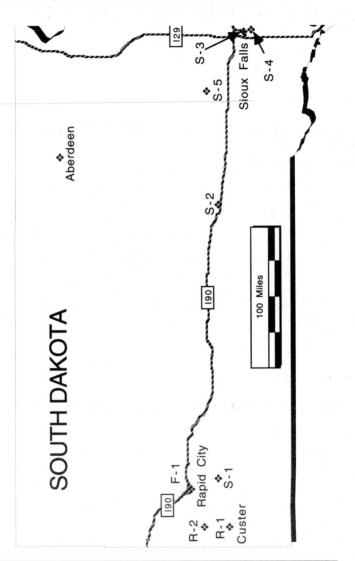

SOUTH DAKOTA

Aberdeen

129

S-3

Sioux Falls

S-4

S-5

S-2

I90

100 Miles

I90

F-1

Rapid City

S-1

R-2

R-1

Custer

Central States Fair F-1	Skoglund Farm S-5
Bunkhouse B&B S-1	TC Ranch R-1
Diamond A Cattle Co. S-2	Happy Hills Ranch/Tack R-2
Meadowbrook Eq. Ctr S-3	
Pineview Farm S-4	

Central States Fair / Rapid City (F-1)

From I-90 take Exit 60. 30 wood/metal 12X12 stalls with bedding @ $7 per night. Vet in Rapid City at ☎ (605) 343-6066. Farrier within 10 miles. These services all within 3 miles (Rapid City).

♱ *P.O. Box 2560 , Rapid City, SD 57709*

☎ **(605) 342-8325**

Bunkhouse Bed & Breakfast / Rapid City Area (S-1)

From Rapid City, go south on Route 79 to Lower Spring Road. As you pass St. Patrick Street in Rapid City, it will be 8 miles to the Lower Spring Creek Road cutoff . At Lower Spring Creek Road (#C 220), go east 4.3 miles. 3 inside stalls @ $5 / @ $3 w/o bedding. No stallions allowed. Nearby ranch has large indoor arena and hosts many horse events. 3 guest rooms and rates range from $20 for a single to $70 per night for a deluxe double. Located on lovely Spring Creek which has plenty of trout! (but fishing licenses is required). Serve full ranch style breakfast. Dr. Dale Hendrickson in Rapid City at ☎ (605) 342-1368. Several in the area. Closest mechanic is 12 miles away--Glen Johnson at JR's Tire in Hermosa at ☎ (605) 255-4587. Open 8-5. Bottle Creek Station in Hermosa. Gaslight in Rockerville, SD at ☎ (605) 343-9276.

♱ *14630 Lower Spring Creek Road, Hermosa, SD 57744*

☎ **(605) 342-5462**

Diamond A Cattle Company / Kimball Area (S-2)

From I-90 Kimball Exit go 6 miles west, 1 mile north and 1/2 mile west. 3 wood stalls with bedding @ $10 per night. Roping arena with pens. Stallions allowed and require current health papers. Have cabin with shower and primitive sheepherder's wagon for rent @ $25-35 per night. Fishing in the area. Free electric hookups if stabling. Vets in Kimball and Chamberlain. Farriers in Kimball and Chamberlain. Closest mechanic is at Midway Truck Stop in Kimball (7 miles away). These services available in Kimball.

♱ *RR #1/ Box 100, Pukwana, SD 57370*

☎ **(605) 778-6885**

Happy Hills Ranch & Tack / Hill City (R-2)

$$

Call for directions.
$$ 8 stalls ranging
in size from 10 X10 to
10X12. Include shav-
ings @ $10 per night.
Stallions allowed.
Outdoor arena is 100 X
200. Several vets
in the area. Farriers
available. Electric
hookups available @
$10 per night.
Tack shop on the

premises. Discount prices and specialize in English.
HC #87/ Box 67B, Hill City, SD 57745
☎ (605) 574-2326

Meadowbrook Equestrian Center / Sioux Falls (S-3)

$$$

From I-229 take 10th Street Exit, turn left and go 2 miles. Call for final
directions. 38 wood stalls (mostly 10X10) with bedding @ $25 per
night. Outside 20X60 pen @ $15 per night. Current health papers
required and do not allow stallions to layover. Nearest vet is at
Dakota Large Animal Center at ☎ 338-5558. Farrier Narlan
Klinghagen is in nearby Parker. Closest mechanic is 1 mile away at
TMA. Closest fuel at Food-N-Fuel in Sioux Falls. Try the Fry-N-
Pan which is 2 miles away in Sioux Falls.
RR #2, Sioux Falls, SD 57103
☎ (605) 339-3030 or (605) 371-0789

Pineview Farm / Sioux Falls (S-4)

Call for directions and reservations. 3.5 miles off Interstate 829.
6 stalls with bedding. Black Hills to the west. Get advance ok for
stallions. Current health papers required. Vet within 2 miles.
Todd Kennedy 25 miles away. Truck stop at Interstate.
Steakhouse 3.5 miles away.
RR #1, Box 764, Sioux Falls, SD 57032
☎ (605) 743-2828

Skoglund Farm / Canova (S-5)

14 miles off Interstate 90. Call for directions. Stalls with bedding/ no details available. Stallions allowed. No charge for boarding horses if you stay for bed and breakfast.
Camper/RV hookups available. Bed and breakfast includes evening meal and breakfast @ $30 per person for adults, teens @ $20 per person, and children @ $15 per

person. Fishing within 30 miles. Vet in Montrose at ☎ 363-5353. Several mechanics 14 miles away in Salem. Fuel available in Salem or Canova.
Route 1, Box 45, Canova, SD 57321
☎ **(605) 247-3445**

TC Ranch / Custer (R-1)

7 miles south of Custer on U.S. 385, then 1 mile on Rt. 291. Bear left 1/8 mile and turn right. 50X100 and 60X60 corrals and 3 acre pasture with shelter @ $7.50 per night. Stallions allowed. Electric

hookups available--donation appreciated. And there is good fishing in the area. Vet available in Custer at ☎ 673-5344. Farrier available in Custer at ☎ 673-4457. Mechanic at

Dave's Repair in Custer (8 miles away). Open 8 to 6 and Saturday mornings. Fuel available in Custer. Meals available at TC Ranch by reservation (for horse people only). Rooms also available by reservation for horse people only. Contact: Tom Champion.
Route #1/ Box 92 TC, Custer, SD 57730
☎ **(605) 673-3249**

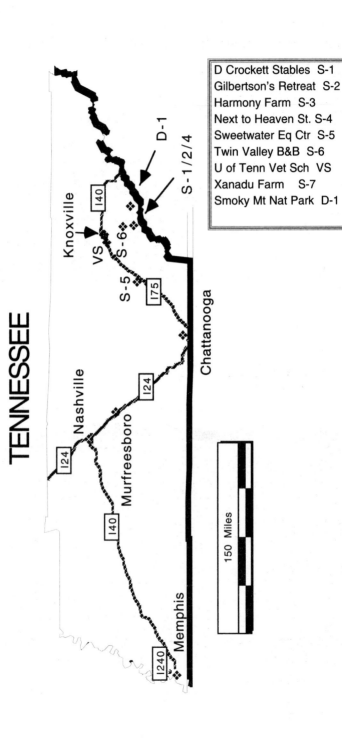

Davy Crockett Riding Stables / Townsend (S-1)

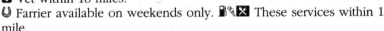

On Highway 73 next to Smoky Mt. National Park (see listing at end of this state section).

12 stalls with bedding @ $10 per night. Stallions not allowed and require current health papers. Contact: J C Morgan.

Campground next to stable. Trout on adjacent river. 60 miles of trails on property, plus the National Park.

Vet within 18 miles.

Farrier available on weekends only. These services within 1 mile.

P.O. Box 161, Townsend, TN 37882

☎ **(615) 448- 6411**

Gilbertson's Lazy Horse Retreat / Townsend (S-2)

Follow Tuckaleechee Caverns signs, 1st road past caverns to the right and then 2nd place on the left. 6 10X10 wood box stalls with

bedding @ $10 per night. $5 per night outside. 80X140 paddocks. Stallions allowed. Current health papers required. 3 rental cabins, ranging from $60 to $75 per night. ⊃ Fishing in the area. ❶ Vet in Maryville at ☎ 984-6660. ♘ Farrier in Friendsville at ☎ 995-2758. ✎ Mechanic within 1/4 mile. George McCampbell at ☎ 448-6206. Open 7 days a week. ❚ Fuel at Parkway Grocery in Townsend at ☎ 448-6276. ☒ Terry's Trout Farm in Townsend at ☎ 448-2290.
✝ *938 Schoolhouse Gap Road, Townsend, TN 37882*
☎ **(615) 448-6647**

Harmony Farm / Bon Aqua (S-3)

On Highway 46, 4 miles south of I-40. Use Exit #172. ▤ 30 wood tie & 10X10 stalls with bedding @ $15 per night. Stallions allowed and require current health papers. ▼ Saddle and Feed Shop on the premises. ❶ Dr. Tom Edmonds in Lyles at ☎ (615) 670-4926. ♘ Farrier on the premises. ✎ Mechanic on the premises. Available 24 hours. a day. ❚ Closest fuel--1 mile. Best priced fuel--10 miles. ☒ Closest food--1 mile.
✝ *Route 2/ Box 240, Bon Aqua, TN 37025*
☎ **(615) 670-4737**

Next to Heaven Riding Stables / Townsend (S-4)

On Highway 331 between Townsend and Pigeon Forge. ▤ Open pole barn with 12 ties and running spring water. Electric hookups available. ❶ Within 7 miles. ♘ On premises. ❘❚☒ These services within 3 miles. Good food at The Timbers.
✝ *1239 Wears Valley Road, Townsend, TN 37882*
☎ **(615) 448-9150**

Sweetwater Equestrian Center Sweetwater (S-5)

Exit 60 off I-75; north on Highway 68 for 3 miles, left on County Road 316 for 7 to 10 miles; located on the right (1065 County Road #316).
▤ 12 10X24 wood stalls with bedding and auto H20 @ $20 per

night. Horse shower in the stable with hot and cold water. Stallions allowed and current health papers are required. ≋ Fishing in the area. ✚ Vet in Sweetwater at ☎ (615) 263-5812. ☉ Farrier in Etowah at ☎ (615) 263-5812.✎ Closest mechanic within 1/4 mile by name of Shoemaker. ☎ (615) 337-3750 and available 24 hours a day. ▮ Fuel at either Exxon or Tiger Mart in Sweetwater. ✖ Good food at Cracker Barrel in Sweetwater ☎ (615) 337-3722.

⚑ *1065 County Road #316, Niota, TN 37826*
☎ **(615) 337-2674 or (800) 662-4042**

Twin Valley Bed & Breakfast Horse Ranch Walland (S-6)

4 miles from Highway 321. Call for directions. ≋ 10 tie/10X10 box stalls w/o bedding. ≋ Vet in Maryville at ☎ 984-6660. ☉ Farrier in Maryville at ☎ 983-1201. ✎ Closest mechanic 1.5 miles at Clyde's on Cold Springs Road at ☎ 983-7699. Open 6 days a week 8-6. ▮ Closest fuel at Amoco in Walland. ✖ Mill House Restaurant in Walland.

⚑ *2848 Old Cilhowee Road, Walland, TN 37886*
☎ **(615) 984-0980**

University of Tennessee College of Veterinary Medicine / Knoxville (VS)

Emergency horse care. Call only for emergencies! May require referral from a vet. NO STALLS FOR TRANSIENT BOARDING. Located at 2407 River Road..

⚑ *P.O. Box 1071, Knoxville, TN 37901-1071*
☎ **(615) 974-5702**

Xanadu Farm / Murfreesboro Area (S-7)

13 miles east of I-65 (take the Franklin/ Murfreesboro Exit). Go 13 miles east towards Murfreesboro to Highway 31/41 (Horton Highway). Turn south. Xanadu Farm is about 1 mile on your right. If you come from the east, 15 miles west of I-24, take a left onto Highway 31/41, go

south about 1 mile and Xanadu will be on your left.

 28 12X12 wood stalls with bedding @ $12 per night w/o feed or @ $15 per night with feed.. Stallions allowed. 🛏 The farm has a nice cottage which goes for $75 per night single or double occupancy and includes a continental breakfast. Each additional person @ $7.50 per night. 🎣 Fishing in the area. ✚♞ Vet in Lewisburg at ☎ 359-3599. Farrier in Goodletsville at ☎ 851-1715. 🔧🗙 Several mechanics within 15 miles. Fuel available in Triune. Many good restaurants in the Franklin/ Murfreesboro area.

🚩 *8155 Horton Highway, Triune, TN 37014.*
☎ **(615) 395-4771**

Great Smoky Mountains National Park Gatlinburg (D-1)

Courtesy NPS

850 miles of trails, many of which are available to horses. Horses restricted to designated trails (which can be found on National Park maps which are available at any of the information centers in the park. There are 5 auto access horse camps-- reservations can be made through the back country reservations office in the park. Horse camps are: Anthony Creek, Big Creek, Cataloochee, Round Bottom, and Towstring. And their capacity averages about 20. Grazing is prohibited and horses must be cross tied.

🚩 *107 Park Headquarters Road, Gatlinburg, TN 37738*
☎ **(615) 436-1231**

Courtesy NPS

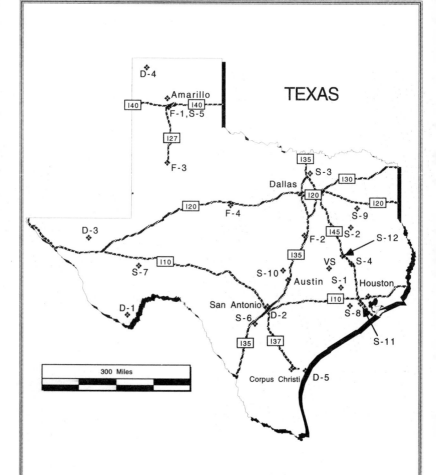

TEXAS

Brittania Farms	S-1
Cedar Crest Stud Farm	S-2
Classic Manor	S-3
Camp Coyote	S-4
Bill Cody Arena	F-1
Cottonwood Stables	S-5
Heart O' Texas Fairgrounds	F-2
Madisonville Best Western	S-12
Majestic Oaks Eq. Club	S-6
Merrell / Ann Daggett	S-7
Panhandle South Plains Fair	F-3
Pecan Tree Farm Stables	S-8
Pine Lake Stables	S-9
Spiritwood Riding Center	S-10
Taylor County Expo Center	F-4
Texas A & M Vet School	VS
Tisdale's Stables	S-11
Big Bend National Park	D-1
Brackenridge Park	D-2
Guadalupe Mt. Nat. Park	D-3
Palo Duro Canyon St. Park	D-4
Mustang Riding Stables	D-5

Brittania Farms / Waller (S-1)

From I-10, go 5 miles north on Highway 6. 100 metal stalls with bedding. 2 Camper/RV hookups available.

☥ *Route 2/ Box 431H, Waller, TX 77484*

☎ **(713) 855-3943**

Cedar Crest Stud Farm / Palestine (S-2)

3 miles out of Palestine on #84 East. No vacancies during breeding season, so call in advance. On space-available basis. No. of stalls unknown. Boarding, breeding, mare care, and lay-ups. Current health papers required. ✚ Managed by Steve Hicks, DVM. On premises.

✖ Best Western Palestine Inn. From Palestine 1 mile southwest on U.S. #79 (1601 West Palestine Ave.) ☎ (903) 723-4655.

☥ *Route 1/ Box 1669, Palestine, TX 75802*

☎ **(903) 729- 4898**

Classic Manor / Dallas Area (S-3)

35 miles north of Dallas-- 10 miles off I-35. Call for directions. 50 stalls. 10 covered, 40 covered mare motels. All with bedding. @ $12 per night. Boarding, breeding, layups, mare care. Current health papers required.

✚ Managed by Dick Shepard DVM. On premises.

☥ *RR # 2/ Box 288A, Aubrey, TX 76227*

☎ **(817) 387-3390**

Camp Coyote / Huntsville (S-4)

9 miles north on Route 75. Call for directions. Must call in advance! 10 wood stalls w/o bedding @ $12.50 per night. Current health papers required. ✚♞ Vet and farrier available in Huntsville.

✖ Sam Houston Inn. Junction I-45 & FM 1374, Exit 114. ☎ (409) 295-9151. Or Waterwood National Resort & Country Club. 16.5 miles east on U.S. 190, 6 miles north on Waterwood Parkway. On Lake Livingston and many recreational things to do. (409) 891-5211.

☥ *P.O. Box 276, Huntsville, TX 77342*

☎ **(409) 294-9338**

Bill Cody Arena - Tri State Fairgrounds Amarillo (F-1)

≋ ⊖⊕⚒▓☒ $$

1/2 mile off I-40 East at 3rd and Grand Streets. ≋ 294 10X10 stalls w/o bedding @ $10 per night. Bedding available @ $5 per bag. Stallions allowed. ⊖ Electric hookups available @ $10 per night. ⊕ Vet available at ☎ (806) 373-7454. ▓ All of these services available within 5 miles. ☒ The Country Barn Steak House. Jct. I-40 & U.S. 287 exit 75 on Lakeside Drive, 1 block north. ☎ (806) 335-2325 or Big Texan Steak Ranch. From I-40 take Lakeside Drive (Exit 75) and go 1 block north. ☎ (806) 372-6000.

⌂ *P.O. Box 31087, Amarillo, TX 79120*

☎ **(806) 376-7767**

Cottonwood Stables / Amarillo (S-5)

≋ ⊖⊕⚒▓☒ $$

From I-40 exit south to Ross-Osage (7 miles), go right on FM 1151 for 1/4 mile. ≋ 51 12X12 metal stalls with bedding and auto H20 @ $15 per night. This outstanding facility was built by the mayor of Amarillo in 1982. Stallions allowed and current health papers are required. ⊖ 1 electric hookup @ $5 per night. Also have showers. ▓ Mechanic 7 miles away at Plains Chevy on 2200 I-40E at ☎ 374-4611. Open Mon- Sat. 7 a.m.-6 p.m. ▌ Closest fuel 1/4 mile east at ☎ 622- 3535. ☒ Within 1/2 mile. See prior listing.

⌂ *Route 7/ Box 640, Amarillo, TX 79118*

☎ **(806) 622-3034**

Heart O' Texas Fairgrounds / Waco (F-2)

≋ ⊖⊕⚒▓☒ $$

Take New Road Exit off I-35. Must call ahead for space! ≋ 350 stalls with H20 and w/o bedding @ $10 per stall. Shavings available @ $5 per bag. ⊖ Camper/RV hookups @ $10 per night. ⊕⊙ Vet and farrier in Waco. ▌▓☒ These services available within 1 mile.

⌂ *4601 Basque Blvd., Waco, TX 76710*

☎ **(817) 776-1660**

Madisonville Best Western / Madisonville (S-12)

≋ ▌▓☒ $$

I-45 and Highway 21. ≋ 8 stalls behind motel @ $10 per night. Check for availability ahead of arrival. ▌▓☒ These services available.

⌂ *3305 East Main Street, Madisonville, TX 77864*

☎ **(409) 348-3606**

Majestic Oaks Equestrian Club
San Antonio Area (S-6)

≣≣ ⊶➊◊◊ ✎ ✖ $$

3 miles from Interstate 10. 20 miles from San Antonio. From Interstate 10 West take Exit 557 (Boerne Stage/ Leon Springs). Left turn at stop sign. 3 miles on Boerne Stage Road. Left turn at 4-way stop. ≣≣ 50 12X12 stalls with cedar shavings @ $12 per night. Require current health papers and stallions allowed. ⊶ Showers available. ➊ Vet in Boerne at ☎ (210) 249-3073. ◊ Farrier in Boerne at ☎ 755- 2524. ✎ Closest mechanic 4 miles away in Pico. ✖ Fuel in Pico. ✖ For dinner try Rudy's BarBque.

⌖ *25785 Boerne Stage Road, Boerne, TX 78005*
☎ **(210) 698-1111**

Merrell & Ann Daggett / Fort Stockton(S-7)

≣≣ ⊶➊ ✎ ✖ $$

4 miles north of I-10 at Fort Stockton Exit. Call for directions. ≣≣ 7 14X14 metal stalls with runs and w/o bedding @ $15 per night. Bedding available at extra charge. Stallions allowed and current health papers are required. ⊶ Electric hookups available @ $5 per night. ➊ Vet in Stockton at ☎ 336-2208 or 336-5291. ✎ Closest mechanic 6 miles away. On call. ✖✖ These services available within 6 miles.

⌖ *Route 1/ Box E , Fort Stockton, TX 79735*
☎ **(915) 336-5490 or 336-6670**

Panhandle South Plains Fair / Lubbock (F-3)

≣≣ ⊶➊◊ ✎ ✖ $$

Take Exit 4 off I-27. ≣≣ 100 wood stalls with sand bedding @ $10 per night. ⊶ Camper/RV hookups available.
➊◊ Vet and farrier available in Lubbock.
✎✖ These services available. Good food at the Santa Fe, Sheraton, or Holiday Inn.

⌖ *P.O. Box 208, Lubbock, TX 79408*
☎ **(806) 763-2833**

Pecan Tree Farm Stables / Houston Area (S-8)

Call in advance and for directions. 40 wood stalls and a 1-mile training track. Stallions allowed. Vets and farriers in the area. These services nearby. There is a Red Lobster fairly close.

⌂ *1031 Hagerson, Sugarland, TX 77479*

☎ **(713) 499-2475**

Pine Lake Stables / Tyler (S-9)

Off I-20 between Dallas and Shreveport. Call for directions. 50 wood/metal stalls @ $10 per night. In business 25 years. Provide total service and these are friendly folks! Stallions allowed and neg cog/ current health papers required. Advance notice for Camper/RV hookups required. Glenwood Animal Hospital (Steve Wilson). It's 6 miles away. Closest fuel is 1.5 miles away. Recommend the Golden Corral Restaurant which is 6 miles away and has a 30' buffet with 150 different items! ☎ (903) 534-0281. For Mexican food try Papacitas on South Broadway ☎ (903) 581-7433. Ranch is close to the world-famous Rose Garden which has close to 500 different kinds of roses.

⌂ *11015 Pine Lake Blvd., Tyler, TX 75709*

☎ **(903) 592-8075**

Spiritwood Riding Center / North Austin Area (S-10)

From I-35 take Exit 256, go west on #1431 to County Road 178. Go north (right) 2 miles on twisting road to our sign. Phone ahead and we will meet you.

▅▅ 19 10X12 wood stalls with wood shavings @ $15 per night. Stallions not allowed and require neg cog/current health papers. Spiritwood is a family- oriented facility offering top quality boarding and riding instruction in a quiet private setting. Stables built in 1989 and include 20 acres of land, large pastures, running creeks and a schooling arena. Insect/fly spray system and indoor wash rack with hot and cold water. Boarders receive 3 personalized feedings a day. ▄▆ 2 electric hookups @ $7 per night and toilet in the barn. ✚ Vet in Round Rock. ♘ Plenty of farriers around. ✎ Closest mechanic at Love's on North Bell in Cedar Park (6 miles) at ☎ (512) 335- 5093. Open Mon.- Fri. 7:30-6, and Sat. 7:30-12:00. ▐✎✖ These services available in Cedar Park.

✝ *Route #7/ Box 11-AB, Leander, TX 78641*
☎ **(512) 259-1717 or 259-5310**

Taylor County Expo Center / Abilene (F-4)
▅▅▄▆✚▐✎✖$$

From Interstate 20 take Exit 36 and go south 4 miles on #322. Must call ahead for reservations! ▅▅ 600 wood/metal stalls @ $10 per night. Current health papers required. ▄▆ Camper/RV hookups available @ $10 per night. ▐✎✖ These services close by.

✝ *1700 Highway #36, Abilene, TX 79602*
☎ **(915) 677-4376**

Texas A & M College of Veterinary Medicine / College Station (VS)
⌂

Emergency horse care 24 hours a day, 7 days a week. Call only for emergencies! May require referral from a vet. NO STALLS FOR TRAN-SIENT BOARDING. Take University Drive to Raymond Stetzer Parkway. Get final directions when you call.

✝ *College Station, TX 77843-4461*
☎ **(409) 845-3541**

Tisdale's Stables / Houston (S-11)
▅▅✚✖

Call for directions. 2.5 miles off Gulf Freeway. ▅▅ 38 20X20 wood stalls with bedding. ✚ Vet 15 minutes away (Pasadena). ✖ Good food at the Golden Corral (5 minutes away).

✝ *8706 Alameda Genoa Road, Houston, TX 77075*
☎ **(713) 991-9803**

Big Bend National Park / South of Ft. Stockton (D-1)

This 740,000 acre park is located on the big bend of the Rio Grande River. There is a back country horse camp some 5 miles from Park headquarters-- but you have to take in all your water and feed for the horses.

Courtesy Texas Dept of Highways

Reservations for this camp site can be made up to 10 weeks in advance. There are over 100 miles of trails open to horses. There is also a primitive 51 mile long road that roughly follows the Rio Grande. It's called the River Road. Fall and winter can be good times to do a trail ride in this Park. Lot's of 4 wheelers in the Spring and the Summer can be hot. Photo courtesy of the Texas Dept. of Highways.

⚐ *Big Bend National Park, Big Bend, TX 79834*
☎ **(915) 477-2251**

Brackenridge Park / San Antonio (D-2)

This 300 acre-plus park off Hildebrand and Broadway is the city's largest park, and some of the equestrian trails take you along beautiful sections of the San Antonio River. For further information call the Brackenridge Stables at ☎ (210) 732-8881 or call the Convention and Visitors Bureau. ☎ **(210) 270-8748**

Courtesy Texas Dept of Highways

Guadalupe Mountains National Park / Carlsbad, NM Area (D-3)

Courtesy Texas Dept of Highways.

55 miles southwest of Carlsbad, 110 miles east of El Paso, this isolated National Park does not draw many visitors. But for a true wilderness experience, it's in a class of its own! It is a meeting of the Rockies and the Chihuahuan Desert and over 50 different mammals live here. Deer, bison, bighorn sheep, foxes, coyotes, and mountain lions are just a few of the local residents. Most of the park trails are open to equestrian use--mainly the north-south ridges in the center of the park. Riders must obtain a free use permit before going into the park. There are horse pens with water near the park visitor center and also one at Dog Canyon. At the visitor center you can obtain a free copy of *The Saddle Stock Access Guide* which rates trails for horses. Make sure to take along a snake bite kit! Photo courtesy of Texas Dept. of Highways.

⌂ *HC 60, Box 400, Salt Flat, TX 79847-9400*
☎ **(915) 828-3251**

Palo Duro Canyon State Park / Amarillo Area (D-4)

Featuring a long canyon (100 miles plus) that is 1200 feet from rim to floor, you will see interesting rock formations and the

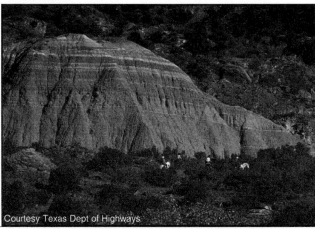

Courtesy Texas Dept of Highways

Lighthouse Hiking/Equestrian Trail takes you along the Prairie Dog Fork of the Red River. There are park stables next to the Goodnight Trading Post and the park has 6 camping areas, some of which are multi-use sites with water, showers, and electricity. Campsite reservations can be made by calling the number below.

✆ *Route 2, Box 285, Canyon, TX 79051*
☎ **(806) 488-2227**

Mustang Riding Stables / Port Aransas Area (D-5)

🐎 North of Mustang Island State Park you can rent horses for beach riding or take your own. For further details call the stables at ☎ (512) 749-5055. Or call the Port Aransas

Courtesy Texas Dept of Highways

Chamber of Commerce.
☎ **(512) 749-5919 or (800) 452-6278**

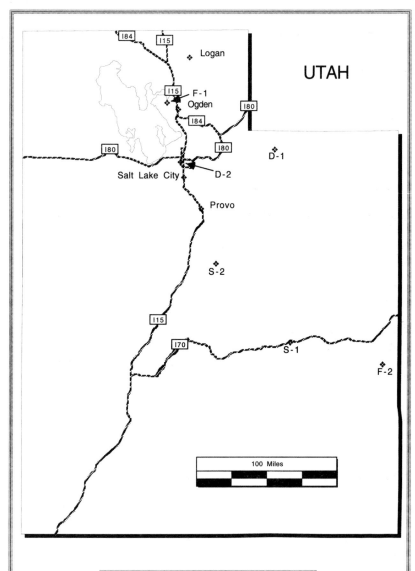

UTAH

Logan

F-1
Ogden

D-1

Salt Lake City

D-2

Provo

S-2

S-1

F-2

100 Miles

Golden Spike Arena F-1
Valerie Newland   S-1
Old Spanish Trail Arena   F-2
Z Arabians   S-2
High Uintas Wilderness   D-1
Pony Express Trail   D-2

Golden Spike Arena Events Center / Ogden (F-1)

▤ ▥ 🚐 🕀 🔱 🔧 ✖ $$

Leave I- 15 at Exit 349, go west toward the mountains and follow the signs. ▤ 385 10X10 stalls with bedding @ $15 per night. Indoor and outdoor arenas, 3/4 mile racetrack, and warm-up arena. 🚐 Within 4 miles of 2 full service RV parks. 🕀🔱 Many vets and farriers close to events center. 🔧✖ Within 5 miles of Ogden City center-- plenty of services.

⚕ *1200 West 1000 North, Ogden, UT 84404*

☎ **(801) 399-8798 or 399-8544**

Valerie Newland / Green River (S-1)

▤ 🔧 ✖

Call for directions. ▤ Have a motel in Green River and at press time Newlands were putting in stables behind the motel. 🔧✖ These services available in Green River.

⚕ *P.O. Box 327, Green River, UT 84525*

☎ **(801) 564-8237**

Old Spanish Trail Arena / Moab (F-2)

▤ 🚐 🕀 🔧 ✖

Must book ahead! 4 miles south of Moab on Highway 191. ▤ 100 stalls. Indoor and outdoor arenas. Easy access. First class facility and set up for horse shows. Controlled atmosphere and concession facilities. 🚐 KOA Campground next door. 🕀 Vet 1 mile from facility is Dr. Len Sorensen. 🔧✖ These services available in Moab.

⚕ *125 East Center Street, Moab, UT 84532*

☎ **(801) 259-6226 or 259-7339**

Z Arabians / Fountain Green (S-2)

▤ 🚐 🛏 🕀 🔱 🔧 ✖ $$

From I-15 take Nephi Exit 225 and go 16 miles east on Utah 132. Facility is on the west side of Utah 132. ▤ 4 12X12 stalls with bedding @ $10 per night. Stallions allowed and current health papers are required. 🚐 2 Camper/RV hookups available @ $15 per night and there are showers available. 🛏 Bed and breakfast available for $45 per couple per night. 🕀Vet is available in Spring City at ☎ 462-3182. 🔱 Farrier available in Wales at ☎ 436-8441. ✎ Mechanic 2 miles away at Beck Auto in Fountain Green at ☎ 445-3454. Open 7:30-6 6 days a week. 🔧 Beck Auto. ✖ Try the Robin's Nest in Fountain Green.

⚕ *P.O. Box 68, Fountain Green, UT 84632*

☎ **(801) 445-3567**

North American Horse Travel Guide

High Uintas Wilderness / East Utah (D-1)

Beautiful high country with many lakes and good fishing. Maximum of 15 horses/14 people per group but USFS strongly recommends smaller groups for less environmental impact on campsites. From Kamas, use High line or Mirror Lake trailheads. If you want to leave horses at home try Piute Creek Outfitters Inc., M Ranch Route # 1, Kamas, UT 84036 ☎ (801) 783-4317.

✝ *USFS, P.O. Box 68, Kamas, UT 84036*
☎ **(801) 783-4338**

Pony Express Trail / North Central Utah (D-2)

The Pony Express Trail covers some 133 miles of the original route across Utah. In 1860-186, riders covered between 60 and 120 miles per day, changing horses and taking rest breaks every 60 miles. Those riders had to average a lean 125 pounds and couldn't top out with mail and sidearm at more than 150! You don't have to be so lean, but this could be a long hot ride for the soft at heart! ⤟ Take Interstate 15 south from Salt Lake city to Lehi. Go west on #73. The trail starts 5 miles south of Cedar Fort at Stagecoach Inn State Park (which was a stop on the Pony Express Trail). Milepost 0. Trail goes southwest through the Dugway Range, Fish Springs Range to Callao (mile 104). Then it swings northwest and west to Ibapah (mile 133). At mile 41, Simpson Springs Station has good water and there is a BLM campground just east of the station. For further details contact the BLM. Remember to bring plenty of water and gas! No permits required.

✝ *BLM District Office, 2370 South 2300 West, Salt Lake City, UT 84119*
☎ **(801) 977-4300**

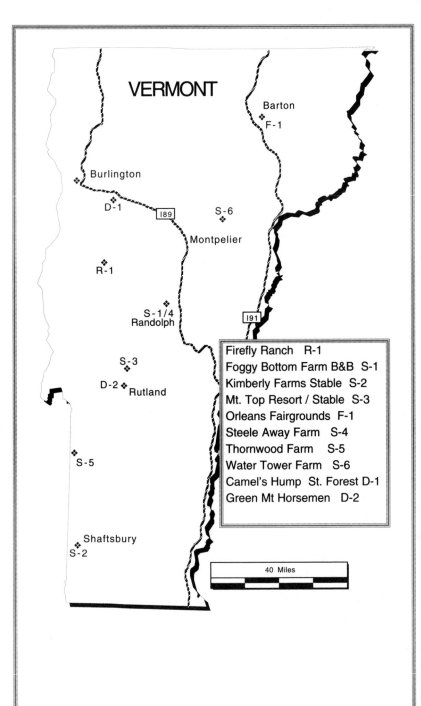

VERMONT

Barton
F-1

Burlington
D-1   I89   S-6
Montpelier

R-1

S-1/4
Randolph   I91

S-3

D-2 Rutland

Firefly Ranch R-1
Foggy Bottom Farm B&B S-1
Kimberly Farms Stable S-2
Mt. Top Resort / Stable S-3
Orleans Fairgrounds F-1
Steele Away Farm S-4
Thornwood Farm S-5
Water Tower Farm S-6
Camel's Hump St. Forest D-1
Green Mt Horsemen D-2

S-5

Shaftsbury
S-2

40 Miles

Firefly Ranch / Burlington Area (R-1)

16 miles northeast of Middlebury. 26 miles from Burlington Airport. This is a ranch country inn, catering to adults (or children of 14 or more if family has at least 4 members). No more than 6 people at a time May through October. And owner Marie Louise Link makes you feel like a member of her family. Super German-American food and 4 languages spoken. American plan only. Require reservations for horse and rider. From May through October, $135 per person per day/ $20 per day extra for single person. Guests can bring their horses (confirm ahead of time if there will be an extra charge for your horse). They provide the feed. Run-ins and 20 acres of pasture. According to the owner, "This is purely a riding ranch and we prefer intermediate to experienced riders. The rides run from 4 to 6 hours. We eat, ride, and sleep at this ranch." Discover 250,000 acres of the Green Mountain National Forest, with over 1,000 square miles of hilly country, beaver ponds, woodlands, and scenic mountain peaks.

P.O. Box 152, Bristol, VT 05443

☎ **(802) 453-2223**

Foggy Bottom Bed & Breakfast / Randolph (S-1)

From I-89 take Exit 4 and follow Route 66 1 mile to Route 12 north- 6 miles from Interstate. Foggy Bottom is on Route 12. Look for large blue sign. 9 12X12 stalls with shavings @ $15 per night. Stallions allowed and current health papers required. 1 Camper/RV hookup available @ $15 per night. Fishing in the area. Call for details and depending on which direction you come from, they can give you specific directions. Vet in Broomfield at ☎ 276-3111. Farrier in Royalton at ☎ 765-4360. Mechanic within 5 miles. Fuel at Rinker's Mobil in Randolph at ☎ 728-3442. Try the August Lion in Randolph at ☎ 728-5043.

P.O. Box 121A, Randolph, VT 05060

☎ **(802) 728-9201**

Kimberly Farms Riding Stable / Shaftsbury (S-2)

1.7 miles west on 7A, 40 miles east of I-87, and 40 miles west of I-91. Call for directions. 20 10X18 wood stalls with bedding @ $20 per night. No stallions allowed and require neg cog/rabies/current health papers. Electric hookups or guest house (which sleeps 4) @ $10 per night. Fishing in pond on the property. Vet in Shaftsbury at ☎ (802) 447-7723. Farrier Tim Wall is in Shaftsbury at ☎ (802) 823-4674. Closest mechanic is Jim Howe (1 mile away) at ☎ (802) 447-7040. These services available in Shaftsbury.

P.O. Box 345, Shaftsbury, VT 05262

☎ **(802) 442-4354**

© Jerry LeBlond/Mt. Top Inn

Mountain Top Resort & Stables / Rutland (S-3)

5 miles off U.S. # 7. North of Rutland. Call for directions.

40 stalls/22 box and in different sizes. Call for rates. No stallions allowed and require current health papers. This is a deluxe resort with many different meal plans and deluxe accommodations--great place for a vacation for you and your horse! Rates for a room range from $49 per night in Spring or late Fall to $90 in Summer and Fall. And the add on for American plan is $30 for each adult. There are many different packages--recommend you write for details.

Over 80 miles of trails on adjacent forest land. Vet in Chittenden at ☎ (802) 483- 9318. Farrier Carl Alexander in Rutland at ☎ (802) 775-4676. These services within 10 miles.

Restaurant on the premises. Also you might try The Countryman's Pleasure Restaurant which is in a 19th century farm house ☎ (802) 773-7141. Or The Grand Finale Restaurant ☎ (802) 775-1853.

☏ *Mountain Top Road, Chittenden , VT 05737*

☎ **(802) 483- 2311**

Orleans County Fairgrounds / Barton (F-1)

From I-91, take Exit 25 and go 200 yards on Route 16N. Take a left and follow the signs. Must call ahead for permission to use this facility! It's open 3rd week of May through October 1. There are several horse shows and cattle auctions every summer. So can be booked up at any given time. ➤ 30-40 stalls with water.

⌂ *Barton, VT 05822*
☎ **(802) 525-3555**

Steele Away Farm / Braintree Area (S-4)

Call for directions. Bob and Sandy Steele run a ma & pa operation and provide individual horse transport. They can also provide emergency services for the horse. Do local and long distance horse moving. ➤ 28 wood stalls with bedding @ $6 per night. Stallions allowed and neg cog/current health papers are required. ➕ 3 vets within 1/2 an hour. ◑ Farrier within 1/2 an hour. ✎ Closest mechanic within 1/2 a mile. ⬛ Several within 6 miles.

⌂ *RR #1/ Box 227M, Randolph, VT 05060*
☎ **(802) 728-4879**

Thornwood Farm / West Pawlet (S-5)

Call for directions. Contact: Ken & Eli Noman. ➤ 13 wood stalls with sawdust bedding @ $10 per night. Must have current health papers. Do horse transportation and lay-ups. ➕ Vet within 3 miles. ◑ Farrier on premises. ⬛✖ These services available within 4 miles.

⌂ *RR #1, Box 830, W. Pawlet, VT 05775*
☎ **(802) 645-9224**

Water Tower Farm / Marshfield (S-6)

Call for directions. 3/4 mile from Marshfield on Route 2. ➤ 4 stalls with shavings @ $10 per night. Stallions allowed and require neg cog/current health papers. 🚐 Camper/RV hookups 5 miles west/several available.

Sometimes a room at the farm is available @ $10 per night. Electric hookup at the farm can be arranged @ $10 per night. ➕ Dr. Sanford in Greensboro at ☎ 766-2222. ◑ Farrier Butch Kimball in Worcester at ☎ 223-2258. ✎ Closest mechanic is at Larry & Son

1 mile away at ☎ 426-3560. Open weekdays. 🅱 Closest fuel at Maplewood Convenience Store in Montpelier. ❌ Several good restaurants in Montpelier. 2 restaurants on Elm Street, the Elm Street Cafe and the Tubbs Restaurant, are operated by the New England Culinary Institute.

⚲ *U.S. Route 2/ Box 225, Marshfield, VT 05658*
☎ **(802) 426-3781**

Camel's Hump State Forest / Waterbury- Richmond Area (D-1)

In Chittenden County, a horse trail has been developed in the Honey Hollow area with the assistance of the Vermont Department of Agriculture. For further details contact GMHA (see next listing).

Green Mountain Horseman's Association / South Rutland (D-2)

This association is the key to trail rides in Vermont. Most rides require that you be a member, but rates are not that high for individual or family memberships. Distance riding's oldest 100 mile ride originates here and there are fall foliage rides, twilight rides, and a 3 day midsummer pleasure ride. ▤ Horse accommodations at the GMHA grounds or at Highbrook Stables next door ☎ (802) 457-3393. 🚐 Kedron Valley Inn ☎ (802) 457-1473 or Woodstock Inn ☎ (802) 457-1100 offer deluxe accommodations and food. ❌ Try either the 1812 House or the Skunk Hollow Inn.

☎ **(802) 457-1509**

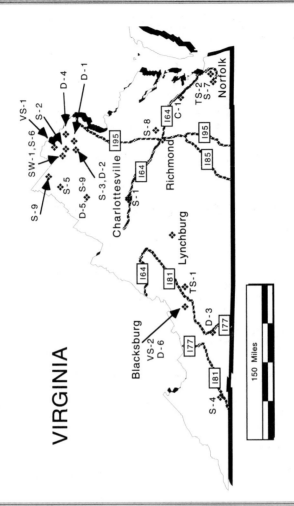

VIRGINIA

150 Miles

Norfolk
TS-2
S-7
C-1
164
195
195
185
S-8
195
Richmond
164
164
S-1
Lynchburg
181
TS-1
164
D-3
177
Blacksburg
VS-2
D-6
177
181
S-4
D-4
D-1
VS-1
S-2
SW-1, S-6
S-3, D-2
D-5, S-9
S-5
S-9
Charlottesville

Aberdeen Acres S-9	Rose Hill Stables S-8
The Barracks S-1	Virginia Tech Vet School VS-2
Hermit Stud Farm S-2	Bull Run Regional Park D-1
Jordan Hollow Farm Inn S-9	Manassas Battlefield Park D-2
Lazy As Farm S-3	New River Trail St. Park D-3
Maplewood Farm B&B S-4	Rails to River Trail D-4
Marion DuPont Vet Center VS-1	Shenandoah Nat. Park D-5
Middleburg Eq Swim Ctr. SW-1	Jefferson Nat. Forest D-6
Monte Vista Stable S-5	Bridles 'N Bits TS-1
Paper Chase Farms S-6	Quiet Shoppe Saddlery TS-2
Pine Grove Farm S-7	Busch Gardens C-1

Aberdeen Acres / Stephenson (S-9)

1.5 miles from Rt. 321. Or go 2.5 miles on Route 11 from Exit 317/ I-81. Call for detailed directions. 3 stalls (1 16X32 and other 2 16X16. They have sawdust and cost $8 per night. Stallions not allowed and current health papers required.. No hookups but showers available. Vet in Winchester at (703) 665-3030. Farrier on call. Mechanic at Ronnie's Garage in Winchester (703) 662-0057 (24 hour a day wrecker). Good fuel prices in Clearbrook at (703) 662-4492. Good food in Winchester (3 miles away).

P.O. Box 220/State Route 836, Stephenson, VA 22656
☎ **(703) 667-7809**

The Barracks / Charlottesville (S-1)

Call for directions. Near Route 81 and 64. Within 5 miles of Charlottesville. Ask for Bugsie. 10 wood stalls with bedding. Stallions allowed and require neg cog/current health papers. Vet on premises. 5 farriers nearby. These services all within 5 miles.

Route 5 / Box 417, Charlottesville, VA 22901
☎ **(804) 293-6568**

Hermite Stud Farm / Aldie (S-2)

Call ahead to confirm space available and for directions. Ask for France. 1.8 miles south of Route 50/15 Intersection (Deerburg Corner). Big silo at entrance. 2 wood stalls with bedding. Stallions allowed and require current health papers. These services available nearby.

P.O. Box 34, Aldie, VA 22001
☎ **(703) 327-6464**

Jordan Hollow Farm Inn / Stanley Area (S-9)

This is a deluxe hideaway for horse and rider! 6 miles south of Luray. From Luray, take Route 340 (Business) 6 miles. Then take a left on Route 624, then a left onto Route 689 and a right on to 626. Call for final directions. 14 10X12 wood stalls

with bedding @ $10 per night. Health papers required and stallions are allowed. 🚐 21 guest rooms available- all with private bath. ✚ Vet in Luray at☎ (703) 778-7387. ✎ Recommend Louis Bosley in Stanley at ☎ 778-3286. He's open Mon.-Sat. 8-5. 🛢 For fuel try Exxon in Stanley at☎ 778-2983. ✖ Good restaurant at the Inn. It features "country cosmopolitan" food and is in a historic colonial farmhouse. There is also a pub in a renovated stable. For reservations call the number below.
⌂ *Route 2/ Box 375, Stanley, VA 22851*
☎ **(703) 778-2285 or FAX (703) 778-1759**

Lazy As Farm / Manassas Area (S-3)
🚍🚺✚☲∪✎🛏✖$$
From I-66 take Exit 43B and go 1.5 miles to 5571 Pageland Lane. Follow that 2 miles to farm on right. 🚍 5 12X12 wood stalls with bedding @ $15 per stall. Stallions allowed and require current health papers. Also have 2 paddocks. ✚ Vet in Centreville at ☎ (703) 631-9133. ∪ Farrier in Centreville at ☎ 266- 7608. ✎ Closest mechanic 5 miles away at Battlefield Texaco in Manassas/open 7 days a week. 🛢✖ These services available in Manassas.
⌂ *5571 Pageland Lane, Gainesville, VA 22065*
☎ **(703) 754-4880**

Maplewood Farm Bed & Breakfast / Abingdon (S-4)
🚍🚻🛏☲∪✎🛏✖$$
From I-81 take Exit 17 and go 5.5 miles on S75. Turn right onto 665. Go .7 miles and Maplewood Farm will be on your left. 🚍 5 12X12 wood stalls with bedding @ $15 per night. Stallions allowed and

require current health papers. 🛏 This is a bed and breakfast facility. Call ahead for reservations. ⚓ Fishing in the area. ✚ Vet in Abingdon at ☎ (703) 628-6861. ∪ Farrier in Bristol, TN at ☎ (615) 968-1638 ✎ Closest mechanic is 6 miles away at Taylor Truck Repair in Abingdon at ☎ 628- 3221. Open weekdays 8-4:30. 🛢 Fuel at Jimbo's (6 miles) in Abingdon ☎ 628- 6215. ✖ Try the Starving Artist in Abingdon at ☎ 628- 8445.
⌂ *Route 7/ Box 461, Abingdon, VA 24210*
☎ **(703) 628-2640**

Marion duPont Scott Equine Medical Center / Leesburg (VS-1)

This is a state of the art veterinary health care facility operated exclusively for horses. With 67,000 square feet of space it includes intensive care facilities for five patients and in hospital accomodations for an additional 24 patients. Call for emergencies only! NO STALLS FOR TRANSIENT HORSES. May require referral from a vet.

☎ **(703) 771- 6800** (Mon.-Fri., 8-5) or if emergency **(800) 453- 7074**

Middleburg Equine Swim Center / Middleburg (SW-1)

Call for directions, rates, and availability of stalls. This is a full boarding, therapy and conditioning facility for horses. It includes 1 swimming pool and 2 small hydrotherapy pools for horses. ⚏ 3-4 stalls with bedding usually available. ✚ Vet next door. ♘ Farrier on the premises.

✝ *Route 1/ Box 194, Middleburg, VA 22117*
☎ **(703) 687-6816**

Monte Vista Stable / Middletown (S-5)

Off I-81 take Exit 302. Go west on 627 to stop sign. Take a right onto U.S. 11. 1.3 miles to stable. ⊨ There are motels and bed & breakfast places within 6 miles of the stable. ⚓ Fishing in the area. ⚏ 6 wood stalls with bedding @ $25 per night. Stalls all 14X20 or larger. No stallions allowed and current neg cog (12 months)/health papers required. ✚ Vet on premises. ♘ Farrier next door at ☎ 869- 3045. ✎ Closest mechanic is at Exxon (1.5 miles). 🛢 Fuel within 1/2 mile. ✖ Restaurants nearby.

✝ *8183 Valley Pike, Middletown, VA 22645*
☎ **(703) 869-4621**

Paper Chase Farms / Middleburg (S-6)

On Route 50. Call for directions, availability of stalls. ⚏ 47 wood stalls with bedding. No stallions allowed. Indoor/outdoor lighted arenas. Complete training, riding center.

✝ *Route 50, Middleburg, VA 22117*
☎ **(703) 687-5255**

Pine Grove Farm, Inc. / Chesapeake (S-7)

Call in advance for directions and availability of stalls! 5 minutes from Route 664. 4 wood stalls with "turnkey" bedding. Stallions not allowed and require current health papers. 3 full time employees at this facility. Vet and farrier available.

1649 Dock Landing Road, Chesapeake, VA 23321

☎ **(804) 488-6638**

Rose Hill Stables / Mechanicsville (S-8)

Off I-295. Call for directions. Must make reservations--call ahead! 33 wood stalls with bedding @ $11 per night. Pasture per horse per night @ $9. Require current health papers. This is a schooling, breaking, training facility and has a sand ring with jumps. Vet and farrier 20 minutes away. These services all within 10 minutes. Recommend the Prairie Schooner nearby or the Smoky Pig in Ashland.

6112 Rose Hill Drive, Mechanicsville, VA 23111

☎ **(804) 746-5906**

Virginia Tech / Univ. of Maryland College of Veterinary Medicine / Blacksburg (VS-2)

Emergency horse care 24 hours a day, 7 days a week. Call only for emergencies! May require referral from a vet. NO STALLS FOR TRANSIENT BOARDING. Located on Duck Pond Drive on the Virginia Tech Campus.

Blacksburg, VA 24061

☎ **(703) 231-4621** or after hours **(703) 231-9041**

Bull Run Regional Park / Centreville (D-1)

5 miles of trails in hilly and flat terrain. Camp sites available, including water and rest rooms. Fee or permit required.

7700 Bull Run Drive, Centreville, VA 22020

☎ **(703) 631-0550**

Manassas Nat. Battlefield Park Horse Mounted Operation / Manassas (D-2)

20 miles of trails in hilly terrain. Maps available and fee or permit required.

6511 Sudley Road, Manassas, VA 22110

☎ **(703) 754-8694**

New River Trail State Park / Austinville (D-3)

42 miles of trails on flat terrain. Horseshoe Campground connects to Trail 32 and has water and campsites. ☎ (703) 980-0278. This state park has maps, water, rest rooms and campsites.

✝ *Route #1, Box 81X, Austinville, VA 24312*
☎ **(703) 699- 6778**

Rails to River Trail / Reston Area (D-4)

6 miles of trails in hilly and flat terrain. Camping allowed and water and rest rooms available. Connects to Trail 64.

✝ *18108 Michael Faraday Ct., Reston, VA 22090*
☎ **(703) 471-5415**

Shenandoah National Park / Luray Area (D-5)

Miles of trails in hilly, mountainous, and flat terrain. Maps available. Camp sites, water, and rest rooms. Fee or permit required..

✝ *P.O. Box 727, Luray, VA 22835*
☎ **(703) 999-2266**

Jefferson National Forest / Blacksburg Area (D-6)

200 miles of trails in mountainous, rocky terrain. Maps available. Camp sites, water and rest rooms available. Forest includes the White Pine Horse Camp.

✝ *110 South Park Drive, Blacksburg, VA 24060*
☎ **(703) 552-4641**

Bridles 'N Bits / Roanoke (TS-1)

"We stock all your riding and stable needs." Mon.-Fri. 10 to 6, Sat. 10-4. After hours leave message at ☎ 772-4409.

✝ *Southwest Plaza Shopping Center, 2050 Electric Road #122, Roanoke, VA 24018*
☎**(703) 772- 4409 or (800) 347- 4509**

Quiet Shoppe Saddlery / Hampton Roads (TS-2)

Riding apparel and equipment. Horsy antiques. 1/2 block off Route 17 /Churchland. Wed.-Sat. 10a.m.-5 p.m.

✝ *3935 Poplar Hill Road, Chesapeake, VA 23321*
☎ **(804) 483-9358**

Busch Gardens / Williamsburg (C-1)

From Washington take I-95 south to I-295. South at Richmond. I-64 east to Exit 242A and follow the signs. See the Clydesdales as part of your tour.

♈ *Busch Gardens Blvd., Williamsburg, VA 23187*

☎ **(804) 253-3039**

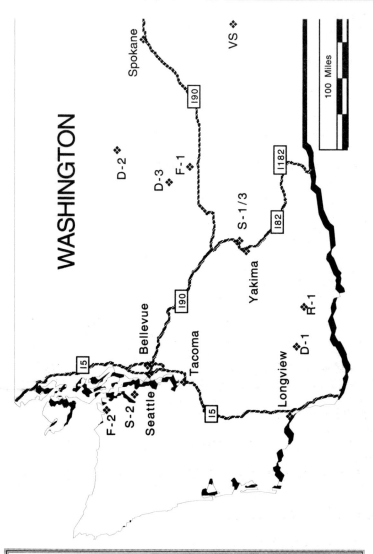

WASHINGTON

Spokane

VS

D-2

D-3   F-1

S-1/3

Yakima

Bellevue

Tacoma

R-1

D-1

Longview

Seattle

F-2 S-2

100 Miles

190

1182

182

190

I5

I5

Flying L Ranch R-1
Grant Fairgrounds F-1
Jefferson County Fair F-2
Lawrence Redman Stable S-1
Sandamar Farm S-2
Washington St Vet School VS
White Burch Stables S-3
Battleground Lake Rec. D-1

Steamboat Lake St Park D-2
Sun Lakes State Park D-3

Flying L Ranch / Glenwood (R-1)

Call for directions. 100 miles northeast of Portland. 6 stalls at adjacent facility (Lazy Daisy at ☎ (509) 364-3481. This is an ideal B&B setup with doubles ranging from $65 to $80 per night and you can board your horse at Lazy Daisy. Features full ranch breakfasts, spa, lounge, ranch trails, and unlimited use of common kitchens. Great views of nearby mountains (especially Mt. Adams) and 160 acres of private meadows. A great place to take your horse for a vacation!

⚐ *25 Flying L Lane, Glenwood, WA 98619*
☎ **(509) 364-3488**

Grant County Fairgrounds / Moses Lake (F-1)

2 hours west of Spokane, close to Highway 17. Call for directions. 100 stalls w/o bedding @ $5. Bedding @ $2 per bag. 300 spaces for electric Camper/RV hookups @ $8.60 per night. Vet and farrier in the area. These services available in Moses Lake.

⚐ *3953 Airway Drive, Moses Lake, WA 98837*
☎ **(509) 765-3581**

Jefferson County Fair / Port Townsend (F-2)

Ferry from either Seattle, Anacortes, or Highway 101. 1 mile west of Port Townsend. 100 wood stalls with bedding @ $5 per night (but you must clean up next morning). Camper/RV hookups available. Vet and farrier in Port Townsend. These services available in Port Townsend. For Italian food, try Lanza's Ristorante/Pizzeria on 1020 Lawrence Street. ☎ (206) 385-6221.

⚐ *P.O. Box 242, Port Townsend, WA 98368*
☎ **(206) 385-1013**

Lawrence Redman Stables / Yakima (S-1)

Off I-82 take Nob Hill Exit, and you will find next to race track. Check first for stall availability. Call ahead! 40 wood stalls with bedding. Hot walkers. Carole Redman does custom embroidery for horse people and has clothing for sale. Vet and farrier available. These services available in Yakima. For food try Marti's (located on the Yakima River) ☎ (509) 248-2062 or Santiago's Gourmet Mexican Cooking at 111 East Yakima Avenue ☎ (509) 453-1644.

⚐ *1701 Dalton Lane, Yakima, WA 98901*
☎ **(509) 452-5101**

North American Horse Travel Guide

Sandamar Farm / Poulsbo (S-2)
≈🚙≋⊕♾️✕$$

From Highway 3 turn east on Bond Road. Go 2.5 miles and turn right on Anderson Road. Go 1 mile and ranch will be on your right. ≈ 10 12X12 wood stalls with bedding @ $10 per night. 🚙 3 electric only Camper/RV hookups @ $5 per night. ≋ Fishing in the area. ✚ Vet in Poulsbo at ☎ 779-1001. ♾ Farrier in Poulsbo at ☎ 697-3133. ♾✕ All of these services available in Poulsbo (4 miles away).

� 4499 NE Gunderson Road, Poulsbo, WA 98370

☎ (206) 779-9861

Washington State School of Veterinary Medicine / Pullman (VS)
⬟

Emergency horse care. Call only for emergencies! May require referral from a vet. NO STALLS FOR TRANSIENT BOARDING.

� McCoy Hall, Stadium Way, Pullman, WA 99164- 6610

☎ (509) 335-0711 or 335-3063

White Birch Stables / Yakima (S-3)
≈⊕♾️✕$$

On Route 82/97 north of Yakima take Exit 29 (east Selah) and call for directions. ≈ 40 wood stalls with bedding and feed @ $15 per night. 50 outside runs, 2 large outdoor arenas, 1 indoor arena, and 2 hot walkers. Roping, cutting cattle, conditioning, and sales. Close to Yakima Meadows. Contact: Roger, Sue, or Willy Hart. ✚♾ Vet and farrier within 3 miles. ♾✕ See Lawrence Redman listing previous page.

� 151 Ray Symmons Road, Yakima, WA 98901

☎ (509) 452-3184

Battleground Lake Recreation Area / Vancouver Area (D-1)
🐎

20 miles east of Vancouver and 3 miles east of Route 503. Trails to back country horse camps.

� Skamania Chamber of Commerce, P.O. Box 1037, Stevenson, WA 98648

☎ (206) 479-3594

Steamboat Lake State Park / Grand Coulee Dam (D-2)
🐎

8 miles south of Grand Coulee Dam on Route 155. Riding trails in nearby Northrup Canyon. Dam is quite dramatic when lights on at night. Call park for further information.

☎ (509) 633-1304

Sun Lakes State Park / Coulee City Area (D-3)

6 miles south of Coulee City on Route 17. Park has several lakes and sandy beaches. Good horseback riding and ⛺ campground has 209 camping sites with hookups.

☖ *300 Beach Street E, Soap Lake, WA 98851*

☎ **(509) 246-1821 or 632-5583**

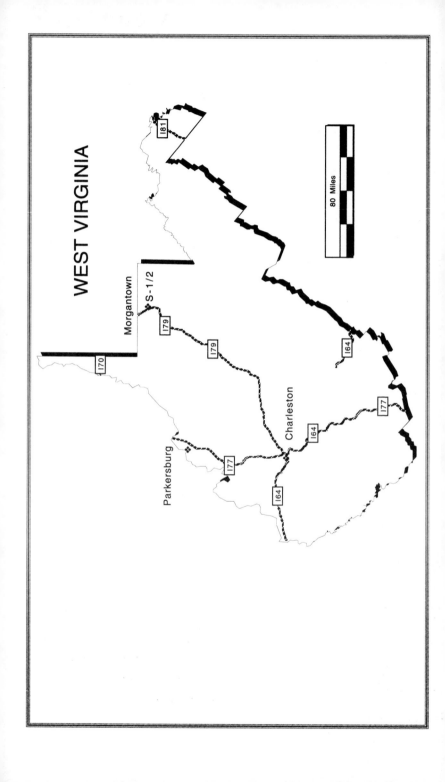

Hunterwood, Inc. / Morgantown (S-1)
▰◨♘➍

Call for directions. 5 minutes from Route 68 or 79. ▰ 25 wood stalls with bedding. No stallions allowed. This is a hunter jumper facility. ◨♘ Vet and farrier available. ➍ These services within 10 minutes.
⚐ *Route 10, Box 161D, Morgantown, WV 26505*
☎ **(304) 296-1979**

Mountain View Farm / Morgantown (S-2)
▰🐎◨➍✖$$

4.5 miles off I-68. Also close to I-79. ▰ 5 10X12 wood stalls with bedding @ $15 per night. Stallions allowed if well behaved. Current health papers required. 🐎 Nice trails through the mountains. ◨ 2 good vets in Morgantown. ➍✖ Morgantown has a good mechanic and other services can be found on the interstate.
⚐ *RR #7/ Box 233A, Morgantown, WV 26505*
☎ **(304) 296-8941**

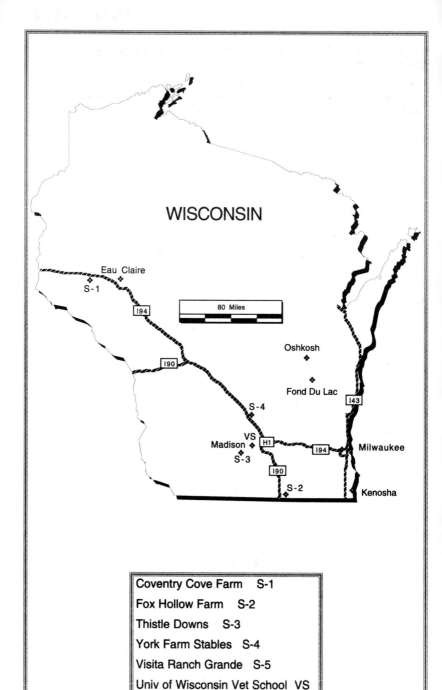

WISCONSIN

80 Miles

Eau Claire
S-1
I94

Oshkosh

I90

Fond Du Lac

S-4

I43

VS
Madison H1
S-3 I94 Milwaukee

I90

S-2

Kenosha

Coventry Cove Farm   S-1
Fox Hollow Farm   S-2
Thistle Downs   S-3
York Farm Stables   S-4
Visita Ranch Grande   S-5
Univ of Wisconsin Vet School   VS

Coventry Cove Farm / Menomonie (S-1)
≋❂☉☒$$

6 miles from I-90. Take exit to Highway 25--go south 1 block, turn right on 12W and then north on Route 79. Call for final directions. ≋ 2 wood stalls with bedding @ $10 per night. Stallions allowed and require neg cog/current health papers. ❂ 2 vets in the area. ☉ Farrier available. ☒ The Bolo Country Inn, in Menomonie, has a la carte entrees from $4-26. ☎ (715) 235-5596.

⚑ *RR # 6/ Box 113, Menomonie, WI 54751*
☎ **(715) 235-6260**

Fox Hollow Farm / Beloit Area (S-2)
≋🚐❂🐾☒$$

Call for directions and availability of stalls. ≋ 34 wood stalls with bedding @ $10 per night. Require 30 neg cog and current health papers. Stallions allowed. 🚐 Electric hookups might be available. ❂ Vet on call. 🐾 These services available in Beloit which is 5 miles away. ☒ For a nice dinner try the Butterfly Club which is 1.5 miles east of I-90 Exit 185B on I-43. It's 1/2 mile east of I-43 exit. ☎ (608) 362-8577.

⚑ *7926 East County Highway W, Clinton, WI 53525*
☎ **(608) 676-5224**

Thistle Downs Sports Horses / Verona (S-3)
≋❂☉🐾🔧$$

Call for directions. ≋ 30 wood stalls with bedding @ $15 per night. Stallions allowed and require current health papers. This facility has dressage and combined training. ❂ Vet at Madison Equine Center at ☎ 256-3410. ☉ Dean Johanningmeier is on call. 🔧 Mechanic and fuel in Verona (4.5 miles).

⚑ *7771 Riverside Road, Verona, WI 53593*
☎ **(608) 845-7719**

Visita Rancho Grande / Sharon (S-5)
≋❂🛏$$

3.5 miles south of I-43 near Darien. Call for directions. ≋ 11 stalls @ $12.50 per night. Can also board cattle. Feed extra. Require current health papers. ❂ 2 vets available. 🛏 Bed & breakfast @ $45 per night and kids/dogs allowed if enough rooms available for the former. The owners, Miriam and Jim Stauffacher, raise Corriente cattle. Campgrounds and motels in the area.

⚑ *W434 Townhall Road, Sharon, WI 53585*
☎ **(414) 736-4081**

York Farm Stables / Poynette (S-4)
▰▰▰❏

Off I-94 take Exit 115. Must book in advance. At same time pick up final directions. ▰▰▰ 3 wood stalls with bedding. Stallions not allowed and current health papers are required. ❏ Nearest vet is Dean Meyer (12 miles away) .

⚐ *N 3299 McMillan Road, Poynette, WI 53955*

☎ **(608) 254- 2811**

University of Wisconsin School of Veterinary Medicine / Madison (VS)
⌂

Emergency horse care 24 hours a day, 7 days a week. Call only for emergencies! May require referral from a vet.

NO STALLS FOR TRANSIENT BOARDING. Must make an appointment first. Facility located at address shown below.

⚐ *2015 Linden Drive West, Madison, WI 53706*

☎ **(608) 263-7600**

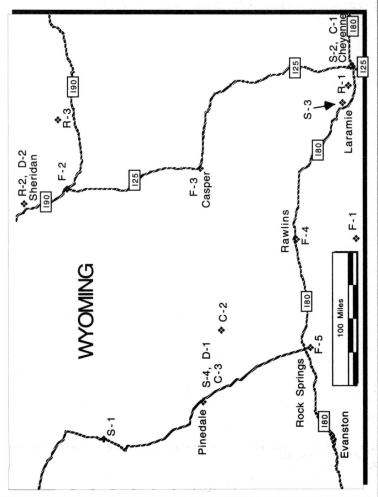

WYOMING

Dixon Arena F-1	Stonehouse Stables S-3
A Drummond's B&B R-1	Sweetwater Ev. Complex F-5
Grand Teton KOA S-1	Wind River Qtr. Horses S-4
Johnson County Fairground F-2	Bridger Wilderness D-1
King Bros. Ranch R-2	Cheyenne Frontier Days C-1
Natrona County Fairgrounds F-3	Cloud Peak Wilderness D-2
P Cross Bar Ranch R-3	Oregon Trail (see listing)
Rawlins Arena F-4	South Pass City C-2
Sheridan Fairgrounds F-6	Green River Rendezvous C-3
Singletree Stable S-2	

Dixon Arena / Baggs Area (F-1)

2 miles east of Dixon, which is about 15 minutes east of Baggs on WY 70. Arena is adjacent to the airport which is on north side of highway. If any problems, call Harry Russell who lives nearby ☎ (307) 383-2640. ⚏ 10 catch pens and large outdoor arena. ☎ There is a pay phone between hangars on south side of airport (200 yards west). Mechanic at D&L Tire in Baggs at (307) 383-7735. Fuel at Conoco in Baggs ☎ (307) 383-6580. Food at the Drifter's Motel in Baggs ☎(307) 383-2015

Drummond's Ranch Bed & Breakfast / Cheyenne- Laramie Area (R-1)

Halfway between Cheyenne and Laramie. 1/4 mile off State Highway 210 which parallels and intersects with I-80 and I-25. Call for detailed directions! ⚏ 4 stalls with straw/shavings @ $15 per night. (@ $12 per night for 2 or more horses). Stalls range from 12X12 to 12X14. Stallions allowed and require current health papers. ⊨ 2 rooms with showers available and have outdoor hot tub. Serve family style breakfasts. Lunch and dinner with advance notice. Waffles on Sundays. ≋ Good fishing nearby. Near Curt Gowdy State Park and 5 minutes to Medicine Bow National Forest.⊕ Nearest vet in Cheyenne at ☎ 634-3080 or 632-6392. ☉ Nearest farrier is Ken Peterson in Cheyenne at ☎ 634-8673. Camper dump available within 2 miles. ✎ Nearest mechanic is 22 miles away (either Cheyenne or Laramie). Flying J on I-25 in Cheyenne. ☒ Cafe Jacques in Laramie. ☏ 399 Happy Jack Road(Highway 210), Cheyenne, WY 82007 ☎ (307) 634-6042

Grand Teton KOA Campground / Moran (S-1)

6 miles east of Moran Junction on U.S. 26/287. ⚏ 6 12X12 portable pens. Ask for Harry Washut. 68 Camper/RV hookups, showers, and water starting at $16 per night and up. ≋ Fishing nearby. ⊕ Vet in Jackson. ☒ Fuel and food on the premises. ☏ P.O. Box 92, Moran, WY 83013 ☎ (307) 543-2483

Johnson County Fairgrounds / Buffalo(F-2)

On north edge of town- head north on main street. ⚏ 100 wood stalls. 150 Camper/RV hookups. Contact: Jerry Ruby. This facility includes arena and adjacent pastures. ☒ These services available in Buffalo. ☏ P.O. Box 911, Buffalo, WY 82834 ☎ (307) 684-9379

King Brothers Ranch / Sheridan (R-2)
▰▱⌖◑⚒🗙$$$

Within 3 miles of Meade Creek Exit off I-90. On Highway 87. Call for final directions.

▰▱ 16 18X30 stalls with bedding @ $18 per night. Stallions allowed and they require current health papers. ⌖ There is a vet in Sheridan (8 miles) at ☎ 672-5533. ◑ Farrier in Sheridan at ☎ 674-5827. ⚒ Closest mechanic at Exxon on Coffee Ave. in Sheridan (10 miles). ▮ Gas Mat on Coffee Ave. 🗙 Perkins Restaurant in Sheridan.
⛢ *3102 Highway 87, Sheridan, WY 82801*
☎ **(307) 672-5354**

Natrona County Fairgrounds / Casper (F-3)
▰▱🚐⚒🗙$

From I-25 take Poplar Street Exit, go south to 1st Street. Turn west to bar (Beacon Club). Then turn left. (1700 Fairgrounds Road).
▰▱ 350 stalls w/o bedding @ $5 per night. ⌖◑ In Casper.
▮ Fuel within 500 yards. 🗙 Within 1 mile (Sizzler, Adam's Rib).
⛢ *1700 Fairgrounds Road, Casper, WY 82604*
☎ **(307) 234-1864 or 235-5775**

P Cross Bar Ranch / Gillette (R-3)
▰▱⌖◑⚒🗙$$

On Highway 14-16 20 miles north of Gillette. ▰▱ 6 wood/metal

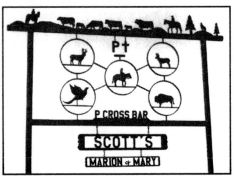

stalls with bedding @ $12 per night. Stalls range in size from 10X20 to 30X40. This is a working cattle ranch. ⊨ " Try our Horse Motel. Our accommodations are clean and modern. Meals are served family style with the family." Bed & breakfast @ $23 per person, and @ $40 per couple. Sack lunch @ $6. Evening meal @ $7. ⛢ *8586 North*
Highway 14-16, Gillette, WY 82716
☎ **(307) 682-3994**

Rawlins Arena / Rawlins (F-4)

On east side of Rawlins. Southwest of the airport on 523 Rodeo. 80 wood stalls @ $3 inside. Outside stalls free. Contact: Caretaker at ☎ (307) 324- 8101. These services available in Rawlins. Try the Country Kitchen.

⌂ c/o County Fair Board, 523 Rodeo, Rawlins, WY 82301

☎ **(307) 324-6866 or (307) 324-8101** (caretaker)

Singletree Stable / Cheyenne (S-2)

From I-80 take Exit 364 and go north through 4 stop lights. Turn right on to Thomas Road (4715 Thomas Road). 10 12X12 wood stalls with bedding @ $15 per night. Feed on request only. Require health papers and stallions are allowed. ✚ Vet in Cheyenne at ☎ 634-3080. Farrier on the premises. Nearest mechanic at Sapps/ Flying J. These services available nearby.

⌂ 4715 Thomas Road, Cheyenne, WY 82009

☎ **(800) 336-0287 or (307) 635-6010**

Stonehouse Stables / Laramie (S-3)

From I-80 exit to Snowy Range Road, go west 1 mile on Route 230, then north 1 mile on Highway 130. 5 stalls available for transient horses @ $20 per night. Require health papers and stallions are allowed.

≋ Good fishing nearby on the Laramie River .

✚ Vet in Laramie at ☎ 745-4383. Farrier available in Laramie at ☎ 742-6952. Closest mechanic is at Markle's Truck Repair (5 miles) at ☎ 742-3708. 24 hour road service at I-80 and Curtis. Fuel at Foster's in Laramie at ☎ 745-7331. The Beanery in Laramie at ☎ 742-0869.

⌂ 3070 Snowy Range Road, Laramie, WY 82070

☎ **(307) 742-7512**

Sheridan Fairgrounds / Sheridan (F-6)

Take Exit 23 off I-90 and go west of the hospital on Fifth Street. It's on the west edge of Sheridan. 150 stalls @ $5 per head per night. The stalls are of pipe, rock or wood. The rock stalls were built in the 30's by the WPA! Bedding available @ $3 per bale. Vet within 2 miles and farriers in the area. Camper/RV hookups free for boarders. These services available. ☎ **(307) 672-2079**

Sweetwater Events Complex / Rock Springs (F-5)

Take the Yellowstone/ Pinedale Exit (191) going north and look for 3320 Yellowstone Road. 400 metal stalls w/o bedding @ $5 per night. Available from June and through August only.
Good fishing in Flaming Gorge Reservoir or Pinedale. Vet across the street. Farrier available. These services all available in Rock Springs. For good food try the restaurant at the golf course.
3320 Yellowstone Road, Rock Springs, WY 82901
☎ **(307) 382-3075**

Wind River Quarter Horses / Pinedale (S-4)

Call for directions. Ehman Lane goes directly off Highway 191. 3 miles from Pinedale. 6 25X50 wood stalls w/o bedding @ $5 per night. Require health papers and stallions allowed. Camper/RV hookups in town. Wind River Range close by. Has some spectacular country and great fishing! (See entry later in this section). 4 vets in Pinedale at ☎ 367-4752. Farrier in Pinedale at ☎ 367-2602.
All of these services are available in Pinedale.
219 Ehman Lane, Pinedale, WY 82941
☎ **(307) 367-4547**

Cattle Drive in Sheridan
© Bruce McAllister

Bridger Wilderness / Pinedale / Lander Area (D-1)

This is the 2nd largest national forest outside of Alaska and has varied topography, interesting geology, and excellent fishing. Many high alpine lakes and even golden trout in some. The Wind River Range has to be one of the most spectacular in all of North America--and one of the most remote. It can have its own weather systems. But it is well worth the effort! There are 9 trailheads from the Pinedale side of the Wind Rivers and the Pinedale Ranger District can help out with maps, directions, and issuing the necessary stock permits (limit of 25 horse/people combined).

⚑ *Pinedale Ranger District, P.O. Box 220, Pinedale , WY 82941*
☎ **(307) 367-4326**

Courtesy Wyoming Travel Commission

Cheyenne Frontier Days / Cheyenne (C-1)

Every year the last full week in July. America's premier western rodeo is a 10-day cowboy's dream and family oriented to boot! Well worth a stop if you have the time.

P.O. Box 2477, Cheyenne, WY 82003-2477

☎ **(800) 227-6336 or FAX (307) 778-7213**

Courtesy Wyoming Travel Commission

Cloud Peak Wilderness / Sheridan - Buffalo Area (D-2)

This wilderness honors the highest peak in the Bighorn mountains. It features towering, sheer vertical walls and has good fishing. Recommended access points include the following.
Hunter Corrals--5 miles from Buffalo on #16. Turn onto Forest #19, going NW 2-3 miles to trail head. Has corrals and unloading ramps. Circle Park--17 miles on #16--then 2.5 miles west on Forest #20. Hitching post and unloading ramp. West Tensleep Lake Trailhead--17 miles east of Tensleep on U.S.#16--then 8 miles north on Forest #27. Call/write for restrictions, permits.

US Forest Service, 1969 South Sheridan Avenue, Sheridan, WY 82801

☎ **(307) 672-0751**

Oregon Trail

Traverses the entire state, running from Torrington to Cokeville. 487 miles on the main stem route--more than any other state. There are 2 companies which put together wagon train treks across portions of the Trail in Wyoming. Historic Trails Expeditions at ☎ (307) 266-4868 or FAX 237-6010 puts on everything from day trips in one of their wagons to 5 day trips @ $620 if you bring your own horse. They operate out of Casper. Or Trails West at ☎ (307) 332-7801. Trails West charges $350 per adult for a 3 day trip and $250 for children 6 to 12. They supply wagons, horses and food and operate out of historic South Pass City. For further information contact:
✆ *Wyoming Division of Tourism, I-25 at College Drive, Cheyenne, WY 82002*
☎ **(800) 225- 5996**

South Pass City / Lander Area (C-2)

This well preserved historic landmark owed its beginning to the discovery of gold in 1867--the same year overland traffic on the Oregon Trail went into a sharp decline in anticipation of the transcontinental railroad. Before that it was Wyoming's largest settlement. It was first discovered by Robert Stuart and the Astorians in 1812 because it allowed easy passage across the backbone of the Rockies on an easy grade. South Pass City open May through October. To get there, take either Route 28 out of Lander or 191 out of Rock Springs to Farson (to link up to 28).
✖ If you get hungry along the way, try the Mercantile in Atlantic City (about 10 miles northeast of South Pass City).

Green River Rendezvous / Pinedale (C-3)

📷

Every 2nd Sunday of July, the town of Pinedale puts on a 2 hour pageant which is considered one of the very best of its kind. Buckskin clad actors recreate those historic fur trade meetings which took place in the old days between the trappers, Indians, and fur company representatives. For further information and dates, contact Wyoming Dept. of Tourism (see Oregon Trail section).

Bringing in the horses.   © Bruce McAllister

NORTH AMERICAN HORSE TRAVEL GUIDE SURVEY FORM

Name of Facility

Directions to Nearest Highway

Address

City/Town   *City/Province*   *ZIP*

Phone (   )   *No. of Stalls*   *Sizes*

Bedding(Y/N)   *Wood*   *Metal*   *AutoH2O*

Stallions Allowed? Y/N   *Cost Stall/Night?*   *Current Papers?*

Vet in Area?   *How Many Miles/km.?*   *Phone(   )*

Farrier?   *How Many Miles/km.?*   *Phone(   )*

Camper R/V Hookups?   *#?*   *Cost/Night?*

Fishing in Area?   *Trails?*   *# Miles/km?*

Type Terrain?

Nearest Mechanic ?   *Phone (   )*

Hours Open ?   *Days Open ?*   *Phone (   )*

Closest Restaurant ?   *Phone (   )*

Closest Fuel Stop ?   *Phone (   )*

SPECIAL FEATURES?

INDOOR/OUTDOOR ARENAS/SIZE

BED & BREAKFAST ?   *COST/NIGHT ?*

CAN YOU SEND PHOTOS? PRINTS OR SLIDES ?   *WILL RUN FREE OF CHARGE IN NEXT EDITION IF FACILITY & PHOTO. ACCEPTABLE.*

SUBMITTED BY:

NAME:

ADDRESS:

CITY/TOWN: *STATE/PROVINCE*   *ZIP*

PHONE NUMBER (   )

RETURN THIS FORM TO:

ROUNDUP PRESS, P.O. Box 109, Boulder, CO 80306-0109

*(If you are listed in current guide, please send any corrections and/
or additions for next edition! Photos help and will be returned if requested–
prefer shots of facility. There are NO CHARGES FOR LISTINGS and we are
always looking for good horse trails as separate entries.*

NORTH AMERICAN HORSE TRAVEL GUIDE SURVEY FORM

Name of Facility _____

Directions to *Nearest Highway* _____

Address _____

City/Town _____ *City/Province* _____ *ZIP* _____

Phone (   ) _____ *No. of Stalls* _____ *Sizes* _____

Bedding(Y/N) _____ *Wood* _____ *Metal* _____ *AutoH2O* _____

Stallions Allowed? Y/N ____ *Cost Stall/Night?* ____ *Current Papers?* ____

Vet in Area? _____ *How Many Miles/km.?* _____ *Phone(   )* _____

Farrier? _____ *How Many Miles/km.?* _____ *Phone(   )* _____

Camper R/V Hookups? ____ *#?* _____ *Cost/Night?* _____

Fishing in Area? _____ *Trails?* _____ *# Miles/km?* _____

Type Terrain? _____

Nearest Mechanic ? _____ *Phone (   )* _____

Hours Open ? _____ *Days Open ?* _____ *Phone (   )* _____

Closest Restaurant ? _____ *Phone (   )* _____

Closest Fuel Stop ? _____ *Phone (   )* _____

SPECIAL FEATURES? _____

_____

INDOOR/OUTDOOR ARENAS/SIZE _____

BED & BREAKFAST ? _____ *COST/NIGHT ?* _____

CAN YOU SEND PHOTOS? PRINTS OR SLIDES ? _____ *WILL RUN*

FREE OF CHARGE IN NEXT EDITION IF FACILITY & PHOTO.

ACCEPTABLE.

SUBMITTED BY:

NAME: _____

ADDRESS: _____

CITY/TOWN: _____ *STATE/PROVINCE* _____ *ZIP* _____

PHONE NUMBER (   ) _____

RETURN THIS FORM TO:

ROUNDUP PRESS, P.O. Box 109, Boulder, CO 80306-0109

*(If you are listed in current guide, please send any corrections and/
or additions for next edition! Photos help and will be returned if requested–
prefer shots of facility. There are NO CHARGES FOR LISTINGS and we are
always looking for good horse trails as separate entries.*

Index

Index

Index

Index

North American Horse Travel Guide

Index